ISLAM AND INTERNATIONAL RELATIONS

Fractured Worlds

Mustapha Kamal Pasha

Routledge
Taylor & Francis Group

LONDON AND NEW YORK

First published 2017
by Routledge
2 Park Square, Milton Park, Abingdon, Oxon OX14 4RN

and by Routledge
711 Third Avenue, New York, NY 10017

Routledge is an imprint of the Taylor & Francis Group, an informa business

© 2017 Mustapha Kamal Pasha

British Library Cataloguing in Publication Data
A catalogue record for this book is available from the British Library

Library of Congress Cataloging in Publication Data
Names: Pasha, Mustapha Kamal, author.
Title: Islam and international relations : fractured worlds /
Mustapha Kamal Pasha.
Description: Abingdon, Oxon ; New York, NY : Routledge, 2017. | Includes
bibliographical references and index.
Identifiers: LCCN 2016056402 | ISBN 9781138644434 (hardback) |
ISBN 9781138646049 (pbk.) | ISBN 9781315627786 (ebook)
Subjects: LCSH: Islam and international relations. | Islamic countries--Foreign
relations--Western countries. | Western countries--Foreign relations--Islamic
countries.
Classification: LCC BP190.5.D56 P37 2017 | DDC 327.0917/67--dc23
LC record available at https://lccn.loc.gov/2016056402

ISBN: 978-1-138-64443-4 (hbk)
ISBN: 978-1-138-64604-9 (pbk)
ISBN: 978-1-315-62778-6 (ebk)

Typeset in Bembo
by Taylor & Francis Books

For Ritu, Ayesha and Tariq

CONTENTS

ACKNOWLEDGEMENTS

This collection brings together my work on the confluence of Islam and international relations. Spread over several years, the various chapters engage common themes arising within different thinking contexts and with varied intent. I am immensely grateful to the publishers for granting permission to use the following copyright material:

Mustapha Kamal Pasha, 'Introduction'
Copyright © 2003 Carfax Publishing. The Introduction draws from 'Fractured Worlds: Islam, Identity, and International Relations', which was originally published in *Global Society* 17(2), 2003. Reprinted with permission from Taylor & Francis Group.
Mustapha Kamal Pasha, 'Exception/Exceptionalism'
Copyright © 2009. This chapter was originally published as 'Global Exception and Islamic Exceptionalism', in *International Politics* 46(5), 2009. Reprinted with permission from Palgrave Macmillan.
Mustapha Kamal Pasha, 'Liberalism, Islam, and International Relations'
Copyright © 2006. This chapter was originally published in Branwen Gruffydd Jones, *Decolonizing International Relations*. New York: Rowman & Littlefield, 2006. Reprinted with permission from Rowman & Littlefield.
Mustapha Kamal Pasha, 'Human Security and Islam'
Copyright © 2007. This chapter was originally published as 'Human Security, Securitization, and Islam', in Giorgio Shani, Makato Sato and Mustapha Kamal Pasha, eds, *Protecting Human Security in a Post 9/11 World: Critical and Global Insights*. Basingstoke, UK: Palgrave Macmillan, 2007. Reprinted with permission from Palgrave Macmillan.
Mustapha Kamal Pasha, 'Islam and the Postsecular'
Copyright © 2012. This chapter was originally published in *The Review of International Studies* 38(5), 2012. Reprinted with permission from Cambridge University Press.

Mustapha Kamal Pasha, 'Globalization and Cultural Conflicts'

Copyright © 2006. This chapter was originally published as 'Globalization, Cultural Conflicts and Islamic Resurgence', in B.N. Ghosh and Hilal M. Guven, eds, *Globalization and the Third World: A Study of Negative Consequences*. Basingstoke, UK: Palgrave Macmillan, 2006. Reprinted with permission from Palgrave Macmillan.

Mustapha Kamal Pasha, 'Fate of Democracy'

Copyright © 2002. This chapter was originally published as 'Predatory Globalization and Democracy in the Islamic World', in *Annals of the American Academy of Political and Social Science* 581(1), 2002. Reprinted with permission from Sage Publishers.

Mustapha Kamal Pasha, 'Leadership in Challenging Times'

Copyright © 2011. This chapter was originally published as 'Global Leadership and the Islamic World: Crisis, Contention, and Challenge', in Stephen Gill, ed., *Global Crises and the Crisis of Global Leadership*. Cambridge: Cambridge University Press, 2011. Reprinted with permission from Cambridge University Press.

Mustapha Kamal Pasha, 'Critical IR and Islam'

Copyright © 2005. This chapter was originally published as 'Islam, "Soft" Orientalism, and Hegemony: A Gramscian Rereading', in *Critical Review of International Social and Political Philosophy* 8(4), 2005. Reprinted with permission from Taylor & Francis.

Mustapha Kamal Pasha, 'Postorientalism and Civilizational Discourse'

Copyright © 2007. This chapter was originally published as 'Civilizations, Post-orientalism, and Islam', in Martin Hall and Patrick Thaddeus Jackson, eds, *Civilizational Identity: The Production and Reproduction of 'Civilizations' in International Relations*. New York: Palgrave Macmillan USA, 2007. Reprinted with permission from Palgrave Macmillan USA.

Mustapha Kamal Pasha, 'Ibn Khaldun and World Order'

Copyright © 1997. This chapter was originally published in Stephen Gill and James H. Mittelman, eds, *Innovation and Transformation in International Studies*. Cambridge: Cambridge University Press, 1997.

INTRODUCTION

> The vanquished always want to imitate the victor in his distinctive mark(s), his occupation, and all his other conditions and customs.
>
> *(Ibn Khaldun,* The Muqaddimah*)*

In an unprecedented display of intellectual philanthropy, the cultural turn in international relations (IR) theory released new zones of engagement with other social worlds and their characteristic imaginings and impulses (Lapid and Kratochwil 1996; Mandaville 1999; Bleiker 2001). On an affirmative reading of this trend, the field was well poised to repudiate Eurocentric constrictions on its self-consciousness. In this improved climate, recognizing other cultural worlds, including Islam and the identities lurking behind that generic label, was not going to be too demanding after all. In a dramatic reversal, however, the optimism warranted by the reflexive tenor in recent conversations in IR and poignantly expressed in appeals to identity/ difference, culture, agency and contingency, appears to have been short lived, deflated by the latest countervailing political and cultural tendencies. On this reading, the reversal is linked to the aftermath of '9/11' and the surge in religiously coded violence in the Islamic cultural zones (ICZs) or Muslim-majority areas informed by transnational subjectivities loosely connecting varied Islamic societies around symbolic commonality, memory and historical experience. The term stresses the plurality of Islamic cultural experience, albeit distinguished by recognizable semiotic markers, without essentializing Islamic identity.

Shattering conciliatory overtures to other worlds and other words, the current climate makes dialogue with difference remarkably limpid, replaced by familiar binary tropes. Although this gloomy sentiment is shared unevenly, the inclination to defeat the political aims of openness in the present context cannot be readily dismissed. The recognition of difference is more conveniently linked to the sins of (relativist) multiculturalism and its reckless disregard for the more enduring features of Western exceptionalism (Huntington 1996; Fukuyama 1992). Conversely, the rising tide of illiberal, anti-Western or 'primitive' currents threatens progress, national security and, indeed, Western civilization itself. These are dark times for Islam, and therefore challenging times for the West. The worlds of Islam today appear menacing; Islam is a *problem of geopolitics*, not an object of cultural understanding. Attempts to recover the complexity, diversity or agency within the heterodox worlds of Islam, therefore, entail insurmountable hurdles. Yet, there are notable observers, like Nilüfer Göle, who see traces of optimism in this context:

> Islam, until now absent from globalization, becomes its active agent. Ironically, the interest in knowing and taming Islam increases the exchanges among different national publics and accelerates the creation of a transnational public sphere. Either interconnectivity between different national publics are intensified or new ones are launched.
>
> *(Göle 2002: 344)*

Unfortunately, Göle recycles the Eurocentric story of globalization. Recoiling to the safer haven of Western civilization, a project Shapiro aptly dubbed 'enclavization' (Shapiro 1999: 2), many influential interlocutors of Western power and thought (but also several erstwhile liberals, radicals and critical thinkers), have sought intellectual refuge in the Manichaean world of the 'West' and 'Islam'. The world of dialogue is severely fractured in the context of an unending 'war on terrorism' and dualism this climate has released. New worries are superimposed upon old ones, not least of them of a political nature in efforts to resume the conversation, especially a conversation based on mutual regard, parity or an ethos of pluralization (Connolly 1995; see also Dallmayr 2002). Rather, the inclination to tame Islam has been ascendant for some time now in large sections of the academy and the social world of Islam. This feature is evidenced in part by the belligerence directed at Muslims in a fast-proliferating cottage industry of experts in IR with direct linkage to the corridors of policy making and state power.

A more historicist reading of the times also yields a verdict of closure in IR, but for different reasons. The relative ease with which familiar tropes concerning Islam are deployed to produce familiar effects suggests more continuity than rupture, stressing the *historical* nature of prevailing consciousness. On this sobering view, perhaps the structure of Western IR is more durable, more resilient, and far less susceptible to alternative perspectives served either by culture, identity or difference, notwithstanding periodic pronouncements of the end of IR theory as we knew it, or its impending demise in its secure borders (Buzan and Little 2001). Only historical amnesia could warrant such belief. The manifest 'love of country' following the tragic events of 9/11 in the IR academy should be placed in context, the sturdiness of received knowledge structures recognized, and their link to statecraft, governmentality and hegemony revealed (Smith 2002a). This exercise may provide some clue to the apparently widening divide between the worlds of 'Islam' and the 'West' (Xing Li 2002).

The suspicion that the IR enterprise is a part of the political world, rather than simply its explanation, focuses our attention squarely in the direction of a more nuanced, historical awareness. Static predispositions to dramatic events become questionable (Calhoun et al. 2002). 'Theories of international relations', as Walker puts it, 'are more interesting as aspects of contemporary world politics that need to be explained than as explanations of contemporary world politics' (Walker 1993: 6). On this view, the insecurities released by the events of 11 September 2001 and the psychic and political closure these insecurities evoked (Zaretsky 2002; Mann 2001; Gray 2002; Benhabib 2002) in the *cultural* West can be read only against the otherness of Islam, one that is historically and culturally inscribed. The term 'cultural West' is consistent with several Islamicist accounts (see Shari'ati 1980), but also underscores the hegemonic effort to separate Islam and the West.

The ontological persistence of Islam as the generalized Other of Western modernity *and its socialized and materialized forms* is a durable obstacle to *glasnost* in IR. To the degree that this intuition is valid, appreciation of difference is merely a first step, secured by self-reflexivity. The claim that the limits of Western IR have a deeper source invites an acknowledgement of the *cultural underpinnings of theory* itself. Calls to 'bring back' culture and identity (Lapid and Kratochwil 1996), therefore, are misplaced. Culture and identity are already there.

The limits of (Western) imagination (including Western IR) lie in the discomforting story of its constitution, consistently imbricated in international practice wedded to power and hegemony (Smith 2002b; Shapiro 2002). A part of that practice is the use and abuse of the figure of Islam as the real and symbolic Other, now as the modular civilization, an equivalent, but mostly as an intimate enemy assuming benevolent, exotic or barbaric forms given the particular historical circumstance (Daniel 1960; Said 1978). With its stable, if uneasy, presence, the world of Islam marks the cultural boundaries of Europe/West, perhaps even helping to constitute them. An historical irony is evident here in the present atmosphere of ahistorical fetishization; the cultural interdependency between Islam and the West (and other zones of civilization) that secures modernity, is emptied out in place of Western provincialism (Connolly 1995). The narrative of a miraculously unhindered rise of the West – without dialogue, learning or mutual borrowing from distant others – returns as the principal feature of cultural hubris (Blaut 1993), with real political consequences.

Against this backdrop, misrecognition of Islam becomes more explicable, both in the image of a distant alterity, or a lowly imitation of the (Western) original. In the first instance, the strangeness of a differentiated faith reduces to singularity; in the second instance, it is placed at the outposts of modernity. On an alternative register, processes of modernization apparently reveal Durkheimian anomie or Freudian pathologies, turned into collective frenzy or barbaric excesses of desperation. Cultural pathologies induced by alien contact subordinate the political struggles within the worlds of Islam. Muslims seem invariably deficient or hostile (or both) to modernization. This sentiment is broadly shared, even amongst modernist Islamic scholars (see Tibi 1990, 2002). That a faith so vast, complex and differentiated in cultural, political, social or personal terms can be demonized as readily, gives the need for historical awareness greater salience and urgency. Western IR cannot escape the burdens of this history. The only consolation resides in the awareness that fractures within the IR enterprise persist; efforts to hegemonize difference may not be entirely successful. Yet it is the hegemonic story one must confront; it cannot simply be wished away with self-congratulatory appraisals, with neither reflexivity nor the surfeit of 'turns' within the discipline.

Islam and Western political imagination

Historical silence on difference lies at the heart of Western IR. The conceptual apparatus of Western IR is built around this silence. Reading this apparatus from the location of ICZs, silence allows the possibility to serve the *liberal-modernist imaginary* as universal reference, not merely within the borders of the *cultural* West, but on a global scale. Certain elements of this imaginary are noticeable for their relatively persistent quality; the idea of progress (modernization), the fiction of Robinson Crusoe (atomistic rational agency); territorially bounded self-enclosed identities (nation); self-referential law and formal rights (negative freedoms and exchange); juridical equality and political rights; and legitimacy (law), to name just a few. Occluded from view is the history of cultural encounters producing exclusions. Islam's Otherness is not natural; it is increasingly naturalized as the exteriority of Western essence. Provincially drawn, this *particular* essence appears as norm, materializing in notions of the ideal-typical wo/man, society, community, social relations, ends of life, movement, and temporality. The apparent incommensurability between the cultural worlds of Islam and the West is a result of a very slow process of differentiation between Self and Other, not simply a cultural, but a deeply political process. Once drawn, divergence is no longer horizontal, but vertical. Western norm, Islamic exception. While divergence is neither timeless nor transcendent, it now serves as the measure of the West's self-image, shaping the repertoire of imagined and real practice globally. The assumed presence/absence of elements of the liberal-modernist imaginary shapes Western encounters of the worlds of Islam.

A key plank of the liberal-modernist imaginary is the idea of the secular, vital to modernization and its socio-political projects. In the present climate, secular fundamentalism offers a perfect counterpart to religious fundamentalism. Religious attachments of any non-Western, but especially Islamic hue, confirm the cultural hierarchy between the West and its others. Forgotten in the frame is the presence of 'secular' impulses within Islam and theological impulses within (Western) secularism. Nor is there an appreciation of the historical presence of *secular* spaces in the ICZs, whether political, social or aesthetic (Lapidus 2002: esp. chapters 5–7). The religious/secular binary possesses the additional quality of homogenizing and consolidating cultural difference. Hence, Muslims harbour no proclivity towards subordinating their religious attachments to modernity, whilst the West struggles to secularize and modernize the Islamic world. Denying the solidifying grip of theological currents within its own liberal-modernist project, the Other's faith becomes the principal hurdle to forging a world without civilizational conflict. On the other side, theological currents within the Western liberal-modernist imaginary are neither inert nor archaic, but continue to furnish notions of subjective morality, salvation, work ethic, freedom and development.

Puritanical variants of the liberal-modernist imaginary draw well-demarcated lines between public and private zones, spaces in which sovereign individuality can be simultaneously unleashed and restrained. The formal place for religion must belong to the private sphere, whilst its real effects can be easily disbursed throughout the social body to the point of opaqueness. Religion thrives, but it must not be visible or audible in the public sphere. Religion's alleged banishment from public life then becomes the basis of political judgement, of evaluation (and indictment) of cultures and societies where this experiment is distorted or merely in its infancy. Politicized appearance of religious sentiments in other spatial worlds only confirms the suspicious presence of primordial leftovers or as 'return' (Lewis 1976). Suppressed in these representations is the restructuring of religion itself (Taylor 2007a), especially its transformation into *ideology*. This process is tied more to the institutional structure of modernity, including the expansion of the public sphere (for India, see Freitag 1996), than the return of religion. Insufficiently acknowledged in extant mappings of Islamic religious resurgence is the *new* idiom of enunciation. Islamicists (and their counterparts in other cultural contexts) communicate with/in modernity to reach the *masses* (Alinejad 2002).

The globalization of the liberal-modernist project further complicates the problem of salvaging an alternative vision within ICZs. Virtually everywhere, communities, polities and people live, work and think in words and worlds produced by the expansion of this project, not only the most ardent proponents in the geographically disbursed zones of economic, political and cultural power, but also its supposed detractors. Paradoxically, its hold on the imagination is most pervasive not only in the *cultural* West, but also *outside*, in the minds of state elites and managers in the Islamic and other non-Western cultural zones, often inspiring mega-projects with disastrous social and environmental effects (Nandy 1988; on technological fetishism in the context of Saudi Arabia, see Sardar 2002).

The binary construction of the social world within the liberal project relegates discordant expressions of modernity as modernity's absence or caricature. Alternatively, these manifestations may suggest the *effects of power* rather than the atavistic reverberations of separate civilizational or cultural worlds. Modernity has severely fractured Muslim societies and their 'alternative' cultural principles. One principal consequence of fracture materializes as infirmity of alternatives. The liberal-modernist project radically reshapes the dominant *syntax* and *grammar* for internal dialogue and contestation in the ICZs. In virtually all areas of the social and political field, entanglement with modernity *conditions* Muslim society: questions over the nature of political community; the structure of economy; ends of government; technological and economic progress; or relations with the outside world. As framing device, the liberal-modernist project shapes and reshapes the *actually existing* context in which alternative social and political projects can be visualized or realized. The limits to the political imagination are, therefore, extended to the alternatives themselves.

The liberal-modernist project rests upon a 'secular' vision to secure that project's principal aims. Despite its failures or feebleness, secular expectations continue to structure political economy, civil society and everyday life. The nation-state in the ICZs remains the principal container of collective societal projects, despite threatening challenges from within and without. Can the liberal-modernist political imagination exhaust the possibilities for politics, good life and social practice in the worlds of Islam? Part of the answer is already available in failures and persistent economic and political crises. The remainder of the answer may lie in understanding the complex challenges engendered by globalization of the liberal-modernist imaginary.

Commitment to the modernist vision for political elites remains firm, not only with those who 'represent' the many who are served least by that vision, but also the marginalized. The struggle to recover fragments of alternative futures and pasts, nonetheless, goes on unabated. This struggle can often assume bizarre, unpredictable, and especially violent forms, given the *modern* apparatuses and modalities of knowledge and power. Seeking an alternative register of enunciation, for some scholars Islam presents an alternative vision to Western modernity, an alternative 'Islamic modernity', underscoring its assumed specificity and cultural distance from the hegemonic narrative (Göle 2000). This vision stands in radical contrast to the liberal-modernist imaginary (Esposito 1983; Euben 1997), within an apparently unified framework sanctioned by the *Qur'an* (Holy Book), the *Hadith* (Sayings of the Prophet), or the *Sunnah* (the conduct of the Prophet or *Ijtihad* – interpretation). However, rival schools and tendencies extend the meaning of terms and traditions (Esposito 1998). The Islamic vision, now reduced in the international public sphere to a revival of a self-annihilating medieval worldview, assumes a multiplicity of contrasting interpretations and claims.

In basic ways, these alternatives depart from the dominant Western imagination with regard to relations between state and society, the individual and community, family life and work, the ends of life and beyond. For instance, without spirituality, the hegemony of scientific reason becomes contestable. Alternative notions can also be found in the deeper recesses of Western historical consciousness, but now reduced to subaltern voices, often fragmentary, and without political support (Nasr 1997). Materialism and its mobile manifestations in consumerism, cares of the self, and the fiction of the sovereign individual all receive reprobation in a more densely layered conception of human agency and purpose (Nasr 1975). The ethical impetus for structuring political community (Barazangi et al. 1996) lies in justice, not legality. Hospitality, civility and generalized reciprocity replace the exchange principle in the conduct of social relations. The human subject is nested and ordained with particular aims in very elaborate systems of philosophical and practical reason, linked to God, the living species and to nature (Nasr 2002; Ibn Khaldun 1958).

Built into these complex systems of ideas is an alternative notion of overlapping sovereignties in which human purpose, intentionality and social life are embedded in concentric spiritual *and* secular pursuits; in family, community, state, the *Ummah* (community of believers) and humanity. Not to be swallowed by the pursuit of happiness or reasons of state, both vertical and horizontal attachments bear moral and ethical content. The philosophical humility remitted by this alternative construction provides better codes of conduct, for interconnectedness and interdependence. It also implicitly underscores the need for an expanded inter-subjectivity. Despite its common representation as the total surrender of reason to the dictates of belief, a conception of overlapping sovereignties in Islamic thought recognizes contingency, dialogue and negotiation in demarcating moral and political boundaries (Ibn Khaldun 1958).

An appreciation of this alternative conception, however, depends upon an ability to transcend the reductionist cartography found in mainstream renderings of the Islamic conception of international relations in the binary construction *Dar al-Islam* (realm of Islam) and *Dar al-Harb* (realm of war) (Zaman 2002).

Thus, the imagined worlds in Islamic thought are quite alien from the secularly inspired vision that has guided modernization drives in the ICZs; they lie outside the dominant discourse of progress, often seen to interrupt its linear march. They are to be found in the struggles for more holistic frameworks of being and becoming, in expressions of hospitality and care for the needy or personal quests to secure a decent existence in a shrinking universe of piety. These worlds also collide with the imagined world of the extremist, the militant, the fundamentalist, whose will to power *conditions* piety, drastically circumscribing the compass of faith and the possibility to procure a virtuous life.

Fractured worlds

The worlds of Islam are fractured, yet dynamic, an instantiation of heterogeneity, difference and change, not the homogenized universe of ossified reason or practice. In sharp contrast to its representation as a unified, static world of believers, Islam provides shelter to a wide range of commitments, weak, strong and uncertain. On balance, Muslim identities are structured less by religion than social circumstance: locality, ethnicity, class, occupation or language. The *religious* component of their identity becomes more visible often in historical contexts where the zeal to institute secular modernity has been the strongest. The process of retrieving selves that appear threatened to the point of annihilation is highly differentiated. Political Islam is only a *part* of that process, not the process itself (Pasha and Samatar 1996).

The domineering presence of the postcolonial state and its projects, contra hegemonic representations, is the only constant in the ICZs. Unable to escape the strictures imposed by modern cartographies (Shapiro 1997), Muslims must negotiate competing claims of piety and material survival within worlds defined by technological and material progress called modernization. In this vein, Islam does not confront the West as much as it confronts the state in its midst, its secular failures and the brutality and repression those infirmities produce.

The failure of the modernizing state in the ICZs is not simply demonstrated in crises of governability, legitimation or economic performance – although these are important avenues of feebleness and discordance. The source of a deeper historical problem lies in the state's denial of its own political unconscious and its reliance upon instrumental rationality to address social questions. State elites and managers who preside over even ostensibly theocratic entities with religious fervour and commitment have tacitly accepted the institutional apparatus of modern statecraft.

The political imagination of modern statecraft is inscribed in the fabric of daily life, constraining, not liberating, ex-colonials in an elusive quest to seek parity with others who have 'left them behind' in material achievement. It is, thus, the secular notion of progress that reworks its way as an absence. The contradiction between the aspirations of the faithful and the available institutional apparatus for their articulation could not have been starker. Here lies the dilemma; the yardstick of material achievement necessitates the impulse to entertain alternative futures. Perhaps this is also the source of extremism, which serves today as the recognizable face of Islam in the economy of meaning and signs.

Contemporary expressions of religious zealotry and its political projects are inherently *modern*. They do not offer, despite claims by its partisans or sympathizers, a different conception of international relations, community or world order. The Manichaean impulse and the will to power that has driven Western cultural encounters with the 'Rest' is equally present in these presumably alternative sites of negotiation and contention. From the worship of brute force (Ray 1999) to an embrace of riches, one is less likely to find sanctuary in renunciation of power or ascetic withdrawal. Hence, neither Islamism nor Hindutva (and their modular cousins) are susceptible to the pre-modern sense of being and becoming. Celebration of alternative visions, therefore, can be a utopian exercise, fraught with more surprises and few certainties.

Conclusion

To the extent that the terms of political discourse either generated or in circulation in Western IR are hegemonic with universal appeal, in *practice* if not in theory, the aim of articulating *alternative* visions of international political space in the world of Islam is a cumbersome exercise. Perhaps the task is two-fold: to demonstrate the limits of extant political imagination and its materialization and *simultaneously* to recover lost fragments of visions within Islamic (and other) cultural zones. Recognition of the cultural trappings of Western IR is to further this move.

The more onerous undertaking, however, is a recovery of alternatives within the worlds of Islam, recognizing both the ascending hegemony of secular liberalism, now hitched to West-centred globalization, and declining state capacity in much of the ICZs (see Chapter 6). Under the new regimes of a global political economy, the scope for autonomous political action has been eroded further, ripening conditions for repression internally and capitulation externally (Pasha and Samatar 1996; Pasha 2000). In its current globalizing version, liberal secularism metamorphizes as the spirit of market theology, reinforced by 'new constitutionalism' (Gill 2002) and the battery of global governance. Key to this spirit is a repudiation (ironically of modernity's invention), namely, national space. ICZs are neither sequestered places to realize alternative collective aspirations nor unified entities to resist the enticements of a 'market civilization' (Gill 1995). Both social and life worlds are fractured. Faith appears to provide the sole effective element of coherence (Nasr 1975). Yet, survival strategies are often mistaken, as in many critical accounts of globalization, as resistance (Pasha 2000).

In a globalizing context, Muslims face a refurbished Protestant/Calvinist compromise as the *only* basis to cultivate democracy, development and modernity. Western political theory has long recognized three 'solutions' to the problem of religion: (1) the Protestant/Calvinist option where religious salvation metamorphizes into a worldly enterprise dedicated to God; (2) ascetic withdrawal; and (3) partition into separate zones of life (Benhabib 2002). Since the fateful events of 9/11, this alternative acquired the status of a new religion with many new converts. Evading questions of historical specificity, elective affinity, or ontology, the theology of liberal secularism reinforces the cultural fault lines that already exist within the ICZs. The 'additional' requirement of secularism to receive full political or cultural membership extends the wedge as *internal others* are further denied basic dignity and respect. Given durable inequalities in the ICZs, this process of *cultural* disenfranchisement deepens the divide, with the palpable effects such injuries often produce.

In this changed and changing context, *Islamic* alternatives can appear more deviant than ever before, now buried under the rhetoric of a cosmopolitan globalizing vernacular. The old dichotomy of civilized/barbarian returns, now dressed in fresh attire. Mere affirmation of the faith takes on the appearance of resistance to globalization, modernity or progress. Intensified secularization becomes the new crusade. The process has already been underway for a long time, but it now acquires global proportions in both scale and intensity. What spaces are then available for religious identities to be realized? With a past of mostly fractured relations between 'the West' and 'Islam', the workings of this logic are not entirely opaque.

Hence, recognition of the real character of these times is a necessary transitional step in accessing the meaning of negotiated alternatives in the ICZs, including the discovery of liberal *and* illiberal variants of those alternatives. This discovery may also help disrupt the dichotomous mentality that services extant knowledge systems, including Western IR. However, the pathways leading to discovery in the midst of dense fog may not be so easily accessible, or linear. The essays that follow seek to tackle the enormous difficulty of overcoming hegemonic thinking, including the fractured character of alternatives. The essays can be read as overlapping reflections on the problem of locating Islam within IR, but also as attempts to disrupt the self-evident verities of Western political imagination that continue to supply IR with frames of capturing Islamic alterity.

PART I
Islamic exceptionalism

1

EXCEPTION/EXCEPTIONALISM

In Islam, it is all different.

(Gellner 1981: 62)

Introduction

Conventional post-9/11 accounts of global distempers offer a remarkable sense of
déjà vu. The reappearance of old cartographies; the recovery of religious binaries;
reliance on familiar tropes of exclusion – all underscore the deeply recursive character
of the cultural encounter with Islam (Al-Azmeh 1996 [1993]: 161–184). From the
perspective of international relations (IR), these recursive patterns reveal the stubbornness of received categories inhabiting the modern imaginary and its source in
theologically coded Western metaphysics. More broadly, they illustrate the presence of serious impediments to transformation in the hegemonic apparatus of
imagining the international. Perhaps less obviously, they show the aporias of
moving understanding to terrains less hospitable to the settled problem of political
identity and culture embedded in Westphalian notions of space-time (Walker
2006a). In this vein, the greater the inclination to offer simplified world pictures of
heterodox social forces – flat world (Friedman 2005), Cosmopolis (Beck 2006), or
some other frame – the greater is the tendency to avoid prickly questions about the
cognitive hold of received conceptions (Walker 1993, 2009). The speed with
which dualisms have returned in the *jihad* against terror, only illustrates how firmly
the infrastructure of exclusions is entrenched in the collective imaginary; how the
Other is conceived and how easily public discourse can be usurped by those *terribles
simplificateurs* (Burckhardt 1955 [1889]: 220).

   A key feature of the intellectual temper in the current global political climate is
its simplicity. Commonplace utterances of an axial shift in the temper of world
politics following the collapse of the Twin Towers in New York and the attack on

the Pentagon swiftly merged into old axioms of the immutability of human nature and its dark contours legitimating imperial expeditions to fight Evil and to defend (Western) civilization (Ignatieff 2005). Familiar responses excavated from the armoury of imperial geography, colonizing mission or more religiously textured exorcisms against Evil typically accompany declarations of an epochal moment. The move from past verities to present formulae appears seamless (Cox 2004b). A crucial facet of hegemonic responses to the current political context is the alterity of Islam, neither localizable nor indeterminate – both deadly and menacing; a form of Otherness that is both distant and intimate. The Islamic cultural zones (ICZs) remain distant, *modernizing perhaps, but not modern.*

To contextualize, the 'Islamic Other' has been central to the formation of Western identity, as some scholars contend (Marr 2006; and Hurd 2003). On this view, despite centuries of contact with the West and its civilizing project, the ICZs have effectively failed to enter the cognitive and institutional zones of 'pure' modernity; in these regions modernity remains incomplete, distorted or mere imitation (Tibi 2002; Lewis 1988; Vatikiotis 1987). Conversely, Islam is remarkably intimate, as everything that needs to be known about it is already known. This sentiment structures orientalism, both as a corporate project and as an enabling frame (Said 1978). For the ideal-typical orientalist, the problem lies above all within the civilizational boundaries of a decadent, but modernity-resisting Islamic religion and the values and institutions associated with it. On the latter premise, there is nothing enigmatic or mysterious about Islam. Familiar tropes – patrimonialism, orientalist despotism, totalizing faith, resentment, envy, rage or patriarchy – provide a ready-made answer to any query. Taken together, the two interlinked frames – remoteness and intimacy – constitute *Islamic exceptionalism* (IE). To be certain, IE is not identical to orientalism, though it is heavily indebted to the latter. The core feature of IE is the notion of the *exceptional* character of Islam, either exoticized or demonized. Orientalism cannot do without either. Hence, it is not necessary to be an orientalist to portray the ICZs as exceptional in terms of assumed democratic deficit, technological retardation or general economic backwardness. Orientalism invariably rests on culturalist logic; IE can invoke political economy, sociological explanation or political analysis without relying on culture as the master variable to account for Islamic woes. The nucleus of IE is Islam's inassimilable difference.

Since the beginning of the 21st century, IE has attained the status of a hegemonic project (Gramsci 1971 [1891–1937]). Rather than merely serve as an inert frame of capturing Islam, in the growing climate of global paranoia and unease, IE furnishes new grounds for exclusions, enclosures, securitization and global exception (GE). The language of GE broadly encompasses a series of practices that produce zones of indistinction; the suspension of normalized rules of governance including international law; new border controls; profiling of populations; surveillance and the arbitrary abrogation of rights under the umbrella of state security.

GE also offers the material elements for a radical restructuring of the ICZs through the projects of secularization and democratization. These projects take the *exceptional* character of Islam as the explanatory axis, both in showing how difficult it is to realize them, but also stressing their necessity. Unlike the civilizing zeal of modernization, a survivalist mentality dictates these projects; the cultural and political domestication of assumed illiberal forces in the ICZs would ward off the threat of terror, violence or Armageddon. The exoticized worlds of Otherness available for display in dominant versions of orientalism tend to wane; the demonic aspects of Otherness take hold of the semiotic and discursive fields. In this context, the problem-solving gaze (Cox 1981) inherent to extant thinking on Islam is singularly transparent.

The aim of this chapter is to explore the field of vision generated by IE; to draw out any possible connections between IE and a presumed globalizing culture of exception; and more generally, to delineate how IE speaks to the limits of IR's engagement with the general political temper in the ICZs. It seeks to explore the nexus between GE and IE, stressing the need to situate GE as a recursive project with historical antecedents, to examine some constraints on the expansive reach of GE, but also to appreciate cultural mappings that nourish GE.

Globalizing exception

In sharp contrast to conventional responses, critical commentary sends a different and heterodox set of messages on the fate of the international, underscoring the contested nature of knowledge claims. Critical accounts question the assumption that theory stands apart from the world. It challenges the sovereign assurance that theory merely explains the world and plays no role in engendering it; these accounts reveal the frailty of positivist mappings nested in a fictitious distinction between value and fact: on a critical reading, the current constellation is inseparable from the enabling frameworks deployed to map it.

Critical commentary operates on two principal registers: reverberations of empire (in its various guises), and GE. In both instances, the invigoration of established modalities of new enclosures, borders and exclusions is apparent (Smith 2002a; Cox 2004a; Coward 2005). Hence, both the colonial present (Gregory 2004) as well as GE generate zones of cultural and political apartheid. Unlike previous claims of an inevitable clash of civilizations (Huntington 1996) – between Islam and the West – which appear vindicated to their proponents, critics of empire (Bhuta 2003) probe the underlying structure of the current Anglo-American design and its presumed neo-imperial ambitions. Implicit in critical discourses on empire is a rebuttal to those who advocate its indispensability, notwithstanding gestures of a kinder, gentler variant (Nye 2004), or support the project of an 'enlightened' imperialism (Lal 2004). On this view, apologists of 'enlightened' imperialism merely solicit new rationales for unilateralist intervention with facile and one-dimensional historical comparisons (Ferguson 2003). Empire's 'finer moments' erase the underside of a spectacularly destructive and violent epoch in human history. A stark example of this thinking is captured in Ferguson's self-affirming defence of empire:

To imagine the world without the Empire would be to expunge from the map the elegant boulevards of Williamsburg and old Philadelphia; to sweep into the sea the squat battlements of Port Royal, Jamaica; to return to the bush the glorious skyline of Sydney; to level the steamy seaside slum that is Freetown, Sierra Leone; to fill in the Big Hole at Kimberley; to demolish the mission at Kuruman; to send the town of Livingston hurtling over the Victoria Falls – which would of course revert to their original name of Mosioatunya. Without the British Empire, there would be no Calcutta; no Bombay; no Madras. Indians may rename them as many times as they like, but they remain cities founded and built by the British.

(Ferguson 2003, cited in Gregory 2004: 4–5)

Critics of received imperial commentary, by contrast, challenge triumphalist claims of the end of history (Fukuyama 1992), claims that justify without restraint or apology the return of Western imperialism under a new guise. Although enfeebled by the spectacle of global terrorism and suicide bombing, triumphalism has merely entered a momentary self-imposed state of hibernation without abandoning its faith in the (inevitable) march of Western Reason. The idea of civilizational superiority remains intact. Hence, Fukuyama reinforces his famous thesis:

We remain at the end of history because there is only one system that will continue to dominate world politics, that of the liberal-democratic west. This does not imply a world free from conflict, nor the disappearance of culture. But the struggle we face is not the clash of several distinct and equal cultures fighting amongst one another like the great powers of 19th-century Europe. The clash consists of a series of rearguard actions from societies whose traditional existence is indeed *threatened by modernisation*. The strength of the backlash reflects the severity of this threat. But time is on the side of modernity, and I see no lack of US will to prevail.

(Fukuyama 2001, emphasis added)

The discourse on GE is premised on the notion of 'the state of exception', an idea that has acquired common currency in discussions on the (political) constellation of our times. Although there are different permutations of the idea, Alain de Benoist offers a compelling description:

In a state of exception, a state finds itself abruptly confronted with an extreme peril, a mortal menace that it cannot face without having recourse to methods, which, following its own norms would be unjustifiable in normal times. The situation of urgency or the state of exception can be defined in other terms as the brutal occurrence of rare events or unpredictable situations, which, because of their menacing character, require immediate response with exceptional measures, such as restriction of liberties, martial law, state of siege, etc., considered as the only suitable responses to the situation.

(De Benoist 2007: 85)

A critique of liberalism in its originary state, the idea of the 'exception' speaks principally to highlight the paradoxes of sovereignty and the ambivalence inherent in the Western liberal political project, first noted by Carl Schmitt (2005 [1922], 1985 [1923]). Failing to reconcile the tension between normalcy and emergency, between law and executive decision, or between the claims of sovereign authority and (human) rights, the liberal order remains vulnerable to arbitrary rule or dictatorship. As de Benoist puts it, '[t]he state of exception is also important because it reveals the original non-normative character of the law. Moreover, it is not the law/right (*Recht*) which is suspended in the state of exception, but only the normative element of the law (*Gesetz*)' (De Benoist 2007: 86).

The language of 'exceptionalism' produces, on Walker's reading, 'renewed distinctions between the saved and the damned in the so-called war on terror and the privileging of security over liberty in contemporary articulations of sovereign authority and the authorization of sovereign authority' (Walker 2006a: 66). Exceptionalism presents a serious challenge to the liberal project:

> Construct the other as enemy, as absolutely alien or absolutely threatening, and the way is open to the declaration of exceptions that affirm the suspension of liberties and the authorization of absolute authority. To exceptionalize at the limit horizontally, at the border of a territorial jurisdiction, is to risk exceptions at the limit vertically where liberal democracy gives way before invocations of sovereign necessity, to the privileging of national security over all other values.
>
> *(Walker 2006a: 76)*

The question of whether a state of exception is inside or outside law remains a constant source of argumentation and controversy. The principal debate on this issue concerns Benjamin and Schmitt. 'While Schmitt attempts every time to reinscribe violence within a juridical context, Benjamin responds to this gesture by seeking every time to assure it – as pure violence – an existence outside the law' (Agamben 2005: 59; for a commentary on the political ontology of Schmitt, see Prozorov 2006; Dean 2006. Prozorov 2005 offers his own variant of the exception). More recently, however, the idea of the exception has become the central diagnostic tool to pinpoint the fragility of the Western liberal order, and in some instances, challenges its plausibility, as captured in Agamben's metaphor of the 'camp' (Agamben 1998), a condition where the exception becomes the rule. This sentiment echoes Benjamin's classic statement:

> The tradition of the oppressed teaches us that the 'state of exception' in which we live is the rule. We must attain to a concept of history that accords with this fact. Then we can clearly see that it is our task to bring about the real state of exception, and this will improve our position in the struggle against fascism.
>
> *(Benjamin, quoted in Agamben 2005: 57)*

With the decay in the Europeanized 'nomos of the earth', the world has entered a precarious epoch in human affairs (Schmitt 2003 [1950]; also see Odysseos and Petito 2007). Ultimately, the idea of the 'state of exception' underscores the impracticality of relegating the political to the normative. Commenting on this Schmittian theme, de Benoist writes:

> [For Schmitt] in suspending legal norms, the exception helps us to understand and appreciate the nature of the political, in the sense that it reveals to us the domain of the sovereign, meaning in this case the concrete capacity to make a decision in the face of an urgent or exceptional situation. The state of exception reveals both who is sovereign and also where sovereignty lies, in the very moment that it makes the decision appear (*Entscheidung*) in its 'absolute purity'. In such conditions, one can see that the politically sovereign instance does not coincide automatically with the state ... the suspension of legal norms in the case of the exception constitutes the ultimate manifestation of political sovereignty.
>
> *(De Benoist 2007: 86)*

Discussions of the 'state of exception' have been consistently linked to the so-called 'war on terror' (WOT), which supposedly institutionalized its permanency (Van Munster 2004). According to van Munster:

> The state of exception is the non-localisable foundation of a political order: the US as the sovereign of the global order ... [allows] the US to exempt itself from the (international) framework of law, demanding compliance by others ... this production of American sovereignty is paralleled by reducing the life of (some) individuals to the bare life of *homo sacer* (life that can be killed without punishment). In the war on terrorism, the production of bare life is mainly brought about by bureaucratic techniques of risk management and surveillance, which reduces human life to biographic risk profiles.
>
> *(Van Munster 2004: 141)*

Liberated from the burdens of international legality, the argument goes, the WOT cracked open the Westphalian settlement with its assumed deference for either norm or law. Unlike most states of emergency that seek temporal finitude, the WOT offered no such promises, hence its permanent installation. However, as Agamben notes, 'while ignoring international law externally and producing a permanent state of exception internally', sovereign authorization 'still claims to be applying the law' (Agamben 2005: 87).

The idea of GE presents an alternative reading of our times, gesturing towards the arrival of a new species of transnational peril unprecedented in content or scope. Insecurity appears unhinged from received vectors of traditional military power, now produced through asymmetrical geometries of networks, flows and mobile agency. A de-territorialized canvass of danger compels and necessitates enclosures on a global scale, superseding national borders. 'At the same time', Bigo suggests, 'it (globalisation) makes obsolete the conventional distinction between the constellation of war, defence, international order and strategy, and another constellation of crime, internal security, public order and police investigations' (Bigo 2006: 5). According to Bigo:

> it is this convergence of defence and internal security into interconnected networks, or into a 'field' of professionals of management of unease that lies at the heart of the transformations concerning global policing.
>
> *(Bigo 2006: 6)*

Bigo challenges the notion of the advent of a securitized globalized world or the arrival of an empire:

> Even if we witness illiberal practices, and even if the temptation to use the argument of an exceptional moment correlated with the advent of transnational political violence of clandestine organisations, in order to justify violation of basic human rights and the extension of surveillance is very strong, we are still in liberal regimes.
>
> *(Bigo 2006: 6)*

The discourse on GE recognizes that a post-Westphalian constellation now reinscribes security at the global level, producing new lines of demarcation between insiders and outsiders. At the same time, the reliance on old strategies of combating the enemy – as the twin wars in Afghanistan and Iraq generally demonstrated – has not diminished. Despite the easy circulation of the notion that the conventional divide between (domestic) political community and (external) anarchy has been redrawn, national imaginaries of (in)security persist. Within these imaginaries, however, some curious innovations to manage collective anxieties seem to be emerging to respond to the new challenges. A key implication of recent trends in securitization is the shift in the concept of security, 'reduced to technologies of surveillance, extraction of information, coercion acting against societal and state vulnerabilities'. In this frame, 'security is disconnected from human, legal and social guarantees and protection of individuals' (Bigo 2006: 8).

The above discussion can be effectively condensed in taking the exception as:

> [T]hat domain within jurisprudence in which decision-making 'cannot be subsumed' ... by existing norms. It is that space in which such norms are held open to suspension or transformation, and where programs of norm-implementation and norm-compliance cease to govern action and decision-making. Accordingly, the exception is synonymous with the attempt to exercise momentarily decisive agency or, as Schmitt puts it, 'principally unlimited authority'.
>
> *(Johns 2005: 619)*

The theme of GE is both diagnostic and disturbing. In the current global political climate, it suggests that the 'state of exception' has transcended national confines to acquire a globalized character. Instantiated by an undeclared global state of emergency, GE disrupts and blurs the lines between international law and unilateral decision, undermining the foundations of the Westphalian settlement and the principle of territorially bounded sovereignty. GE is especially alarming as it removes any restraints – moral or legal – over the exercise of arbitrary power, including military power. As Žižek (2006) notes:

> 9 November 1989, announced the 'Happy Nineties' – the dream of fine de l'histoire foretold by Francis Fukuyama. September 11 is the great symbol of the end of utopia – a return to real history. The Happy Nineties of Clinton have long gone. We are in a new era with new walls being built – between Israel and Palestine, around the European Union, on the Mexican/US border, and between Spain and Morocco. The Berlin Wall is being substituted with new ones. We are in an era of new forms of Apartheid and 'legal' torture.

A similar sentiment is shared by Patman (2006), and recent invasions (Afghanistan and Iraq) have been examined in this light (Gregory 2004). However, whether GE fulfils the Schmittian criteria is questionable. As de Benoist proposes:

> The measures taken by the American government following the attacks of 9/11 are therefore not without precedent. However, they also have particular characteristics, which distance them radically from the Schmittian 'model'. In declaring a war, seemingly without end, in order to confront a danger – global terrorism – the American authorities seem to be leaning towards an institutionalization of these exceptional measures. The state of exception ceases therefore to be an exception, and henceforth becomes permanent.
>
> *(De Benoist 2007: 88)*

In general, the idea of the state of exception is characterized by the 'rhetoric of exclusion' and 'fear of foreigners' with growing securitization of migration. Often, these developments have produced institutional and societal effects. As Huysmans and Buonfino note, a major consequence of the 'state of exception' is an emergent 'politics of exception' and 'politics of unease'. 'Politics of exception focuses on the state of threat to the life of a nation, the legitimacy of exceptional policies justified by the threat and the ensuing trade-off between security and liberty that it produces.' By contrast, 'politics of unease addresses insecurities in a less pronounced way. It does not focus on existential threats to the territorial and functional integrity of the state but connects a wide variety of different policy areas such as welfare provisions[,] counterterrorism and illegal immigration through the discussion of policing technologies' (Huysmans and Buonfino 2008: 767).

GE underscores the central point that the current global political climate replaces assumed notions of Kantian hospitality; multiculturalism – the liberal management of internal difference – with xenophobia. Increasingly, the figure of the Muslim 'immigrant' takes on a menacing presence, a potential threat to ontological security and civilizational survival. Ideas of graded citizenship are not too far behind.

A striking feature of GE is the potential rupture between sovereignty and territory. Exceptions surpass received mappings of sovereign authority. Walker captures this thought quite succinctly:

> When exceptions were conventionally declared at the limits of the sovereign state, qualified by the ordering capacities of a system of sovereign states, enabled by a theory of history marking the modernity of sovereign authorities and inhabited by resistance to imperial and theological order, exceptions are now enacted in ways that exceed official cartographies of sovereign authorization.
>
> *(Walker 2006a: 65)*

This rupture has wide-ranging implications for extant conceptions of ordering political life. The comforting and familiar aspirations for sovereign authorization, within hermetically sealed national spaces, succumb to undisclosed horizons and perils. Some of the most ambitious, yet ambiguous, claims about the arrival of a post-Westphalian world seek answers to questions that arise from an assumed rupture between sovereignty and space without working out the question of the political: the forging of *new* political identities and contestations surrounding it.

For some scholars, the concept of 'the state of exception' is wedded to processes of depoliticization, but more basically it shows the fruitfulness of the terminology to understand politics. As Huysmans notes, 'structuring politics around exceptionalist readings of political power tends to politically neutralize the societal as a realm of multi-faceted, historically structured political mediations and mobilizations' (Huysmans 2008: 166). Couched in this critique is the continued relevance of political struggle as an arbiter of social orders as well as the impossibility of severing the nexus between power and resistance.

The idea of a ubiquitous state of exception also lends itself to contestation and critique on grounds of its ahistorical deployment as well as the denial of the role of culture in the constitution of exclusions. In the first case, discourses on the state of the exception rarely invoke the recursive quality of threat management emanating from the colonial experience (Gregory 2004). The dual face of power in the colony, one that takes the state of exception as a norm *for* the natives, defies the presumed newness of the concept. Remarkably absent in Agamben's reconstructed history of the state of exception, for instance, the colony mysteriously vanishes from the account. In his otherwise brilliant exegesis of the state of exception, Agamben (2005) avoids any discussion of the state of emergency in the European colonies.

Clearly, 9/11 appears as a decisive moment in altering the line-posts of rule. However, an appreciation of the colonial context in which many of the non-European areas have found themselves shows the ever-presence of the exception. Despite the inextricable link between the 'state of exception' and a 'liberal society' – a link that might nullify a transhistorical deployment of the concept – the colony has been *the* principal source for generating the model of exceptionalism and exporting it to the metropolis. According to Williams (2003: 325), the 'colonial laboratory' (as in Ireland's case), served 'as a state of permanent exception for which it was deemed necessary', in the words of Hardt and Negri,

> to grant the intervening authority the capacity to define, every time in an exceptional way, the demands of intervention and the capacity to set in motion the forces and instruments that in various ways [could] be applied to the diversity and plurality of the arrangements of crisis.
>
> *(Hardt and Negri 2000: 28)*

The question of (cultural) difference further qualifies how GE would work, an aspect of the concept not fully explicated in extant discussions. While the resurgence of a religious idiom – of the saved and the damned – significantly textures the GE, the full import of the redeployment of religious cartographies has remained ambiguous. Can the current exclusionary global constellation emerge and cohere without reliance on these cartographies? The 'new enclosures' and new justifications for 'privileging of security over liberty' (Walker 2006a: 66) have been inseparable from classification, surveillance and targeting of specific populations with assumed cultural/religious attachments. In the current climate of unease, the particular cultural/ religious make-up of Muslims cannot be divorced from sovereign authorizations.

Both territorialized and de-territorialized, exclusionary practices tend to rely on presumed cultural (or religious) discriminations. However, as the discussion in the subsequent section proposes, the deterritorialization of the exception (captured in the idea of GE) also reworks IE on registers no longer confined to 'official carto-graphies of sovereign authorization' (Walker 2006a: 65). In turn, the deterritor-ialization of Islamic political projects lends greater credence to GE, presenting them as a singular, homogenized face of rejection.

Revisiting Islamic exceptionalism

> But there does seem to be something about Islam, or at least the fundamentalist versions of Islam that have been dominant in recent years, that makes Muslim societies particularly resistant to modernity.
>
> *(Fukuyama 2001)*

The theme of exceptionalism is neither novel nor remarkable. More generally, exceptionalism has been a preferred frame to account for uniqueness or deviance, both positive and negative. On a positive register, the story of the rise of the West has been portrayed as a unique historical experience afforded by the Enlightenment or particular socio-political settlements, including the emergence of a Protestant ethic, reason, science or secularism (McNeill 1963; Hall 1985; Gellner 1994). The figure of Max Weber is pivotal in advancing the thesis of Western exceptionalism drawn from his comparative historical sociology and study of different religious traditions (Turner 1974). A core feature of this thesis is to recognize modernity, not as an intercivilizational project implicating varied cultural influences, but exclusively as an endogenous Western affair. The secularizing character of the West is particularly important in this design, producing the necessary ingredients of the institutional structure of modernity. In Weberian understandings, what distinguishes Islam – not only in reference to Christianity, but also the 'Sinic' and 'Indian' worlds – is to be 'markedly secularization-resistant' (Gellner 1992: 6). The kernel of IE becomes immediately apparent. However, to metamorphize into a full-blown explanation of Islamic pathologies, IE ransacks the archive of orientalism, albeit remaining vigilant to the hazards of cultural relativism; it must reflexively deploy the comparative method to establish difference. On a comparative reading, then:

> [t]wo primary categories for apprehension of things Islamic – unreason and servitude – posit Islam as a creature in diremption, as the unlikely coexistence of sheer animality on the one hand, and an abstract, hence forever forced and repressive, principle of order on the other. Nothing mediates the relation between the war of all against all on the one hand, and the Leviathan on the other; nothing mediates God and the world; one of them only is triumphant at a given moment. Civil society, the realm where individual needs are rationally coordinated, and that which brings forth the state, is unthinkable.
>
> *(Al-Azmeh 1996: 169)*

In the current political climate, IE serves as a consolidating gaze, both to explain assumed pathologies in the ICZs as well as to highlight the enormous difficulty, if not implausibility, of their assimilation into the 'civilized world'. Nowhere are the constrictions of IE more pronounced than in relation to explaining political projects in the ICZs. With a heightened emphasis on religion, not as a discursive formation – fluid and heterodox – but as an unchanging and homogenized assemblage of dogmas and practices, IE forecloses the pathway to understanding political contestation in the ICZs and its wider social context. Politics, on this reading, merely mirrors religion; it can never be the determinant shaping social life in the ICZs.

An alternative viewing of IE, however, further exposes the main planks of what are essentially culturally embedded theological foundations of Western IR, than mere misrecognition of Islam. The largely Christianized view of the process of secularization is a case in point (Asad 2003). Drawn from reading of the Protestant settlement, the character and place of religion in Muslim society appears both distinctive and pivotal. The ideal-typical story of the Calvinist compromise filters judgement of presumed elective affinities between faith and rationalizing impulses, their presence in Western quarters and absence in the ICZs. No account of secularization is complete without the centrality of the Western Ideal. This sentiment underscores a larger point: interrogations of the ICZs tend to shed less on their political dynamics than reveal the limits of hegemonic wellsprings of Western political imagination.

Those limits appear in two related forms: civilizational hierarchy and 'Universal Reference'. In the first instance, the self-congratulatory cult of civilizational superiority (Connolly 1998) assumed in Western IR, is effectively mobilized to combat the 'new barbarians' (Al-Azmeh 2001). Popular accounts of 'Islamic terror' congeal this sentiment. An obvious effect of this structuring process is the denial of co-evalness to Islamic Otherness. The strategy to subsume heterodox worlds in the ICZs under the capacious tent of 'Islamic terror' is not coincidental. Rather, it reveals fixed patterns of capturing Islam and its resistance to the liberating horizons of West-driven modernity (Daniel 1960). Related to civilizational hierarchy and serving as its premise, is the idea of 'Universal Reference' (Bourricaud 1985). No hubris is necessary here to feed the political unconscious of IR. The Western story of the emergence of the 'international' serves as the master copy in mappings of the modern world. Ideas of the state, sovereignty, secularism, nationalism, citizenship, civil society – virtually all the political categories of extant imagination – are drawn from the European experience, with negligible or non-existent contact with Europe's others and their organizing logics. The ICZs are interrogated on these terms, only with a nominal reference to Muslim aspirations, imaginings and deficiencies. A key justification for this received practice is the reliance on what can be termed as 'originary' logic, the notion that modular political forms *first* developed in Europe, and only later diffused through the expansion of international society. The idea of Universal Reference rationalizes key elements of hegemonic thinking: the primacy of modernity in shaping the world; the centrality of *modern* social forms in conditioning political imagination and practice; and the difficulty of sustaining alternatives without serious engagement with *modern* discursive and semiotic worlds.

Despite its attractions, however, there are obvious difficulties in sustaining 'originary' logic. An implicit corollary of this logic is the erasure of the political world outside the West, either as a subject of IR or as a significant accomplice in shaping modernity. Through the entire passage of the rise of the West, the non-Western world remains inconsequential. In relation to the ICZs, especially, no significant innovation in political practice is acknowledged. In this familiar story, culture replaces politics as the defining feature of the ICZs. Indeed, if politics does enter the stage, it dons the garb of oriental despotism or its functional equivalent. A second problem lies with the hermetic assumption, one that disallows the presence of any meaningful contact between cultures and societies *before* the advent of colonialism. Cultural exchange, if recognized, would decidedly unsettle the naturalized world of West-centred transformation (or modernity). It would also endanger the radical possibility of entertaining alternative sources for the origination and consolidation of modernity.

A third source of disquiet springs from an appreciation of the productive capacities of cultural adaptation, but also mimicry and translation (Bhabha 1994). Without embracing the notion of functional equivalence, one that would at least nominally accord similar tasks to disparate cultural units in the name of universalism, the historical experience of cultural transitions compellingly suggests heterogeneity, not homogenization. Built into the recognition of heterogeneity is a repudiation of a linear curve that links distinct societies, or takes one as the source of accounting deviance in others.

The burden of the above reservations to the hegemonic forms for recognizing the ICZs is colossal. In the first instance, tales of civilizational supremacy would then confront temporality or the transitional character of human institutions, with an acknowledgement of finitude. The denial of the political to other worlds in favour of culture forecloses the option of recognizing elements that drive those worlds: struggles over the limits of action; questions of justice/injustice or the issue of authority in general. In addition, heterogeneity would allow an appreciation of alternative sources of authority or the establishment of lines of inclusion/exclusion, as well as an understanding of apparent repudiations of Europeanized notions of politics, *not* modernity.

The rejection of a linear storyline would present new possibilities to better comprehend the attractions of particular versions of ethics, justice, rule and authority in place of the assumed certitude of a cultural lag that prevents societies from attaining freedom, democracy or wealth. This is not to privilege cultural relativism, but to acknowledge the limits of a cultural project that projects itself as the Universal Reference.

The problematic location of the ICZs in established IR cartographies is well known. Post-orientalist critique highlights the imbrication of knowledge with power: it is virtually impossible to find neutral contexts for the production and spread of wisdom about Islamic Otherness. Yet, strategies to deal with this Otherness are heterodox, with the management of difference now nourishing countless cottage industries. In the corridors of power, in particular, to engage with Islam is principally to offer better *management* options.

The issue is not merely one of historical prejudice, but the problem of assumed Muslim resistance to the expansion of international society, its norms and practices. It also concerns the assumption of Islamic resistance to the expansion of international society, despite decades of development and modernization. On this reading, 'Muslim rage' (Lewis 1990) is a violent expression on the self-same spectrum of rejection. Strategies to manage Islam emanate from the unease that the task of assimilating Muslims is either too hard or unworkable. The failed promise of eventual membership realized through development and modernization gives the present constellation the character of an incomplete project.

Before interrogating the nexus between IE and GE, it might be fruitful to reconstruct some of the key elements of IE in the current global environment of unease. Three interlocking themes appear to structure the discussion: (1) the recurrent image of Islamic Otherness; (2) a terrain of Otherness that is outside modernity or precariously situated at modernity's edges – captured in strategies of spatio-temporal distancing; and (3) the domestication of Islam.

The first theme draws and refurbishes the repertoire of orientalism. Recovering Islam's 'essential' qualities in the area of belief, character, psychic state or behaviour (and relations between and among these elements) allows commentators to generalize about Islam and its cultural and political projects. Hence, the assumed rigidity of Islamic belief provides an explanation of resistance to reason or science. This sentiment is not restricted to Western commentators on Islam, but is shared by Islamic modernists (Tibi 2002; and Hoodbhoy 1991). It is also relates to the notion of Islam's failure to evolve through history (Lewis 2002). In turn, resentment or envy offers roadmaps to investigate Islamic encounters with the West. As Pipes argues in his polemical book, militant Islam has less to do with economics and more to do with Muslim frustration and the question of identity (Pipes 2003). Devji (2005) offers an alternative, if equally orientalist, account. The psychic state of Muslims is a favourite object of scrutiny, giving clues to Islamic self-destructiveness and collective self-mutilation or anomic behaviour, a view challenged by Euben (2002b). The principal cumulative effect of these accounts is that they suppress recognition of the political and its relation to Islamic subjectivities.

The precarious location of Islam in relation to modernity presents familiar pathways. On modernity's highway, the ICZs are laggards. The story of progress tying the various knots in modernization claims is an unhappy one for the ICZs: Islam cannot fully modernize. However, this is a story not of absence, but incompletion, one stressing deficiency. It is also a tragic story, since the end is already foretold. On this hegemonic narrative, the ICZs are simultaneously timeless and historicist, trapped in their own historical imagination drawn from an unchanging belief system.

The phantasmal modern and global exception

> All significant concepts of the modern theory of the state are secularized theological concepts not only because of their historical development – in which they were transformed from theology to the theory of the state, whereby, for example, the omni-potent God became the omnipotent lawgiver – but also because of their systematic structure, the recognition of which is necessary for a sociological consideration of these concepts. The exception [*Ausnahmezustand*] in jurisprudence is analogous to the miracle in theology.
>
> *(Schmitt 2005 [1922]: 6)*

As noted, commentaries on Islam consistently take Western modernity as the 'Universal Reference' (Bourricaud 1985). In discussions of democracy, civil society, gender relations, development, science or culture, the standard theme is the exceptionalism of Islam. The common assumption in these accounts, however, is not entirely rigid, stretching from the notion of Islam's incompatibility with mod-ernity to the idea of a time lag in realizing modernity's promise. Multiple inter-mediate positions on the relation between the two traverse the discursive field. In the first version, Islam and modernity are based on opposing logics, one sanctifying faith, the other reason; the former privileging community, the latter the individual; Islam as a totalizing system with no differentiation; modernity inconceivable with-out differential spheres of human action. In sum, an elaborate inventory of binary universals divides the two worlds.

On the obverse side, the notion of incompatibility between Islam and modernity is contested. However, several roadblocks are introduced that produce a similar effect. These barriers are temporal in nature. Over time and proper social engineering, the ICZs can attain full membership into international society. These barriers are differentially distributed across the spatial universe of Islam: greater compatibility to modernity in the non-Arab ICZs compared to the stultifying cultural worlds of the Arabs. A typical example of this distinction can be found in the special forum on democracy in the Middle East in a leading journal (see especially contributions by Ghalioun 2004; Lakoff 2004; and Stepan and Robertson 2004), or in an earlier formulation (Kedourie 1992). What begins as a sociological argument metamorphizes into a *culturalist* argument, stressing the particularism of the Arab world. The initial opening to a historicist reading of the relation between Islam and modernity returns to the verity of warmed-up cultural essentialism served with orientalist condiments.

Paradoxically, the figure of modernity remains a mere phantasm, invading the social field with impunity without showing its complete face. The ICZs are over-determined by Islam. In the balance between the two, the explanation of Islamic distress rests mainly with religion. Modernizing hypotheses face a similar problem: the resistance to modernity comes primarily from faith. The terms of discourse are set by modernity, but only superficially; the source of all predicaments lies with Islam. One instance of the phantasmal quality of modernity is the classification of Islam into various tendencies, each tendency drawn in relation to modernity. A classic statement in this regard is presented by Voll (1982), a leading scholar of Islam in his notion of 'styles of action', which all relate to Islam's relation to Western modernity. The world of Islam remains an inhospitable stage on which modernity can merely cast phantasmal presence.

The field of vision harbouring IE allows little room for the counter-hypothesis that the ICZs are *constitutive of* political modernity. Even if the historical claim that modernity owes few debts to the ICZs, a claim that bears scant historical veracity, it merits scrutiny that the driving logic in the ICZs could be the shape of the political and, to a lesser extent, religion. The institutional matrix in the ICZs is *modern*, not in the sense of developed or developing, but as the condition of possibility produced in an historically embedded international society. Alternatively, the *outside* of the ICZs is not the West, but their separate and collective sense of the future; the West is deeply woven into the fabric of the ICZs (as can be said about Islam's integral presence in the West), despite Occidental claims of radical alterity or orientalist hubris. The lines of demarcation are arbitrary, above all, *political*; neither historical nor cultural. Exclusionary strategies seek culturalist foundations to establish difference.

Cultural differences are not unreal. Yet, where does one draw the line between collectivities, civilizations? The received strategy in IE is to avoid the question, preferring the rhetorical advantage gained with silence. Reliance on radical and inassimilable difference is a vital part of the political, the contestation over inclusions and exclusions. The missing factor here is obviously the figure of modernity in its relation to the ICZs, which remains phantasmal.

IE treats modernity as an outside, Western. Built into this frame is the temporal distance (Fabian 1983) separating the West and the ICZs, notwithstanding the unified plane of international society, or global political economy. The paradox lies in the inability to reconcile the diachronic register of progress with the synchronicity of international society. One solution to this paradox is to build a dual carriageway of development, which allows some entities to move at a different (faster) pace than their slower counterparts do. The story of development theory can be written on these terms. Alternatively, the solution lies in assigning fixity, with the expectation of potential trouble this may produce: resentment, anomie, violence and terror. The latter appears to be the principal inference IE draws.

Both solutions misrecognize the universal, if uneven, character of the global modern. The presumed effects of lagging behind are not about resentment – which certainly has a place even in the seemingly more advanced sectors of international society – but *closure*. An unrecognized aspect of political distempers in the ICZs is the growing awareness of closure, the possibility or certainty of being locked out. Established imaginaries conflate the future with the West: the common aspiration in humanity to emulate its experience, achievement and rewards. Alternatively, it is a *modern* aspiration to produce alternative futures, ones that are not trapped in fixity and repetition. On this score, the appeals of *political* variants of Islam are patently modern.

In the current global setting, the failure of IE to recognize the ubiquitous presence of the modern in the ICZs takes the form of new projects to change their cultural character in the form of secularization, promotion of procedural democracy, with due sensitivity to guarding the boundaries of a fortified West. In the first instance, secularization drives take the Calvinist settlement as a prototype, misrecognizing either the functional or substantive character of faith in the ICZs – not merely as a totalizing order but heavily textured by its institutional instantiations and performative aspects. The project to democratize the ICZs, in turn, fails to acknowledge the centrality of the historical appeal of notions of justice and fairness in Muslim society. A one-dimensional spotlight on building procedural democracy in the ICZs cannot easily displace the grip of those notions.

Several visible lines of contact emerge between IE and GE. In the first instance, IE can release the state of exception from the scaffold of sovereign Muslim spaces and acquire global presence. Unhinged from territory, but embodied, Islamic otherness invites exclusions at points of circulation, not fixity. Recent practices to restrict, monitor or control Islamic otherness tend to confirm the shifting lines of insecurity and securitization. Borders are not where they used to be (Balibar 2002). Otherness carries with it the constant risk of being excluded. Embodied, otherness can remain despatialized.

Second, projects to transform the ICZs collide with the mobility of a self-subsistent Islamic otherness. Unbounded, the mobile figure of Islamic otherness no longer lends itself to sovereign civilizational management within sequestered national boundaries. Inherently embedded in fixed cartographies, projects of democratization or secularization, for instance, appear meaningless in contexts of deterritorialization. The latent failure to tame Islamic otherness is likely to produce a global culture of unease and attendant rationales to globalize exclusion. The latter (GE) would be an impossible undertaking, but the former (politics of unease) acquires a distinct presence.

Paradoxically, GE can reinforce movements towards a deterritorialized, if defensive, Islamic self-awareness as a new form of resistance. The task of challenging a global state of siege and lifting the embargo on borderless borders engenders despatialized identities; it can also spark reckless and violent schemes designed to undo the effects of GE. Heterodox projects to connect distinct points in the ICZs become explicable on these registers, schemes to forge both communities of belonging and rejection. Translocal, these communities further embolden the claims of IE and rationalize GE.

In short, there are no easy or self-evident pathways connecting IE to GE. IE summons a wide variety of justifications and rationalizations. However, there are also insurmountable hurdles to globalize the 'state of exception' through established strategies of sovereign authorization. Available ideological accoutrements offer hints of overcoming some of these hurdles, but also the potential to incite the need for reproducing old imaginaries. In turn, rationalizations for GE strengthen the claims of Islamicist rejection. Drawn from the latter's own variant of IE in which a totalizing faith offers a comprehensive solution to all the ills of West-driven *Jahilliya* (ignorance) (Qutb 1990 [1964]), attempts to globalize the state of exception only confirm the separateness of Islamic Otherness.

Conclusion

Extant commentary is symptomatic of bigger disorders in mapping the ICZs and their location in the political imaginary. Yet, the issue is not merely one of ideology or a question of misrecognition. The over-simplifying reach of these accounts concerning Islam may not be readily transparent once they enter spaces of common sense. Once naturalized, these narratives spurn complexity in favour of *simplificateurs*. More sober accounts offer alternative possibilities, but they also suffer from similar ailments, notably 'the problem of difference' and in the present instance 'the problem of Islam'. A central feature of that problem is the difficulty of eschewing implicit strategies of erasure or assimilation. The global culture of unease has contributed immensely to the enlargement of that problem despite (or because of) elaborate strategies to appropriate Islam. The strength of these strategies lies in the convenience with which hegemonic understandings recoil into policy and practice. With massive expenditures of intellectual energy now devoted to devising presumably new ways of capturing the psychic and cognitive worlds of Islam, the tacit knowledge that informs understanding is neither politically irrelevant nor purely a passing phase. Ideas are not mere representations, but materially constitutive of the social world. The scopic regimes (Jay 1988) of appropriating the ICZs are durable; they also *condition* both the form and content of the relational flow towards those zones and towards peoples inhabiting them. With sizeable populations of Muslims living in the Western zones, the effects of these scopic regimes acquire immediacy and greater political salience. *The Islamic world is not somewhere else.*

Scopic regimes (see Chapter 9) can be self-reproducing and relatively autonomous from facticity. The naturalization of particular truths as universals allows frames of appropriation to endure. As postcolonial critique has suggested in the context of orientalism, the imagined worlds of Otherness are not fictitious, but real. The act of naming ensures that specific descriptions circulate – familiar binaries and received distinctions. This is made possible by power: the power to name, discriminate. Unsurprisingly, hegemonic classifications between 'good' and 'bad' Muslims, as one example, arise out of these given heuristics (Mamdani 2004; policy recommendations follow Friedman 2002).

IE legitimizes recent cognitive mappings of Islam and strategies of its political and cultural domestication. The specificity of Islam as a 'secularization-resistant' force or as an atavistic anti-modern global adversary with totalizing aspirations directly feeds into projects to alter the cultural face of the ICZs. These projects merge and consolidate into a unified scopic regime of IE. Seemingly, there are softer and harder variants of IE, defined by their respective colouring with orientalism. Historical and sociological analyses can often promise alternatives to IE. Closer scrutiny, however, suggests otherwise: to the degree that religion is perceived as *the* distinctive marker of variance in the social and political experience of the living worlds in the ICZs, the grip of IE can be loosened. Rather, if the condition of modernity, alongside its apparatuses – both real and symbolic – is placed in a determinate role, accounting for practice, new openings for capturing the career of the political in the ICZs may become more likely. That possibility appears closed in the climate afforded by GE.

A key implication of the preceding discussion hints at the necessity of avoiding the temptation of abstracting the GE without its particularized instantiations, both in abetting exclusionary practices, but also limiting its scope to specific populations with distinct and recognizable marks of Otherness. Paradoxically, in seeking to conquer a nebulous world of globality, exceptionalism rests heavily on reinforcing IE. The current global mood concerning Islam and its borderless scope can be read on these terms.

2

LIBERALISM, ISLAM, AND INTERNATIONAL RELATIONS

> Each universal ideological notion is always hegemonized by some particular content which colours its very universality and accounts for its efficiency.
>
> *(Žižek 1997: 28)*

The last two decades of the 20th century saw an invigorating process of contestation, critique and construction of alternatives within the field of international relations (IR). With the arrival of a so-called cultural turn (Lapid and Kratochwil 1996) the world of IR had seemed astonishingly reflexive and heterodox. The promise of new encounters less encumbered by supremacy and prejudice, the softening of hard orientalism with awareness and apprehension of difference (Inayatullah and Blaney 2004) and growing critical awareness of the question of identity in IR (Thies 2002) offered new openings. No singular worldview fully ordered things or was the order of things.

Yet in times of crisis, assumed danger, or emergency, these autonomous spaces in IR can swiftly shrink and recognizable patterns of convergence or complicity with power return. In the post-9/11 climate of political closure, the tenuous character of alternative voices becomes self-evident. Without much resistance, securitization resumed hegemonic status, with political realism redefining the tenor of IR with renewed vigour. Neorealist orthodoxy, only recently facing challenge from a wide variety of locales within the IR community, made a spectacular comeback, showing an erstwhile imperviousness to questions of identity and difference or the compulsions of political economy. The promise of diversity and openness offering prospects for a more ecumenical discipline were apparently short lived. Buttressed by an ethos of xenophobia seeing legitimation in a reputed 'clash of civilizations' (Huntington 1996), a reversal seemed to be materializing.

The apparent resecuritization of IR and growing closure to multivocality and difference in the wake of dramatic recent events underscore the enormous difficulty of sealing off discursive from non-discursive worlds. The pervasive militarization of public space Gregory (2004) and normalization of the state of exception (Agamben 2001) parallel an all-encompassing *mentality of securitization*. This mentality is expressed more tangibly in the hardening of borders and political closure in the centres of global power (Levy 2005; Keebel 2005; Huysmans 2004; Slater 2004; Bigo 2002), with a simultaneous attrition is sovereign claims for independence or autonomy in the peripheral zones of the global political economy. A dual framework of dispensation crystallized with the subsumption of sovereignty by empire. The Third World lay porous and vulnerable in the face of declining multilateralism within a fractured post-Westphalian order minimally authenticated in international law and organization. By contrast and increasingly, the centres of global power (mainly in the West) were sealed off from threatening populations from the South, mostly the Islamic world (Howell and Shryock 2003). Securitization also manifested in a pervasive great psychosis from alleged enemies of civilization (Zaretsky 2002): the binaries of the civilized and the barbarian or the saved and the damned conditioned the Western social milieu.

To be certain, though, the extant politics of closure suggests deeper hegemonic tendencies now easily provoked by power. While no one-to-one correspondence exists between the world of IR and the world it seeks to interpret, the fusion of the two worlds suggests deeper tendencies *within* IR to respond to events in particular ways. These hegemonic tendencies emanate from particular negotiations with otherness, both cultural and intellectual. It is these deeper historical tendencies within IR that form the central concern of this chapter, as their recognition is central to the possibility of decolonizing IR.

The resistance of Western IR to alternative forms of knowledge is not a question of malice, conspiracy or ignorance, or a sudden reaction to unprecedented events. Rather, the current response to recent developments exposes the limits of the canon drawn principally from durable cultural imaginaries and patterns. The dependence of IR on these imaginaries and patterns directs inquiry away from presentism or primitive functionalism to an appreciation of historical and ideological strands. In the first instance, Western IR congeals the burden of historical encounters with otherness. Despite appeals to universalism, the hegemonic proclivity to deny alternatives legitimacy and a simultaneous quest either to annihilate opposition or to assimilate otherness conditions the historical past of the discipline. In the second instance, the mystification of a particular story as *the* story remains the durable plank of Western IR. In this ideological construction, Westphalia parades as the foundational moment of IR, as a preamble to the canon. In either historical or ideological terms, Western IR shows an elective affinity to the career of modernity in a culturally embedded form. The official account of IR (as with the history of modernity) appears largely as a biography of Western triumph, of encounters premised on a consolidation of Western power, not weakness.

Within this framework, this chapter sees IR *as an instantiation of Western liberal modernity*, a set of mutually overlapping mappings, performances, and engagements with the social and political world. What are the implications of hegemonic thinking for apprehending the world of Islam? IR personifies the career of spatially determinate social forces in relation to perceived and actual Otherness. IR carries the baggage of historical encounters, including established patterns of discrimination and classification, definite ways of addressing the mundane and the metaphysical, discernible rules for separating the inside from the outside, discrete symbolic economies of representation, discrete trajectories of what is regarded as the proper character of social or political life, and in typical cases an implicit self-awareness among social agents that their framework or model of organizing the social world is the natural order of things – legitimate, superior and paradigmatic. Given the hegemonic status of Western (notably American) IR (Smith 2002b), other practices appear deviant, inferior and illegitimate. Islam falls on that register.

Western IR is a particular realization of the liberal modernist imaginary. Durable attributes give Western IR its distinctive character: the Westphalian legacy (including a preference for secularism); a modernist confidence in progress (initially secured within the framework of the modern state but also obtainable within secure spaces of a pacific international community); the ontological primacy of the individual above society; and the innate superiority of capitalist exchange (as the principle of allocating resources and preferences and structuring social interaction and cohesion). In terms of basic philosophical orientation, these attributes help structure a unified field of engagement with the world, emerging from actual historical experience and the presumed ascent of the West (McNeill 1963).

The salience of cultural encounters is paramount to a fuller recognition of the cultural limits of Western IR, particularly in the materialization of the principal elements. Through interaction with other worlds, notably the Islamic civilization, the self-image of Western IR has evolved and consolidated. It is not only against the idea of a state of nature that a particular (liberal) notion of social organization has emerged, but through competition with the social order conditioned or pro-visioned by Islam (Daniel 1960). The putative deficiencies of Islamic civilization provide the backdrop to an evolving Western self-confidence and hubris.

A mere glance at the career of popularly recognized competitor fields furnishes the measure to assess the centrality of Western liberal modernity to IR. Comparative politics or area studies, for instance, tend principally to record the scope of variance from archetypal attributes of Western experience. Hence, whether the Westphalian imaginary has fully captured the hearts and minds of ex-colonials remains a persistent theme in extant analyses (Jackson 1990). The normative discourse on 'failed states' (Bilgin and Morton 2004) is yet another reminder of the hegemony of 'Westphalian common sense' in IR (Grovogui 2002). Similarly, secularism and its presence marks the boundaries of 'civilization' based on reason against others that allow irrational forces to occupy salience in societal interaction (Hurd 2004). On this view, mod-ernist belief in material progress within the secure confines of a sovereign nation-state distinguishes the West from societies that subordinate the drive toward acquisition to nonmaterial ideals or entertain alternative conceptions of the 'good life'. The primacy of the unencumbered individual is yet another crucial feature of the liberal modernist imaginary. Societies in which community, group or family is privileged, appear necessarily deficient against the normative supremacy of the autonomous self. Closely linked to this facet, of course, is the hegemony of disembedded capitalist exchange, both as an ideal-typical modality of social connectivity as well as for organizing society itself. Emerging out of the particular historical experience of the rise of capitalism, the modern state and bureaucratic rationalization, these attributes provide the West with an ideal-typical benchmark and norm to evaluate non-Western performance in all social fields. The rigidity of commitment to these elements undergirding IR can also help account for the enormous difficulty of according legitimacy to alternative modes of thinking and behaviour. Typically, alternative cultural priorities and life patterns appear either deviant or they are simply reflective of a 'primitive' stage of development.

To the extent that mainstream IR remains intrinsically *Western* in its articulation, its claim of universality must be placed in relation to its cultural limits. If this intuition has any merit, then the task of decolonizing IR begins with an appreciation of those limits. Provincializing the West then becomes a necessary step toward a counter-hegemonic discourse (Chakrabarty 2000). Recognition of the cultural underpinnings of the canon, nevertheless, is only a first step toward a calibrated process of deconstruction and reconstruction. This task is made more difficult by the hegemonic status of Western culture globally but also by the hegemony or domination of modern rationality and its institutional manifestations almost everywhere. What spaces are available to visualize and materialize alternatives in the context of domination and hegemony? Those alternatives may themselves contain significant traces of hegemonic thinking and practices or symptoms of conditions of domination. The globalization of liberal modernity compounds the process of recovering new perspectives more attuned to heterodox conceptions of the social and life world. Few spaces remain 'outside' the imperium of capitalism or the modern state. The logic of exchange and rationalities of modern power deeply condition the syntax of social existence. To propose otherwise, as in orientalist constructions of Otherness, is to deny the burden of colonial impact or unequal power relations in the postcolonial setting and especially the ubiquity of the modern.

The quest for alternatives, though decidedly complex, must nonetheless proceed from an accounting of tensions, paradoxes and contradictions within hegemonic thinking to release new spaces of enunciation and counter-hegemony. There is no firm assurance that self-correcting mechanisms of co-optation within IR will not contaminate any alternative that might emerge. As recent re-workings of constructivism in IR theory bear out, neorealism has efficiently incorporated the language of constructivism without yielding to the latter's logic (see especially Wendt 1999; for an overview of the so-called constructivist turn, see Checkel 1998). This elementary caution can guard against exaggerated hope of a discursive turn or, more optimistically, revolutions of a Kuhnian kind (Kuhn 1970). In the final analysis, alternatives are tied to social forces and their capacity to generate new and durable political options. Theory is a necessary and indispensable complement to meaningful transformation, but an appreciation of the historicity of IR is central to any decolonizing exercise. It minimally allows the option of challenging the natural authenticity of certain forms of knowledge and their claim to universalism. Similarly, historical consciousness can lend temporality to otherwise timeless understandings of human nature, social organization and connectivity. To that end, a mapping of some key paradoxes within the canon, made more explicit in the recent response to dramatic events, can be a helpful beginning.

Securitization, liberalism and Islam

Three dimensions of the impulse toward securitization provide a mapping of central paradoxes that define an essentially liberal canon of IR: first, the historical burden of Western encounters with Islam; second, the necessary limits of liberal tolerance; and third, the quest for cultural hegemony through secularization.

The securitization impulse arises most immediately from the popular image of a threatening political Islam. The relative ease with which old symbols have been effectively deployed to evoke predictable responses directs inquiry, as mentioned, toward the historical sources of IR. The first claim to be explored is therefore the intimate relationship between the *securitization* of contemporary thinking and historically conditioned knowledge structures drawn from encounters between the West and Islam (Daniel 1960), which have produced the fiction of deeply felt incommensurable differences between the two worlds (Lewis 1976, 2002).

Second, securitization is not the antithesis of liberalism but, in fact, its underside. The emergence of a 'siege' mentality in the wake of recent events, which seemingly departs from the natural terrain of liberalism, is neither as radical as it seems nor unprecedented. There are historical parallels with other times when the barricades have gone up and xenophobia has been promoted. Recurrence is a normal state, keeping in view encounters with particular ethnic or religious minorities. The reaction to Islam, however, is distinctive. It draws upon deep historical currents implicating an intimate enemy, admired, reviled, pitied and feared under different historical circumstances. In the zone of politics, the reaction to Islam brings to the surface enduring fault lines within liberalism, always perched uneasily between the contradictory promise of freedom and sovereign demands. In times of emergency, hospitality gives way to self-preservation. This is not a departure from but a necessary continuation of liberalism.

Third, a crucial plank linking securitization and liberalism is the aspiration of creating homogenized cultural space, which remains the fundamental aim of hegemony. Difference – especially incommensurate difference – may offer productive uses to create domestic hegemony, but it can potentially undermine a more international (or global) quest. The enemy outside can help solidify the 'nation' or 'civilization' (the extant expression), but undermines liberalism's claim for overcoming a bifurcated world. There are no obvious resolutions to the dilemma. In part, though, the global drive toward secularization becomes explicable in this context. Secularization seeks to transform the world in the image of the West. This claim redirects focus on secularization, best seen as the 'softer' variant of securitization.

Paradoxically, the drive toward secularization heightens the necessity for securitization as threatened cultural and religious communities may choose to resist. On the other hand, securitization may diminish the appeals of liberalism (and secularism), principally showing the 'beastly' side of liberalism. In either case, the failure or inability to recognize difference *on its own terms* reveals the constrictions of liberalism as a framework of tolerance. In the case of Islam, these constrictions become recognizable as both secularization and securitization confront Islam's cultural and political expression – Islam as an alternative design to organize the social world or to tame liberal modernity. Although largely unsuccessful, as the conclusion to this chapter argues, so-called resurgent Islam is both a container of modern politics and an oppositional force. Misrecognition of 'political' Islam as an atavistic throwback or as a reactive social phenomenon merely recycles orientalism, but it also challenges the liberal conceit of cultural hospitality and mutual tolerance. The uses of Islam, as negation, underscore the ambivalences inherent to liberalism. Islam represents all that liberalism ostensibly negates: Islam's assumed closure, irrationality, belligerence and bigotry. On the other hand, liberalism's open-door engagement with difference, tolerating the otherness of Islam, is repudiated in attempts to extend its own version of reason to the cultural worlds of Islam.

Islam as the radical Other

The orientalist apprehension of Islam is central to the self-construction of IR and Western identity through marking a boundary between civilization and pathology. This section explores the relationships between the Western perception of Islam as radical Other and the various reactions that take the form of securitization in an apparent abandonment of liberal norms.

The intensity of reaction to religiously coded violence offers few surprises. However, the pervasive securitization that has followed, especially the targeting or profiling of Muslim populations to secure Western civilization, betrays deeper motivations and motives. The reappearance of the 'Islamic peril' bears historical resonance, Islam being an unwelcome familiarity, a fact scarcely concealed in the erasure of even nominal appeals to mutuality and cultural interdependence. To the extent that a sharp religious separation between Christendom and the world of Islam (Al-Azmeh 1993) has drawn the cultural boundaries of the West, the current mood congeals *religious* tendencies despite presumed Western secularization.

Furthermore, the hegemonic image of a monolithic, homogeneous Islam draws from a *longue durée* of encounter between Christendom and the worlds of Islam. Although there is considerable fluidity in the actual encounter, the hegemonic image is one of divergence, of incommensurable difference between Islam and the West. What defines the contours of this image is the notion of a uniform Islam devoid of contradictions in its vast, heterodox worlds. With orientalist efficiency, the signature of Islam is one of an undifferentiated, unchanging radical Other. As Al-Azmeh puts it, '[t]he evil which was Islam became a want, a deficiency in the natural order of things which was this order itself seen, from the Enlightenment onwards, as the culmination of universal history. Islam once Evil vying against Good, thus became an anachronism, a primitive stage in an emergent historicist notion of things' (Al-Azmeh 1993: 16). The notion of a singular, radical Other renders Islam as an outpost of modernity. Discrete cultural boundaries sharply mark off the modern from the traditional, the latter as 'deficient, if modernizing, other'. A key implication is the equation of (Islamic) politics with pathology.

The idea of Islam as boundary marker, of both the West and modernity, spatializes difference, but to guarantee that boundaries are not relaxed, time offers the most economical resource (Fabian 1983). Outside progress, the world of Islam remains a 'medieval' oddity, unyielding to centuries of Western contact and its positive impact. Colonized by politics that manifests itself as a social pathology of a religious world unwilling to secularize, Islam's quest for modernization is mired in futility. Hence, the absence of secularism accounts for Islamic extremism, gender oppression, irrational politics, and economic stagnation or misery. With secularism, moderation would prevail. Freedom from the stranglehold of religion would relax gender relations in the direction of greater equality. Politics, in turn, would reflect reasoned dialogue and deliberation, not passionate attachments coloured by religiosity. Similarly, religious taboos would be lifted which persistently serve as impediments to a self-expanding market economy. In sum, secularization holds the only promise for a better life.

Compounded by the return of binary tropes and the injection of a totalizing religious idiom of enunciation in popular consciousness, the otherness of Islam now appears absolute. Hospitality yields to apprehension, difference fully materialized in strangeness. Secularization or the evacuation of Islam from its public settings now works as an essential precondition for full membership into civilized society. On the other hand, securitization ensures attending the failures of secularization. In the economy of representation, extremist Islamic currents take on the appearance of archetypical pathology of atavistic rage (Lewis 1990) as a generalizable feature of Muslim society. This sentiment is strengthened by deeper anxieties of peril for Western civilization both inside its confines in the shape of the suspicious Muslim immigrant who defies assimilation and outside in the form of evil (Blair 2005). Similarly, the veiled woman appears as a social nuisance, disrupting the 'modern' character of Western society.

At the core of securitization is the question of (Western) identity, how to secure it in the face of barbarism. The inscription of danger (Campbell 1998) characterizes securitization, strengthening the inside/outside divide (Walker 1993), and naturalizing an irreconcilable friend/enemy distinction (Schmitt 1996). The primal necessity of survival and self-preservation subordinates other liberal values emanating from morality, cosmopolitanism or international obligation (Kant 1983; Doyle 1983). The return of the coercive aspects of the state, allegedly tamed by liberalism or relaxed to accommodate the whims of globalization and the promises of a rising global civil society, becomes explicable on this account. The state fortifies its hold on the mind, pushing to the sidelines other societal actors. The radical otherness of Islam necessitates civilizational framing, or 'strategies of containment', but only the state can harden the boundaries and keep the intimate enemy at bay. The notion of 'homeland security' captures this paradox, its terminology having crossed the Atlantic to Europe, drawing together 'the people and agencies who detect, protect and respond to threats' (Homeland Security 2006).

Popular imaginaries rarely escape the effects of hegemony. As Gramsci noted, common sense betrays its imprint (Gramsci 1971) in everyday life, pervading the entire social body. The apparent hostility towards Islam can be read as the recessive side of the liberal West; its current manifestation is nothing new. Hence, the consolidation of a 'natural attitude' (Benhabib 2002) toward Islam demonstrates not only the effects of securitization but also, in a deeper sense, the determinate boundaries of cultural cartographies. Both state and civil society in Western polities share these cartographies to generate predictable responses to recurrent Islamic threats. The state and civil society often compete to maintain those cartographies. The Islamic cultural zones (ICZs) have been rebranded as zones of danger, presenting a menacing geopolitical presence and requiring barricades and surveillance. Despite the pronounced coming of a 'flat' world Friedman (2005), civilizational lines that are neither fixed nor so rigid are once again fortified to split humanity into conflictual zones.

The rise of Islamophobia (with resemblances to anti-Semitism) becomes intelligible in this context. Islamophobia ensures that the enemy *inside* is recognizably more treacherous than the undifferentiated Other outside. Polite racism has easily succumbed to blatant expressions of prejudice and hatred. The figure of the 'Muslim' provides ready nourishment to a pervasive climate of paranoia as recent hate crimes in Western polities with renewed ferocity show. Neither tolerance (a concession to permissive, if insurmountable, difference) nor recognition (appreciation of its legitimate cultural existence and agency) is now the preferred option of social contact and interaction between 'liberal' majorities and 'illiberal' Muslims, or between 'good' Muslims and 'bad' Muslims (Mamdani 2004).

Securitization as liberalism's backstop

We have seen how Western fear of Islam as the radical Other generates responses of securitization that apparently entail abandoning normal commitments to liberal norms. Securitization, however, has always been an inherent and necessary component of liberal modernity, a contradiction that reveals liberalism's own orientalist foundation. The apparent proclivity of mainstream IR to succumb to cultural hubris so readily suggests the presence of determinate limits that are not functionally reducible to presentist currents. Despite its differentiated practice in distinct spatial and temporal zones, liberal thought is trapped with those limits. Against the backdrop of these limits, the fiction of universality can only be ideological. Liberal modernity and its project of rationalization of the globe cannot proceed without the ideological rationale of universality. Securitization may provide psychic certainty, but it is unable to generate modernization, help produce wealth and freedom, or emancipate humanity from barbarism and misery. In hegemonic thinking, only under a liberal dispensation can the assumed deficiencies of the ICZs be removed. However, imminent dangers pose serious impediments. Hence, the present constellation reveals contradictory tendencies within liberalism.

To the degree the foremost function of the state is to secure the 'inside', there is no contradiction between universalism and its particular instantiations. Liberty can never be absolute in the presence of sovereign demands; it must accede to the Leviathan. The uneven spread of civil liberties within the imperium (or the modern state) is a constant reminder of the fateful paradox inherent to the Enlightenment. Without eliminating real or potential threats to sovereign power, the 'good life' is a phantom quest. Securitization rests on this liberal paradox. Some values are more sacrosanct than others. In Schmittian terms, the base of sovereign power lies in its capacity to distinguish friend from enemy. Freedom, on this view, is contingent and conditional. Hence, negative, *not* positive, freedoms within a liberal social order are not coincidental. Limits on sovereign authority are inherently provisional and in a state of emergency, non-existent. Captured in the principle of sovereignty, securitization structures the fabric of the liberal order. The persistent unease noticeable amongst liberal circles concerning the alleged erosion of civil liberties in the 'defence of the realm' is therefore misplaced. Liberals tend to ignore the inherently tenuous footing of the liberal project, at once accommodating of difference but repelling its advances. The undeclared global state of emergency presents in stark proportions the liberal paradox. Exceptional circumstances require exceptional procedures.

Tensions within liberalism, however, run deeper. In the first place, the chief aim of the Leviathan to desecuritize the polity (and its international instantiation) assumes demarcations between the market and state and the evacuation of security from civil society (Buzan et al. 1998). This fictitious separation between the realms of economics and politics is readily exposed in international space. In a neo-mercantilist world, the assumed disjointing evaporates. In an ideal liberal world of market hegemony, the separation appears opaque, concealed by hegemony and its instantiation. Yet, hegemony guarantees market conquest. The founding moment of hegemony is violence.

In the second place, hegemony is not established in neutral space. The lines dividing the 'inside' from the 'outside' often breached cannot be fully transcended. The post-Cold War constellation, it is widely conceded, was an uncertain time in world affairs despite the assumed triumph of Western liberalism and its model of structuring social and political life (Mearsheimer 1990).

In hegemonic policy circles, political Islam, the principal idiom of stateless barbarity and successor to totalitarian communist savagery, simply extended the scope of uncertainty following the demise of the Second World War. Yet the particular ways in which IR thought and practice have metamorphized recently go beyond ideology to culture. More stable orientalist dispositions seem to be implicated. Familiar answers to a global peril have been discernible, but deeper historical forces may be involved. The crucial element giving established modes of response particular definition is the deployment of recessive anti-Islamic sentiment.

Against the liberal paradox between sovereignty and liberty, the mood of the times becomes explicable. The refrain that 'everything has changed' disguises fault lines within Western liberalism. Although the utterance commands us to acquiesce faithfully to a self-evident truth given its elegant rhetorical economy, it fails to show why particular choices have emerged. The despatialization of violence in a world stoically committed to a post-Westphalian imaginary ends up producing a strictly statist reaction. It was argued earlier in this chapter that the invocation of religiously charged vocabulary, with references to evil, arises from cultural wellsprings that can help mobilize passion and policy against an unconventional (stateless) enemy. It is, however, the deployment of sovereign power against known and hidden adversaries that offers ultimate security.

The fault lines within liberalism exposed in the current conjuncture of global emergency have always been more visible beyond the West: the non-Western world is usually exempt from the application of liberal principles. The exception is the rule in that context. Historical practice has shown that tensions within liberalism – between universal freedom and its partial instantiation, claims of sovereignty and demands of liberty, secular public space and private religiosity, or thin and thick cosmopolitanisms – afflict the liberal mission, if not altogether eroding grounds of legitimation. The new rules now being assembled to structure the self-acknowledged impossible task of assimilation of Muslim minorities are extracted from past colonial practice. Today in the West, as in the former colonies, liberalism suppresses its universalistic claims of liberty in favour of security, order, discipline and punishment. On balance, though, these developments in hegemonic centres only faintly mirror the military terror unleashed in the ICZs. Liberal pretensions secured at home are easily abandoned to fight evil abroad. In those hapless areas, the fury of Western power acknowledges few limits.

Colonial practice provides ample testimony to uneven and unequal application of liberal principles in the realm of economics, law or politics, as well as the realization of the Westphalian promise. The unevenness and contradictory application of liberal principles in colonial contexts raises deeper questions concerning their origins and intent. In many instances, liberal governmentality is a progeny of colonial practice, brought from the colony to the metropolis and not the other way around. The colony, on the other hand, rarely experienced the brighter face of liberalism. Recall Frantz Fanon's depiction of the colonial context:

> In the colonial countries ... the policeman and the soldier, by their immediate presence and their frequent and direct action maintain contact with the native and advise him by means of rifle butts and napalm not to budge. It is obvious here that the agents of government speak the language of pure force. The intermediary does not lighten the oppression, nor seek to hide the domination; he shows them and puts them into practice with the clear conscience of an upholder of the peace; yet he is the bringer of violence into the home and into the minds of the native.
>
> *(Fanon 1967: 29)*

There seems to be implicit recognition that liberal principles apply only to (Western) liberal societies; the colony is perpetually in a state of emergency, though at different levels of threat.

It is now a truism in post-orientalist accounts that the reduction of Islam to an ideology of closure and violence emanates from orientalist underpinnings of liberalism. Orientalism, however, has historicist and non-historicist forms (Said 1978; Abaza and Stauth 1990; Salvatore 1996; Halliday 1993).

The latter, a clumsier articulation of strategies of dealing with Otherness, as in the case of racism, assigns fixity to the Other. A subtler, perhaps more effective form is the historicist variant that views otherness temporally. Western orientalist constructions of Islam for the most part have oscillated between the non-historicist and historicist versions, often mixing the two. Despite its avowed commitment to univeralism, liberalism rests on orientalist constructions of geopolitical and cultural space: the fluidity and changeability of the West measured against a rigid 'East' resistant to both reason and material progress. Political economy essentializes this Kiplingesque divide, qualified by a story of progress through time. Without Western contact and input, goes the argument, the non-West is condemned to varying degrees of barbarity. Relations between the West and Islam are an essential part of that story.

Despite celebrations of past Islamic achievement, an evolutionary, teleological liberalism has rigidly assigned ICZs a lower position on the totem pole of social development with the story of stagnation readily on offer. Once a great civilization, the script goes, the Islamic civilization was unable to generate orientations with elective affinity to things patently modern (Lewis 2002).

Endogenous factors ultimately account for Islamic stagnation in this script, with the role of exogenous forces (notably imperialism) aiding, not undermining, modernization in the ICZs. Eventually, though, these regions will 'catch up' and modernize. Time can bring the worlds together, yet, paradoxically, it helps establish distance between civilizations in the first place. The kinship between orientalism and liberalism is palpable in this account, the former providing the diagnosis, the latter the remedy.

Orientalism, though, also serves another important purpose. Tied to hegemony, it serves as a backstop to liberalism. Given the unbridgeable gulf between claims of liberty and sovereignty that have plagued liberal thought, in times of crisis, the progressive inclinations within liberalism can be repressed in favour of a stage theory of development. Conversely, the 'outside' world can be allotted the status of an outcast beyond the pale of civilization. Both tendencies can be found in the practice of Western liberalism in relation to Islam.

Creating homogeneous cultural space

The tightening of boundaries and the coercive construction of security and order have always been inherent to, rather than the antithesis of liberalism, above all in the colonies and in the historical encounter with Islam. Securitization has discernible limits, however. Conceived centrally as a response to exceptional circumstances, its temporal horizon is constricted. A state of emergency is not consistent with the drive for capitalist accumulation (for a different view, see Roberts et al. 2003).

If the 'good life' hinges on wealth creation in a monetized exchange-driven economy, the coercive features of liberal modernity can only be transient. Hence, securitization cannot be assigned permanence. Rather, self-seeking and internalization of its logic alone can ensure the fulfilment of the liberal dream. There is the additional problem of dealing with Islamic heterogeneity. A binary separation between 'us' and 'them', in itself arbitrary and capricious, leaves out zones of entanglement between Islam and the West. Neither annihilation nor assimilation can deliver civilizational security. The compulsions of global capitalism accentuate the problem. The ICZs are an integral part of the capitalist world, obeying its dictates but also servicing its key sectors. Although peripheral, the ICZs are not marginal to processes of world accumulation – hence the tension between securitization and the demands of capitalist reproduction on a world scale. This tension accounts for alternative modalities of securing the 'volatile' ICZs. The temporal limits of securitization require a more enduring solution: a hegemonic quest to create a homogeneous cultural world through secularization. Needless to say, these modalities – securitization or secularization – are not strategic or policy options but corollaries of a particular field of vision.

In liberal thought, the more similar the rest of the world, the more secure it is. An implicit assumption guiding Western orientations toward Islam is the belief that a secular world is freer and more peaceful. This belief is first a legacy of savage European experience, an experience of brutality and war wrought by religion. Universalizing the secularization thesis, the post-Westphalian order has aptly sought freedom from religion in realizing the principle of sovereignty. Second, this view solidly rests on the assumption that religion has been expelled from public life in the Western world, replaced by reason. The presence of religion in non-Western regions, notably the ICZs, undermines the process of establishing a social order sheltered by rational principles. The essentialization of ICZs as regions possessed by religious sensibility to the exclusion of any compulsions of political economy, material considerations or nonreligious ideals directly flows from this (orientalist) mapping.

The liberal belief in equating progress with secularization, however, rests on amnesia and erasure. Liberalism tends to disown its own theological underpinnings. As Asad argues, '[i]n much nineteenth-century evolutionary thought, religion was considered to be *an early human condition from which modern law, science, and politics emerged* and became detached' (Asad 1993: 27, emphasis added).

Liberalism rests on theological elements, including subjective morality, salvation and the work ethic. It is inconceivable to separate 'modern' notions of subjective morality and religiously sanctioned conduct. The idea of salvation, in turn, has been crucial to establishing a determinate linkage between particular behaviours and conduct, and the teleological promise of reward, both worldly and otherworldly. Without necessarily embracing Weberian rationality in its fullness, the underlying principles of work ethic are not simply drawn from lay experience but the proximity of religion to quotidian practice. Finally, a capitalist economy is inconceivable without trust in exchange. Again, the idea of trust draws heavily from both religious thought and practice. Similarly, secularism rests on a sharp demarcation between public and private spheres. Yet, in practice, the formal place of religion becomes the private zone, while its real effects can be disbursed throughout the social body to the point of opaqueness. Once religion is seemingly exiled from public space, it serves as a basis to make political judgement of cultural zones outside. Presence of religion in the public sphere, therefore, signals a problem, a maker of premodernity or incomplete instantiation of modernity. Forgotten in this hegemonic discourse is the place of religion within Western liberalism, its ties to notions of subjective morality and ethics. Moreover, silent in this discourse is the transformation of religion into ideology qua modernity.

Secularization can guarantee the creation of a homogenized cultural space but also advance the aims of security. The presumed threat to civilization comes from political communities and their inhabitants who are unable to separate worldly from religious affairs. The epithet 'fundamentalism' is often used to designate phenomena reflecting fusion between the two. On this account, secularization and progress become indistinguishable. Missing in this conversation is the contradictory nature of Western secularism and its paradoxical relation to religion but also the propensity of generalizing the transition from Christendom to Westphalia beyond Europe (and later North America). Absent in this discourse also is the historical context of the formation of modern non-Western states, particularly in the ICZs. Invariably, the latter process has been consummated under colonial or semicolonial arrangements, conditioning the content, character and form of sovereignty and negotiations between religious and lay authority. These silences permit transparent yet distorted answers to complex historical processes. The quest to create a homogeneous cultural space qua secularization disguises the implicit religious underpinnings of the project. To the extent that secularism is a particular resolution to the problem of sovereignty (the transition from heaven to earth) in actually existing (Western) cultural zones, it cannot avoid transmission of specific values and orientations. These values and orientations are inescapably trapped in a logic promoting cultural particularism. Secularization, on this view, is an enunciation and realization of Western strategies of addressing the emergence of new subjectivities released by capitalist modernity and the rationalization of politics.

Conclusion

The urgent task of decolonizing IR knowledge requires, as a first step, recognition of its own cultural form and limits, a step that will undermine IR's pretension to universal validity. This chapter has argued that the limits of IR are intrinsic to its historical constitution, rooted in practice under the shadow of Western power and hegemony. Theory sprouts not from nowhere but from determinate if spatially dispersed societal currents (Cox 1983).

Neither power nor hegemony is simply an empty signifier; it is impregnated with actual historical material. On this reading, post-9/11 IR offers a useful site to re-examine contradictory impulses. Particularistic norms and practice challenge professions of universality, and commitments to inclusion are subdued by exclusionary performance or 'enclavization' (Shapiro 1999) into civilizational fortresses erected to ward off the infidel or the barbarian despite assertions of the 'end of history' (Fukuyama 1992) and the arrival of a global civil society. On the face of it, these tropes underscore the inextricable nexus between theory and history but in a more durable sense suggest the presence of unresolved tensions within IR and its philosophical homeland, liberalism. Although Western liberalism (on a hegemonic reading of history) has triumphed as the first secular global religion, dampening prospects of alternative visions of organizing international social life, the fault lines persist and may even have widened.

To the extent that the liberal modernist imaginary is globalized, it poses serious impediments to pacific relations between political communities less enamoured of exiling religion from public life and Western polities that have evolved a particular resolution to the public-private question. Crusading secular attempts to eliminate thicker forms of religious attachments embody a fundamentalist logic of closure to difference. The assumption that there is an absence of internal friction and fracture within the ICZs, to evolve new pathways between spirituality and material life or religion and politics, serves the liberal mission well. Appreciation of discord and dialogue would greatly diminish the certainty that missionary zeal requires to secure the Holy Land. The failure to recognize fractures also misrepresents the scope of modernity's presence within the segmented world of the ICZs. To be sure, the grammar of internal dialogue and contestation within ICZs remains intrinsically modern, recognizable in contestations over the nature of political community, the structure of the economy, ends of government, technological and economic progress, and IR. Recognition of this facet, as well as appreciation of the form and content of liberal modernity in the social worlds of Islam, defies the obverse orientalist conception of the self-constitution of ICZs. History appears at three levels. First, liberal modernity enters the ICZs with established images of otherness, as a civilizing force against stagnant or stagnating barbarism. Although many empathetic orientalist protagonists do not embrace the colonial project, the framing context is decidedly of a missionary kind. Salvation or modernization appear as its principal goal. Second, Western military and economic power against weaker adversaries conditions liberal modernity – adversaries who are unable successfully to resist. To reiterate, securitization has always been inherent to liberalism, especially in its historical encounters beyond the West. The texture of liberal modernity as well as resistance captures the one-sided effects of power. In important ways, power reinforces and rationalizes the missionary spirit. On the other hand, the colonial project provides power with its *raison d'être*. Given nobility of aims, the exercise of power appears just and legitimate. Echoes of the past seem to persist in the colonial present (Gregory 2004). Finally, in the ICZs liberal modernity retains the mixed effects of the colonial project, institutionalized principally in the character of the postcolonial state. The latter plagiarizes the myth of progress via modernization but also the self-conception of colonial paternalism. Hence, the dominant classes in the ICZs – and the state that ensures their economic and political fortune – face Muslim masses as subjects, not as citizens. The structuration of differentiated citizenship remains one of the principal legacies of the colonial project and its postcolonial instantiation as modernization. The consolidation of a rentier sensibility in the arena of global political economy further sustains this larger context.

Voices of resurgent Islam (Esposito 1983) appear in two principal forms, first as a plea for inclusion into global cultural space and second as a protest against rejection. In the former instance, there is an aspiration to participate in globality with sensitivity to its particularism. In the second case, resurgence appears as a reminder to a fateful resistance to difference. Clearly, there is considerable variance in resurgent Islam, but in its diverse expression, there is a common quest for participation in modernity. To the degree that political Islam seeks a resolution to the problem of sovereignty, it embraces the logic of modernity, institutionalized either as political economy or as the nation-state. Although the idiom of enunciation betrays signs of pre- or antimodern temperament, the desire to bridge heaven and earth remains an intrinsically modern quest. Political Islam is ensconced principally, if not exclusively, in national space, notwithstanding its popular representation as a global and globalized phenomenon (Ayubi 1991). Islamicists seek to capture or transform the *modern* nation-state against moral or ethical claims drawn from presumably an alternative (religious) source. On the other hand, the dismissive repudiation of Islamicists by secular nationalists as 'traditionalists' or enemies of modernization strengthens their belief in the totalizing closure of the modern world to an alternative (Islamic) mapping of the social world. Rejectionist Islam, therefore, records a protest against modernity. The political aims of 'transnational' Islam tend to betray the political itself.

To recapitulate, IR has consistently portrayed Islam, the radical Other, as a pathological form beyond the pale of modernity. Political Islam is inherently modern. First, it aims to resolve the question of authority within the framework of sovereign power. Compulsory references to the scriptures provide a framework for accountability, but there is no escaping the secular import of the state and its institutional accoutrements. The centrality of the modern state to the establishment of a just social order defies the image of a self-sustaining community of believers successfully negotiating a City of God. Second, modern rationalities of governance and governmentality, of technical reason and bureaucratization, invade the political horizon of political Islam. On this view, the fiction of a premodern 'community of believers' quickly evaporates. Finally, political Islam is a *particular* resolution to the question of a new form of subjectivity informed by the emergence of the modern economy, family and civil society. The compulsions of exchange, privacy and intimacy secured in a bourgeois mode, and individual pursuits enabled by non-familial social ties, speak to the modernity of the social world of political Islam.

Finally, IR's orientalist apprehension of Islam as a static and homogeneous faith generates an essentialized and tautological understanding of violence. On this view, religiously induced violence is inherent to Islam's pathological and traditional otherness. It is, however, the *fractured character of liberal modernity* in the ICZs that largely accounts for trends toward nihilism and violence. Nihilism is an implicit recognition of the implausibility of realizing the promise of either the City of God or the City of Man, an appeal to the most affected sectors within the hegemonic world of capitalism and modern rationality. Hence, nihilism and its realization as terror underscore the death of politics, the inability to forge a future drawn from alternative wellsprings, or the near absence of potential to create parallel political projects. Few spaces remain outside modernity and its Western global expression. Yet the West appears inhospitable to difference. The political closure nourished by difference actively transforms dissent into rejection. The liberal–modernist imaginary and its institutionalized presence in ICZs deeply conditions alternatives, both realized and potential.

3

HUMAN SECURITY AND ISLAM

Recent unsettling events (Calhoun et al. 2002; Smith 2002a, 2002b; Gray 2002) have directed unprecedented foci on the social and psychological worlds of Islam; their constitutive affinity to politics and violence; unspoken pathologies of Islamic culture and collective psyche; and strategies to civilize populations mesmerized by that religion's vast and seemingly irrational appeal. Orientalist modes of capture and recognition have offered, with renewed vitality, familiar taxonomies of Islamic exceptionalism. A consolidated view of Muslim cultural rigidity infused by religion (Lewis 2002) pervades the public sphere as 'common sense' (Gramsci 1992 [1891–1937], 1996). Against the backdrop of global exceptionalism (Agamben 2005; Bhuta 2003), and ongoing processes of neoliberal globalization (Roberts et al. 2003), the worlds of Islam face unprecedented stress.

This chapter maps out the principal trajectories and content of new challenges to human security in the Islamic cultural zones (ICZs), a term suggesting both the putative unity of geographical spaces impacted by Islamic culture as well as the diversity within the Islamic world. Avoiding economistic readings of human security in favour of a culturally embedded account of vulnerability and agency, this chapter reframes mutual connectivities among exceptionalism, neoliberalism and human insecurity. In this vein, the chapter engages structural and historical aspects usually bypassed on a presentist register highlighting dramatic events in extant reflections. Similarly, resisting the urge to produce yet another assemblage of human insecurity in the troubled ICZs, the discussion instead offers a passage to confronting established frames of capturing Islam and their aggressive redeployment in new global enclosures (Walker 2002).

The analysis proceeds with an examination of the limits of mainstream accounts of human security and proposes mutual constitution of exceptionalism(s) and insecurity. It suggests that both liberal and critical variants of the human security discourse have (successfully) evaded basic questions about the structuring logic(s) of international relations. Rather, a reformist agenda honed by persistent attention to the 'effects' of either geopolitics or, more recently, neoliberal globalization, clouds foci on the more durable mechanisms of human insecurity. In the aftermath of new enclosures, the reproduction of human security becomes both more transparent and more opaque. Threats to human security appear more palpable and recognizable with turmoil in the ICZs. On the other hand, the linkage between Islamic exceptionalism and the global exception within a neoliberal imaginary is not so readily visible. The materialization of human insecurity in the ICZs is not a religious/ cultural issue, but a problem of the political, with perennial and new ambivalences surrounding the question of the Other, how to manage it under altered states.

The apparent global distempers are not necessarily the birth pangs of a new order, nor perforce the lingering imprint of a decaying civilization. Instead, they combine features of the old and novel to reveal some of the more blatant contradictions released in the endeavour to manage difference. Human insecurity is affiliated principally with these contradictions.

Revisiting human security

Discourses of human security offer productive avenues to capture dimensions of insecurity beyond statist conceit. Challenging privileged sovereign claims against exposed populations, they allow inquiry and ethics to proceed toward recognizing vulnerabilities generated by the state's own excesses or incapacities to shelter and provision the 'bare necessities' of existence of humans qua humans. On this view, structures of inequality and their malignant effects concealed in discourses of national security, border policing and surveillance, might be exposed. Human security shifts the focus away from the invisible, abstract subject of security, to the concrete, social individual. Occluded or erased in hegemonic discourses, the *human* in security can be reinstated. In the guise of expanding the agenda of security, the particularized universality of humankind can now be approached, no longer an afterthought of high politics, *raison d'être* or statecraft.

Three main themes seem to pervade extant conversations on human security. First, the growing vulnerability of populations propelled by neoliberal globalization. Second, exclusionary state practices toward those caught between necessity and exit strategies (as in the case with migratory flows). Finally, the victims of 'failed states' unable to provision minimal human existence in the areas of survival or security (Hampson et al. 2002; Nef 1999; Thomas and Wilkin 1999; Stoett 1999; Ogata and Cels 2003; Commission on Human Security 2003). On this reading, protections secured by the state in the form of welfare and aspirations of economic development are apparently under severe strain with the erosion of sovereignty and the arrival of predatory accumulation. Neoliberal globalization has weakened state capacity to the degree that citizens must now explore avenues of survival and community in the belly of civil society. The heterodox forms civil society could assume are not relevant in this account, except that civil society is regarded as a preferred alternative to a diminishing state. Material vulnerability exacerbated by neoliberal globalization exposes humans to unprecedented risk, fear and anxiety. Without adequate protections previously furnished by the state, insecurity has apparently deepened.

A second theme in extant human security discourses takes an unfavourable view of the state, chiefly in its relation to cross-border flows of the 'new nomads' of global political economy: migrant labourers and sex workers forced to seek material succour without juridical protection. The discourse of 'failed states' laments the passing of effective sovereignty and the unleashing of new threats to human security (Cooper 2003).

Human security, however, is a contested concept, its meanings shuttling between universalistic aspirations for human betterment and the specificity of historical and cultural contexts conditioning those aspirations. In the first instance, the liberal post-Enlightenment promise of freedom from want and fear seeks materialization through history, undeterred by assumed social and cultural rigidities. Overcoming obstacles to that quest becomes the principal aim of promoting human security. Liberal bias, involving assumptions of plenitude, historicism and evolutionary ascendance, infuses the general literature on this theme. As with the hegemonic universalism of Western human rights discourse, a notion of liberal neutrality or thinness of cultural heterogeneity in the face of emancipatory progress impregnates the prevailing conversation on human security. Secured by rationalized economic and social change, temporality merely qualifies freedom. The great transformation in material and cognitive worlds is likely to propel humanity in a singular direction. Protection of the most vulnerable on this view translates into shielding economically defenceless populations from the scourge of want. In turn, building institutions that harness human capacities can yield the essential prerequisites of a humane order, liberated from strife, violence and destitution, but also successfully absorb market rationality.

In the second instance, human security escapes the constrictions of modularity. On this reading, diverse modalities of culture, locale and identity condition the realization of security, from provisioning material sustenance and safeguarding populations against different instantiations of violence, to the protection of the habitat necessary to sustain and guarantee respect for human dignity and cultural distinctiveness. In this context, human security is not only about negative protections but also about positive aspirations, to preserve and enhance human dignity and forms of (cultural) life in which human dignity is embedded. This is not a plea for legitimating fixity, but an appreciation of both the integrity of life's varied expressions in culturally distinct domains and the indivisibility of material, cognitive and cultural spheres that demarcate the universe of security. Resting on a confluence of materiality and culture, human security on this reading particularizes humankind.

Admittedly, release from the fetters of statist *imaginaire* opens up security to institutional protections in civil society and its elaborate, if heterodox, systems of human protection. Once the monopoly of the state, solidly entrenched in the discourse of sovereignty, security can now encompass civil society and its institutions. This shift, needless to say, is fraught with serious pitfalls. Powerful social interests in the absence of effective state power may potentially appropriate civil society. In turn, civil society may be relatively weak vis-à-vis the state (Keane 2003) to spearhead large-scale efforts to overcome the vagaries of historically conditioned inequities and virtually insurmountable economic hurdles. Salvaging security from the state, therefore, can be a mixed blessing, offering new possibilities for protection, but also exposing society to structural inequalities and excesses (Blaney and Pasha 1993). Both fanaticism (Colas 1997) and unfettered acquisition (Wood 2003) provide instances of a civil society that can be uncivil.

The current global constellation places enormous burdens on extant discourses on human security, particularly in reference to the reframing of sovereignty and the redeployment of orientalist themes to reconfigure the position of the ICZs in the hegemonic imaginary. In the first case, the instantiation of the 'global exception' (see Chapter 1) apparently redefines the world order in attempts to manage Islamic otherness. The consolidation of neo-orientalism, on the other hand, reactivates medieval cartographies on a global scale, a process anticipated before 9/11 by mandarins of empire (Huntington 1996). The marriage of exceptionalisms – global and Islamic – has produced new vulnerabilities for people in and from the ICZs, while deepening previous ones (see Chapter 1). Although threats to human security are unevenly distributed across class, nation, gender or location, the consolidated gaze of neo-orientalism ensures that *Islamic* identity appears as a monolithic label defying space or time.

Islamic exceptionalism

On a hegemonic reading, Islam and the cultural zones bearing its distinctive impression remain outside modernity (Lewis 2002; Pipes 1983). Inherently feeble in reconciling faith with reason (Benedict XVI 2006), violence and a totalizing commitment to the transcendental often working in tandem mark its bloody landscape. 'Islam has bloody borders', as Huntington (1993) proposes. Unlike Christianity, as Pope Benedict XVI asserts, where 'we can see the profound harmony between what is Greek in the best sense of the word and the biblical understanding of faith in God', this is not the case with Islam. 'But for Muslim teaching, God is absolutely transcendent. His will is not bound up *with any of our categories*, even that of rationality' (Benedict XVI 2006, emphasis added). In received hegemonic thinking, the ICZs brook no separation between science and the sacred, politics and the religious (Pipes 1983; Vatikiotis 1987), expunging private arenas of selfhood and self-seeking that must submit to the force of the community, the fraternity of believers and their collectivized sensibility. This reading, laid to rest in the crumbling edifices of post-orientalist critique, has regained consciousness in the current Manichaean climate of binaries, of the civilized and the savage, the modern and the pre-modern. Naturalized in public discourse and policy, the image of Islam, a force singularly resistant to modernity, prevails as common sense. In the midst of other, more malleable grand faiths, Islam is *the* exception. Trapped in the past, it remains unable and unwilling to accommodate change, to embrace the modern and graciously accept its munificent offerings.

Estranged from theological disputation with other monotheistic religions, notably Christianity, the theme of Islamic exceptionalism receives its lay enunciation in theories of modernity and modernization, given especially their 'secular bias' (Eickelman 2000: 119). Aggressive modernizing drives (as Turkey or Iran starkly demonstrate) cannot readily erase the otherness of Islam, nor can strategies of assimilation (as in Europe and North America) absorb it. On this view, lacking vibrant institutions of individuation (Gellner 1994), the modernist impulse lends itself to subordination to a collectivist ethos drawn from Islamic culture.

The sentiment of Islamic exceptionalism is neither novel nor radical, its sediments buried deep in Western apprehension of Muslim otherness. Presumably heretical in originary claims, Islam's power and expansion softened the blatant rhetoric though maintaining abiding commitment to the otherness of Islam now drawn from batteries of alternative imagery. The immutability of hard orientalism metamorphized into the soft orientalism of historicism and meta-narratives of modernization and development. Hard orientalist claims either demonized Islam or exoticized it – Islam as the Devil's own creed or a colossal harem to fulfil Western desires and fantasies (Said 1978; Yeğenoğlu 1998). Softer variants see the world of Islam as a decaying order, a great civilization derailed by authoritarian excess, the triumph of dogma, or political dissension. In either case, an involution places the ICZs in a temporal ditch, awaiting rescue. While other cosmologies have successfully managed to reform and to adapt, the ICZs hold firm to believe in transcendent futures, outside the march of history and its promised frontiers. On this reading, the pathology of our times, congealed in large and small infernos, replicates the logic of rejection. A resurgent orientalism now buttresses the consolidated gaze of otherness.

Islamic exceptionalism covers a wide ideational spectrum, from assumed cognitive deficiencies to profit fully from the innovative *Weltanschauung* of the West, the successes of scientific reasoning, market rationality, to the organization of personal spheres of family, sexuality and procreation. To be sure, it is not merely an orientalist trait to find Islam to be an obstacle to scientific development, but equally a modernist prejudice as well (Hoodbhoy 1991; Tibi 2002). In the hands of modernists, a caricatured faith appears as the Other of progress and modernity. Applying a radically diluted and distorted Weberian lens, the neo-orientalists find Islam to be lacking in the functional equivalents of a Protestant ethic or secularized versions of salvation. Without bearing the fruits of a Reformation and privileging Other-worldly affairs above this world, Islam has presumably cultivated no open spaces to aspire to material paradise, preferring a deferred afterlife. Similarly, the personal realm of the family, notoriously advertised as Islam's public face, gives Islamic exceptionalism its *élan vital*. The image of the veiled Muslim woman stands as the mirror opposite of the liberated Western woman. The former is trapped in communal bondage sanctioned by religion, the latter underscoring the achievements of an individuated society with autonomy and freedom. As with colonial feminism, saving Muslim women now occupies a central place in the economy of Western consciousness concerning the ICZs (Abu-Lughod 2002).

Despite the porous character of the ideational and practical worlds of Muslims, a consolidated gaze affords easy recognition. Now lying at the centre of the current global architecture of world politics, the ICZs confirm the stubbornness of Islamic exceptionalism, its unchanging character through the centuries. Although internally torn, these zones appear as homogenized otherness. The actually existing fractured worlds of Islam (see the Introduction) do not change, on this image, their collective ethos as a unified force resisting modernity.

To be certain, Islamic exceptionalism is not an inert, passive frame of recognition. An orientalist trope, it is an 'enabling' frame, as Said (1978) would suggest. It enables specific instantiations of power and legitimation. Difference must be managed through either erasure or assimilation. In the first instance, its seemingly malevolent forms provide rationalization for the pacification. In the latter case, drives to modernize, but especially to secularize, can alter their *exceptional* character, making the ICZs more like the rest of the Westernized world. The potential impact of the deployment of this framework in the service of global power on human security is not too remote from this vantage point.

Following Carl Schmitt's critique of liberalism as a double-faced discourse of power, which in times of emergency reveals its beastly side, Islamic exceptionalism affords in the context of the global exception its true character. Neo-orientalist reworking of Islamic exceptionalism helps concretize 'the enemy'. The polite language of liberal tolerance yields to the essential reality of the political. As Schmitt puts it, the 'concepts friends and enemy are to be taken in their concrete, existential meanings', a designation reinforced by the us–them distinction, 'not as metaphors or symbols, not mixed and watered down by economic, moral, and other ideas; nor are they to be taken psychologically as the expression of private feelings and tendencies' (Schmitt [1932] 1996: 5–6). Schmitt recognizes even the possibility of advantageous business dealings with the enemy, but the enemy remains 'the other, the stranger' since 'he is, in a particularly intense way, existentially something different, and alien'. On this Schmittian reading, incessant struggles within liberalism to conceal the friend–enemy distinction are readily exposed. In the context of Islamic exceptionalism, the depoliticizing liberal rhetoric vanishes with the reappearance of the accurate face of radical otherness that seeks 'the negation of our existence, the destruction of our way of life' (Schmitt, cited in Mégret 2002: 366).

Islamic exceptionalism makes the ICZs susceptible to new human security threats in three principal ways. The most obvious is the persecution of military might, targeting mainly Islamic states and Muslim populations. Accounts of militarized conflict, the vicious cycles of violence that bear the name of 'insurgency' and attendant pacification or 'collateral' damage of the innocent and their material and cultural habitat suggest a massive rise in all aspects of human insecurity. Drawing its alleged 'legality' from the state of emergency, the deployment of military power has a far-reaching impact, including an increasingly fortified homeland. The state of emergency itself has already exposed populations to a kind of domestic terror. As Mégret points out:

the effects of this state of emergency are already being felt in – and are indistinguishable from – the evolution of the legal order. At the domestic level, there is the familiar danger, under the all-encompassing banner of 'security', of militarization of the polity and a reduction in civil liberties, including proposals for increased wire-tapping, indefinite detention of those suspected of terrorism, racial profiling, various forms of censorship, and the lifting of the taboo – albeit only in the media – on torture. Somewhere on the precarious fault lines of the domestic and the foreign, a long-held ban on the assassination of foreign leaders is overturned and immigration is being held ever more strictly controlled, in a desperate attempt to sanctuarize the 'homeland' cocoon.

(Mégret 2002: 368)

The *cumulative* psychological effect of a universal state of paranoia (Ball 2005), implicating Muslim populations in a rapidly growing culture of surveillance, is less recognizable. Yet, from the perspective of human security, this is perhaps one of the more potent effects of the undeclared state of emergency. A growing assault on religious identity and its cultural manifestations is also recognizable in public spheres of liberal polities. Behind the liberal cover of individual freedom of speech, for example, Islamic identities have rapidly become a favourite target of mockery and ridicule. The rising vulnerabilities, especially of Muslim immigrants in the West, are closely associated with the state of emergency. Citizenship increasingly rests on cultural vectors, not legal personhood. Muslims, in particular, now have an extra burden not only to demonstrate more fully and appropriately their 'love of country', but a willingness to sever their links with established symbols of Islamic identity captured in appearance or attire. Failure to assimilate in the performative zone of Western modernity can easily invite surveillance, both of the state and civil society. The inhospitable gaze of normalcy is a constant reminder to Muslims of the burden of their identity and the enormous difficulty of integration in an alien world. Within this frame, strategies of self-help and seclusion acquire greater sustenance. On this reading, the self-reproducing structure of exclusion and segregation becomes less opaque.

Constrictions of Western notions of secularized modernity (Vento 2000; Kratochwil 2005; Curtis 1996) have been lifted in refurbished drives to democratize and secularize the ICZs. Paradoxically, the increasingly desecularizing polity in the United States throws up no apparent anomalies in the quest to 'liberalize' Islam and to weaken the hold of absolute truths in exchange for procedural democracy (Advisory Group on Public Diplomacy for the Arab and Muslim World 2003) and consumption-driven self-seeking negotiated by a neoliberal global compact (Friedman 1999). For instance, Thomas Friedman, an organic intellectual of American imperial designs, writes:

America and the West have potential partners in these [Islamic] countries who are eager for us to help move the struggle to where it belongs: to a war within

Islam over its spiritual message and identity, not a war with Islam ... a war between the future and the past, between development and under-development, between authors of crazy conspiracy theories versus those espousing rationality ... Only Arabs and Muslims can win this war within, but we can openly encourage the progressives ...

(Friedman 2002)

Global exception

Paradoxically, the current mood has both shifted the terrain of global and domestic politics as well as consolidated established modes of reckoning the ebb and flow of social and political life. The reappearance of religious taxonomies of the saved and the damned or lay renditions of unbridgeable self/other dichotomies of civiliza-tional hierarchies (Euben 2002a) have displaced lines drawn by the principle of sovereignty. Presumably, the inside/outside divide has been redrawn by suspending international law or the invocation of what may be termed the 'global exception' (Newman 2004). The exception, as Johns (2005: 619) explicates, is:

that domain within jurisprudence in which decision-making 'cannot be sub-sumed' [Schmitt, 1922, *supra* note 5, at 13] by existing norms. It is that space in which such norms are held open to suspension or transformation, and where programs of norm-implementation and norm-compliance cease to govern action and decision-making. Accordingly, the exception is synonymous with the attempt to exercise momentarily decisive agency or, as Schmitt put it, 'principally unlimited authority' [Schmitt 1922, *supra* note 5, at 12].

On a global scale, the legitimating rationales for the 'exception' entail both the supplanting of liberal rules governing international society and revising conduct toward certain classes of citizens domestically previously recognized as legal persons by self-referential law. Ambiguous zones of legality either reclassify target members of certain populations or strip them of personhood, 'bare life' as Agamben (1998) puts it. Yet, in most instances, these zones are demarcated with an *a priori* cultural and religious baggage, being Muslim; the instantiating group identity is suggested by the Islamic faith. Hence, Islamic exceptionalism becomes the normative justification to enforce the exception.

Ironically, the exception to the exception is provided by Islamic exceptionalism; the exception is no longer a universal principle with a global scope, but delimited by a classificatory economy in which Muslims are *exceptional*. The recent conversation on the global exception, therefore, needs modification. How *global* is global? A sharp wedge between assumed liberal polities and citizens, on the one hand, and illiberal states and subjects, on the other, materializes the global. To the extent that the current climate tends to blur the line between the inside and the outside (Walker 2002, 1993), the exception is extraterritorial; sovereignty is rescaled to affect potentially *all* zones. In this sense, the global exception is truly global.

However, the instantiations of *the exception impacts some populations more than others*, generally suspending the liberal compact *in toto* in relation to the ICZs and Muslims.

The nominal classification produced by Islamic exceptionalism, however, is not merely nominal, but substantial with a familiar lineage in post-Enlightenment reworking of the great divide between Christendom and Islam. As 'the essential enemy' (Kagay 1999), Islam now reappears in the cartography of the global exception, tempering the latter's ambition. Islam is not necessarily the heretical contender to Christianity, but as the antithesis to an expanding neo-Kantian civilization (Fukuyama 1992). Put differently, the exception is *culturally* impregnated. Islamic exceptionalism both sets the stage for it and qualifies it. The substantiality of Islam gives the global exception a determinate foothold. Decisionism emanates not simply from sovereign prerogative, but from cultural mappings of otherness, baring in essence the contradictions within Western liberalism, but not necessarily in ways Schmitt (1996 [1932]) would suggest.

As with the colonies where liberal values remained suspended in perpetuity, the global exception produces a bifurcated world. Muslim otherness is not a homogenized universe, although it serves as an originary provocation to discriminations. Following Mamdani (2004), there are 'good' and 'bad' Muslims, a classification tied to the ambivalences of sovereignty. The burden of proving to be a 'good' Muslim was a universal burden for *all* Muslims: 'unless proved to be "good", every Muslim was presumed to be "bad"' (Mamdani 2004: 15). Crucially, judgements of 'good' and 'bad' refer to Muslim political identities, not to cultural or religious ones. The world of the exception recognizes politics as the principal source of classification. However, there are few readily accessible criteria to separate politics from culture and religion. Islamic exceptionalism, therefore, remains caught within the vortex of this ambivalence.

The colonial model offers an unimpeded view of the fault lines within Western liberalism, but also the nexus between Islamic exceptionalism and the global exception. Colonial cartography and classification ensured a permanent breach based principally on race:

> This world divided into compartments, this world cut in two is inhabited by two different species. The originality of the colonial context is that economic reality, inequality, and the immense difference of ways of life never come to mask the human realities. When you examine at close quarters the colonial context, it is evident that what parcels out the world is to begin with the fact of belonging to or not belonging to a given race, a given specie.
>
> *(Fanon 1963: 39–40)*

The global exception rests on a religious/cultural divide, though the racial trappings in 'the colonial present' (Gregory 2004) are equally at work. Islam's 'repellent otherness' (Al-Azmeh 1996) is an assemblage of religious, cultural, racial and, above all, political correlates congealed in Islamic exceptionalism. The seemingly indeterminate 'legal' status of prisoners in the global campaign against terrorism is fairly determinate. Inescapably, religious designation subordinates other affiliations. As with the colonial setting, the global exception makes distinctions. Both draw from liberal mappings of the political field. Both conceal and reveal the contradictions of the liberal project.

Exceptionalism(s) and human security

The connection between Islamic exceptionalism and human security appears ambiguous. How do cartographic mappings of sovereignty impinge upon human security in the ICZs? There are no self-evident pathways to see the nexus between the growing propensity to suspend liberal dispensation with regard to Muslims and threats to the fabric of their societies. The global exception has the obvious effect of denying negative freedoms to Muslims via securitization. However, securitization is the context of human insecurity principally for Muslim immigrants, and only indirectly for populations in the ICZs. In the latter context, the main threat comes from intervention and deepening and corrosive effects of neoliberalism.

On the face of it, neoliberalism and securitization are inherently contradictory. The aim to expand the universe of the global economy, to absorb labour and resources from all regions of the world, to facilitate the movement of capital, people and commodities across boundaries, to increase productivity, seemingly collide with border policing, law enforcement and stricter regimes of immigration. Securitization potentially impedes neoliberal globalization. On an alternative reading, the structures of neoliberal global governance necessitate securitization (Roberts et al. 2003). Rather than disrupt the evolution of an ever-expanding and stable order, securitization distributes the risks globally, but also averts large-scale resistance through received strategies of disruption, surveillance and repression (Munck 2007). The willing embrace of the leading sectors of the neoliberal order underscores not simply the conveniences of global alignments, but perceived mutuality between the goals of neoliberal globalization, and global surveillance and militarization. As Roberts et al. (2003: 886) point out, a 'geopolitical vision' is 'closely connected to neo-liberal idealism about the virtues of free markets, openness, and global economic integration'. Neoliberalism and the exercise of organized violence are not poles apart. 'The economic axioms of structural adjustment, fiscal austerity, and free trade have now, it seems, been augmented by the direct use of military force' (ibid., 887).

By way of contrast to previous imperial designs, what distinguishes this moment of neoliberal geopolitics is that the notion of enforced reconnection is today mediated though a whole repertoire of neoliberal ideas and practices, ranging from commitment to market-based solutions and public-private partnerships to concerns with networking and flexibility to mental maps of the planet predicated on a one-world vision of interdependency (Roberts et al. 2003: 889).

At a deeper level, both securitization and neoliberalism afford similar rationalities, though their sphere of influence may not appear as mutually constitutive. The rationalized neoliberal subject and the securitized liberal subject overlap, permeated by technologies of (bio-)power and surveillance. To the extent, however, that those technologies collide with the force of varied forms of cultural life and their alternative wellsprings, the neoliberal, securitized subject remains a mere aspiration of extant governmentalities in the ICZs, but only up to a point.

Certain forms of 'fundamentalism' present a particular form of 'neoliberal' compromise, despite their apparent rejectionist tonality. The conflation of heterodox religious worldviews and practices within Islam, but especially between its 'communal' (or 'traditional') strands and its 'individuated' (Protestant?) nemeses, to put it quite simply, prevents an understanding of the hybrid character of adjustments to neoliberalism. Islamic exceptionalism impedes access to the lived and experiential worlds in the ICZs. While non-fundamentalist strands offer multiple pathways for reconciling the divine with the everyday, lived reality, puritanical variants appropriate the neoliberal quest to unite technical rationality with the regulation of bio-power, synthesizing the rationalized mentality of political and economic management with the management of sexuality. Liberated from traditional religious authority, Puritanism allows salvation in a privatized world of religiosity, but also self-seeking restrained principally by attachment to performative fundamentalism. The latter helps evacuate the density of religious experience from the social and life-worlds of the believers, paving the way for essentially earthly pursuits, including self-seeking in a monetized, exchange, capitalist economy, and the pursuit of political power within the territorial confines of the modern nation-state.

The possibility of a neoliberal compromise implicating various incarnations of so-called fundamentalism is easily spurned in the prevailing context of Islamic exceptionalism. On the latter view, Islam mirrors the stagnant waters of tradition and absolutism of the 'transmundane', to borrow the term from Eisenstadt (1984), not the fluid or the 'mundane'. Some hegemonic readings of Islamic otherness do recognize temporality and heterogeneity within the ICZs, but the usual typologies entertain a familiar binary script. The acknowledgement of temporality allows only a fictitious escape from the prison house of orientalism. In fact, it deepens the cultural divide by linking otherness to time (Fabian 1983).

The story of the advent of the market and its ancillary supports in the ICZs is an old one. Exposure to the logic of exchange has a long trajectory, both in its pre-colonial incarnations, but equally so in the colonial and post-colonial worlds. The ruination of local ways of social reproduction is a well-documented process, an essential part of the folklore of anti-colonial historiography. In its most recent manifestation, however, it is *not the market, but market fundamentalism*, that poses serious challenges in the ICZs as elsewhere. The latter rests on the uncompromising fiction of securing a better future without statist, social or cultural restraints. A diminished state is capable of guaranteeing neither societal good in the form of material development or safety against violence, nor as a unifying force in societies divided by caste, ethnicity, religion or region.

In turn, the denial of the social in favour of atomistic individuality ensures Darwinism on an unprecedented scale. The self-regulating market can only exacerbate hierarchies, now on a faster and globalized scale given time-space compression. It is in the realm of culture, though, that market fundamentalism poses an even bigger challenge than popularly perceived fundamentalisms of another kind. Neoliberal subjectivity is based upon a thin regard for the thickness of cultural life, dislodging embedded social purposes in favour of consumer-driven self-seeking and self-construction. The homogenizing thrust of narcissistic achievement is an enormous force to disrupt culturally heterodox forms of life.

In sum, the consolidation of the neoliberal subject in the ICZs, visualized in market fundamentalism, cannot fully emerge without stripping Muslim society of its distinctive encounters with the social and life-worlds. Read against this image, recent strategies to secularize the ICZs are reminiscent of the colonial project to liberate 'natives' from the grip of irrationality, or the modernization project of the euphoric post-World War Western imaginary. As with the colonial project that produced 'derivative' discourses (Chatterjee 1986), not only of nationalism, but religious revivalism and modernism, neoliberal fundamentalism only fortifies religious fundamentalism, both in its oratorical rejection of modernity, but more precisely, its embrace of the latter's more malevolent aspects.

Paradoxically, the real 'winners' of global exceptionalism and neoliberalism are the 'fundamentalists' who have successfully found reconciliation between the stable world of essentialized belief and the chaotic world of economic globalization. Like innocent bystanders, the real casualties are the ordinary people whose faith remains tenuous and a last defence against a world they can neither tame nor reverse. Despite an apparent 'clash of civilizations', neoliberals and fundamentalists have conjoined identities: market and religious fundamentalism are not as far apart as usually understood (Huntington 1996; Friedman 1999; Barber 1996).

Conclusion

Extant liberal discourses on human security typically bypass questions of culture and identity arising within *politically* conditioned spaces of difference. The vulnerabilities produced by structures of classification, exclusion and discrimination extend beyond economic insecurities, as shown in the invocation of the global exception. Without examining the newly fortified borders of exclusion and corresponding strategies of managing difference, analyses can persistently equivocate. Part of the problem in human security discourses lies in their originary liberal mapping of power, preventing a fuller recognition of global transformations. The fault lines within liberalism, expressed more sharply in its failure to reconcile sovereignty and citizenship, on the one hand, and difference *within* citizenship, especially during times of emergency, mask the modern human condition. Structural tendencies appear as anomalies. However, vulnerabilities arising from the politics of difference are neither ephemeral nor deviant.

A second major problem in human security discourses belongs to its fixation on a 'hierarchy of needs' model and its latent economism pronounced in cataloguing various indices of insecurity. Alternatively, an appreciation of the inviolability of cultural identity to the sustenance of the human condition can help displace the hegemony of economism. Such appreciation need not rest on cultural relativism or essentialism, merely the indivisibility of social life forms. In the current climate, life-worlds placed under sustained political surveillance are not merely addenda to received indices of human insecurity. Rather, culturally fractured life-worlds direct inquiry towards processes and structures of power and their effects.

Twenty-first-century Islamic exceptionalism provides global structures with a new rationale to systemically reproduce human insecurity on a vast and unprecedented scale. The view that the unending 'colonial present' is simply another series in the continuation of historical prejudices against the world of Islam misrecognizes the transformed context in which Islamic exceptionalism is reproduced. The *globalized* terrain radically changes the equation. As central *dramatis personae* in the materialization of the global exception, the fate of most Muslims both within the ICZs and in non-Islamic zones of marginality are irrevocably tied to the fortunes of the liberal project. However, this is a paradoxical affinity. The success of the liberal project simultaneously enhances protections in a presumed state of normalcy and undermines the cultural distinctiveness of Islam. Reinstatement of legality may provide pathways to the enjoyments of benefits of sovereignty and citizenship, both suspended under the global exception. However, liberal intolerance of religiously contingent identity can only heighten under the regime of an unfettered liberalism not appearing fragile.

On the obverse side, the state of exception (Agamben 2005) intensifies thick identities. Under threat, culture and religion can harden. As noted, the global exception chiefly aids the more puritanical sectors of the cultural and religious worlds of Islam. In this context, the principal challenges for extending the conversation on human security in the ICZs lie in overcoming both the fetters of a liberal imaginary as well as resisting cartography of radical difference drawn by the state of the exception.

4

ISLAM AND THE POSTSECULAR

Introduction

The language of the 'postsecular' acknowledges the enduring presence of faith in politics, repudiating secularization theses claiming diminution or privatization of religion in social and political life. In cognitive and experiential worlds, those presumably unfettered by these conceptions (for example, the Islamic cultural zones, or ICZs), the postsecular presents a different order of challenge and possibility. This chapter questions the hegemonic view pervasive in both secular and postsecular theorizing of the fiction of immutability of faith in the ICZs and recognizes its rupture and displacement under conditions of late modernity. The ontological dislocation in the character of religion itself under conditions of late modernity opens up the possibility to account for the assumed resistance of Islam to secular modernity, but also to explain Islam's imbrications in politics read under the sign of political Islam. Paradoxically, under the condition of late modernity, a more homogenized Islam appears to crystallize in the ICZs at odds with an 'open' Islam.

Diverse conceptions of the 'postsecular' have now entered the discursive spaces of Western social and political theory, spaces previously usurped by secular reason. Apparently, the 'postsecular' impulse has come mainly from philosophers, not theologians or sociologists. A burgeoning literature on postsecular theorizing is now available, with notable contributions by leading social thinkers, including Asad (2003), Badiou (2003), Caputo (2001), de Vries and Sullivan (2006), Derrida (2002), Habermas (2008), Irigaray (1993), Joas (2008), Milbank (1991), Taylor (2007a), Taylor (1984), and Vattimo (2002). Also see Blond (1998), Caputo and Vattimo (2007), and Davis et al. (2005). Caputo's insight aptly sums up the 'postsecular' impulse: 'A postsecular philosophy', Caputo explains, 'emerges as a result of the death of God, spelling "the death of any kind of monism or reductionism, *including secularism*"' (Caputo 2001: 133, emphasis added). This is not a new occurrence, but on the heels of a deepening crisis of liberal modernity marked by its historical failures to speak *for* religious contexts of alterity and widespread politicization of religious subjectivities on a world scale (Casanova 1994; Juergensmeyer 2003; Thomas 2005), the 'postsecular' turn promises alternative sites of engagement between politics and religion, renouncing 'religious decline as the telos of history' (Casanova 2006: 18).

These sites provide new thinking spaces, both to dispel the hegemony of secular frames of capture, and to generate new vernaculars more responsive to local religious context. It is, however, unclear how postsecular awareness could shape international relations (IR) as theory and practice. As with secularism, the discursive field of postsecularity remains principally Euro-American. Secularism, as Joseph A. Camilleri reminds us, 'is a distinctly European or Western project, which originates with the Westphalian response to the wars of religion in Europe and eventually adopts the Enlightenment's predilection for reason as the defining principle governing the public sphere' (Camilleri 2012: 1020). A 'derivative discourse' (Chatterjee 1986) in the non-European world, secularism acquired a familiar currency in shaping models to banish religion from politics. The 'postsecular' turn underscores the limits of those secular models. It is important to stress the plurality of secular models, avoiding generic understandings produced by hegemonic variants of secularization theory (Bhargava 1998; Jakobsen and Pellegrini 2008). Casanova cautions against reading secularization as a single theory. Rather, it is best disaggregated into three propositions: '(1) secularization as a differentiation of the secular spheres from religious institutions and norms, (2) secularization as a decline of religious beliefs and practices, and (3) secularization as a marginalization of religion to a privatized sphere' (Casanova 2006: 12). Recognition of limits, however, only changes the perceptual field in which religion can be interrogated, not vitiate its materialization as an assorted practice conditioned by circumstance and context.

Assuming diversity of metaphysical perspectives, the 'postsecular' is likely to diverge from its Euro-American modularity in other cultural contexts: the character of postsecularity would simply mirror *cultural* variance, Islam presenting no exception. On received analysis, the 'return of religion' (captured in the generic terminology of 'resurgence', 'renewal' or 'fundamentalism', with the prefix 'Islamic' attached to it) merely authenticates the resistance of Islam to modernity (or its by-products, including secularism). The deployment of these terms alongside the 'Islamic' prefix fixes heterodox and fluid phenomena into neatly manufactured containers requiring no further need for interrogation or analysis.

The putative failure of secular reason to shape Muslim polity, society or culture offers few surprises; the postsecular on this reading cannot say anything novel about the ICZs; these zones have been *de facto* 'postsecular'. Challenging this normalized perspective, this chapter explores the principal forms in which the 'postsecular' resonates in the ICZs. The postsecular condition, it is argued here, should not be seen as 'a return of religion', but religion's 'rupture' *and* 'displacement'. The former connotes temporal discontinuity characterized by breakdowns in established routine, pattern and sequence. The latter entails a shift (*Verschiebung*) in spatial terrains.

'Displacement' suggests an unconscious redirection from potentially disruptive effects to familiar sites of ontological safety. For present purposes, however, the term is used quite broadly to register the impact of deterritorialization on political identity.

The use of psychoanalytical terms to political analysis is not without its hazards, including the charge of 'methodological individualism'. For present purposes, the deployment is to register principally a *spatial* shift in politics which inevitably entails psychic dimensions, including disorientation and closure. The latter may have significant effects on politics. To avoid methodological individualism, one scholar places these effects under the rubric of 'cultural schizophrenia' (Shayegan 1997). Another problem with a reliance on 'displacement' in the present context is the impression of temporal fixity within the ICZs, compensated only by a spatial shift. Recognizing this problem, the notion of 'rupture' is used to dispel that impression. Hence, 'rupture' and 'displacement' are conjoined to record the specific character of the postsecular in the ICZs. It is not the absence of the postsecular that characterizes the ICZs, but Islam's *particular* instantiation in a globalizing context. A key feature of that process is a pull towards more homogenized expressions of belief to the detriment of multivocality, producing, paradoxically, more fracture than unity, as well as greater reliance on secular reason (including instrumental rationality) to materialize religious desires. Viewed, thus, within a broader geo-epistemic frame, the 'postsecular' is not simply a moment of self-transcendence within Western understandings of religion, but a highly differentiated globalized spatio-temporal condition showing localized cultural markers. Needless to say, in challenging hegemonic frames of understanding the relation between Islam and postsecularity, the discussion follows a more schematic format. The spatial and temporal heterogeneity of Islamic practice cannot obviously survive the bluntness of this choice.

The burdens of engaging Islamic alterity within hegemonic frames are familiar enough: the picture of a religiously *overdetermined* cultural tradition, unyielding either to mutation or transformation. This sentiment is pervasive in both orientalist and post-orientalist (sociologically oriented) interpretations of societal processes in the ICZs (Lewis 2003). Ernest Gellner (1981) is a good representative of post-orientalist mappings of Islam. A key implication is that this representation naturalizes Muslim hostility and resistance to secularity, and by extension, makes postsecularity appear redundant: without experiencing secularization, as is the case with its Euro-American counterpart, the 'return of religion' (Lewis 1976) in the ICZs appears only as a confirmation of the ever-present postsecular. Faith requires no defensive rationalizations to provide alternative idioms to envision politics, sociability or cultural production. This picture of the world of Islam as an unchanging or resistant faith, either outside modern time (Osborne 2010) or operating on a schizoid track defined by a more or less fixed tradition-modernity dyad (Tibi 2002), makes the postsecular condition wholly superfluous, if entirely transparent. According to Ernest Gellner:

> One of the most conspicuous and significant facts concerning our contemporary world is that, while the sociologists' secularization thesis is all in all valid, one

major part of the world remains absolutely secularization-resistant: the world of Islam. Today, the hold of Islam over the societies and the minds of Muslims is at least as great as it was one or two centuries ago; in certain ways, it is probably *more*, not less, powerful.

(Gellner 1990: 318)

Gellner (2000) explicates a similar argument in 'Religion and the Profane'.

This chapter challenges the apparent irrelevance or transparency of the postsecular condition in the ICZs. One option is to refute 'immutability theses' in favour of some variant of secularization theory. Acknowledging alternative secularities (distinct from the Western ideal-type), the return of religion can then appear not as a 'return', but as a rejection of secular reason. This option is not entertained for reasons that become clear later. A second possibility is to rethink the nature of faith itself within the ICZs, outside the 'religious-secular' container altogether. On this alternative reading adopted here, Islamic political, social or cultural desires do not swing between twin poles of religiosity and secularity, but materialize ruptures and displacements within translocal social and life-worlds. First, the meaning of religion and, by extension, the so-called 'religious–secular' divide in Islam, does not mirror its monotheistic counterparts. Both *din* (religion) and *dunya* (world) come under the jurisdiction of faith. This is not a tired, recycled view of a symbiosis between the sacred and the profane in Islam, but a concession to a different cartography: the secular *cannot* exist, but the sovereignty of the sacred allows discriminations between different species of human affairs, on the one hand, and the divine, on the other. What passes as the 'worldly' is essentially the mundane, the everyday, the uneventful quotidian. Its relative autonomy is acknowledged, subject to its compliance to particular rules of performativity. Yet, this is not a world without norms, nor the lack of religion, since it is faith that affords the general principle which states that not all spheres of sociability and human exchange are equal. The 'secular' in the Islamic domain stands *inside* faith. This raises the important question not only about the operational code that defines religion, but the larger issue of the lines separating the sacred and the profane. The notion of piety may offer an opening into this wider conversation. Second, the fractured character of social worlds in the ICZs encompasses belief and the 'religious–secular' divide, producing new forms of religiosity that are given the appellation of 'political Islam' (Esposito 1983; Ayubi 1991; Roy 1994; Kepel 2003; Mandaville 2007; Ayoob 2008).

The discussion proceeds in four short sections to explicate these points. The first section addresses the 'myth' of secularity in IR to help situate the problematic location of Islam in received narratives. This location is sanctioned both by orientalist framings of Islamic alterity as well as IR's self-referentiality as a 'secular' enterprise. This intuition is pursued in the second section, which features the apparently awkward staging of the postsecular in the ICZs. Section three explores ruptures and displacements of religion in these zones under conditions largely *not of their own choosing* (Marx 2001 [1852]: 7). The retrenchment of an 'open' faith in favour of an increasingly 'closed' Islam congeals the effects of rupture and displacement. The final section of the chapter develops the implications of the postsecular turn for IR drawn from the previous sections.

IR and postsecularity

The story of the postsecular in IR is complex and ambiguous, illustrated in part in recent debates over political theology (Odysseos and Petito 2007; Luomaaho 2009; Guilhot 2010). As these debates highlight, the question of religion remains unsettled despite the self-congratulatory claims of secularization theorists. Secularization theorists distort Weber, as Habermas points out:

> The theory of modernization performs two abstractions on Weber's concept of 'modernity'. It dissociates 'modernity' from its modern European origins and stylizes it into a spatio-temporally neutral model for processes of social development in general. Furthermore, it breaks the internal connection between modernity and the historical context of Western rationalism, so that processes of modernization can no longer be conceived of as rationalization, as the historical objectification of rational structures.
>
> *(Habermas 1987: 2)*

It is, however, IR's 'secular' self-image built around specific historical signposts, notably Westphalia, that provides the hegemonic template (Westphalia as the originary moment of the birth of IR, however, is open to question (De Carvalho et al. 2011)). Osiander also shows that *cuius regio, eius religio* was actually stronger in the Augsburg Treaty than in the Westphalian ones already 20 years ago (Osiander 2001). Once attached to power, self-images in any field of inquiry, including IR, can have enormous heuristic and political effects. A potential effect of hegemonic self-imaging is to ensure the erasure or silencing of alternatives (Trouillot 1995). In canonical accounts drawn from secular reason, the 'return of religion to IR', thus, implicitly acknowledges its extended homelessness (Esposito and Watson 2000; Fox and Sandler 2004; Haynes 2009; Hurd 2007; Hatzopoulos 2003; Thomas 2005; Westerlund 2002; for a broader picture of the terrain of 'secularizing' currents, see Appleby 2000; Asad 1993; Berger 1999; Connolly 1997; Norris and Ingelhart 2004).

Notwithstanding its particularistic nature, IR's secular self-image continues to serve as a universal reference. Until recently, the *religious* side of IR has remained marginal (Luomaaho 2009; Guilhot 2008; Philpott 2000). The 'secular' promise of Westphalia was *essentially* a Protestant compromise. Casanova (1994) links the secular to developments within European Christianity designed to preserve the religious autonomy of the 'inside' while spurning religion's 'outside' presence. As Calhoun stresses, '[t]he Peace of Westphalia did not make states secular. It established the principle of *cuius regio eius religio* – who rule, his religion' (Calhoun 2010: 41).

As international relations, however, the Protestant settlement carries with it sizeable religious and cultural baggage. In claims invoking humanity, human rights, sovereignty, ethics or justice, the modularity of this settlement has produced not only specific ideals and repertoires of expectations concerning state building, diplomatic practice, rule making and general international conduct, but also preferred ways of structuring 'domestic' society aligned to the intimations of (Western) modernity – the latter despite assumed Westphalian exemptions for that sphere. The 'secular' character of IR has engendered the fiction of an autonomous, 'individuated' political subject, one who provides the measure to gauge the march of freedom, progress, democracy or development across borders. The exclusionary effects of institutionalized secular expectations are not too remote to unearth (Butler 2008).

Buttressed by orientalist frames of apprehending 'religious' others, secularity rapidly evolves into a 'standard of civilization', both for separating 'insiders' from 'outsiders' in international society, as well as for producing the hierarchicalization of political community (Walker 1999). The confluence of these horizontal and vertical dimensions mediated by orientalism continues to cast its imposing shadow on international practice. The promise and limits of postsecularity, therefore, can be better assessed, not only in relation to the failing fortunes of secular reason, but to orientalism's durability and scope.

The cumulative effect of the 'postsecular' turn on global horizons is yet to be ascertained. Camilleri's (2012: 1028) intervention highlights:

> the need to rethink the simplistic separation of religion and politics and the consequent need to redefine political space and authority; the unveiling of some of the cognitive and normative underpinnings of distrust, verging on rupture, between Islam and the West; and, perhaps, most importantly, the search for a new conception of political pluralism that can more effectively address the challenges posed by rising levels of religious and cultural diversity.

To be sure, the postsecular is linked to the exhaustion of secular modernity marked by recognition of its failures to order social, cultural or political life drawn principally from rationalities ensconced in frames of immanence. Alternatively, postsecularity is attached to sectors of the global condition in which religion resists eviction despite the consolidation of materialist civilization on a world scale. Religion continues to provide cultural defence, escape, succour and a resource of meaning to the majority of the world's population. Paradoxically, postsecular sentiment reflexively confirms both the historical transformation wrought by 'secularizing' processes *and* their absolute limits. The ubiquity of the 'immanent frame' (Taylor 2007a) in contemporary life speaks to the first; the inability of this frame to afford answers to deeper existential questions, to the second. A problem with secularization theory is the assumption, as Taylor notes, that 'the motivation to religious life in human beings is very shallow and not very profound, so that religious life is tied to certain sociological forms that existed earlier. And when these sociological forms are destabilized by modernity, religion disappears as well' (Taylor 2008). Without secularity, no postsecularity; but a secularity that is increasingly unable to explicate the durability of transcendence in human affairs, except the one that is couched in received claims of secular reason: religious attachments as residues of tradition, irrationality or 'incomplete' modernization.

Disguising its religious underpinnings, secular imaginaries have provided much of the philosophical and substantive content of IR, both in its self-understandings as a discipline as well as in international practice. Rational verities apparently purified of religion have continued to structure normative ideals and practical conduct of agents. In disparate arenas of state building, democracy or development, 'secular' rationality authors and authorizes participation in international society to the exclusion of alternative cultural (read 'religious') expectations; 'reasons of state' not 'value rationality' being at the core of relations across borders. The master narrative for IR remains, it seems, the quest for the good life secured within an 'immanent frame'. The arrival of postsecularity does not revive religious consciousness, but places it, on Taylor's reading, alongside secular reason as another option in imagining normative futures and present concerns.

The main effect of postsecularist thinking in IR is the recognition that, as Camilleri (2012: 1028–1029) notes, 'not just the Enlightenment version of secularism but also the Westphalian conception of the state' is under scrutiny. Yet, to the degree that the appeal and constrictions of postsecularity are spatially dispersed, it is unclear whether the Westphalian state is under active reassessment *everywhere*. Rather, discussions of the character of secularity in the public sphere have mainly sought understandings of a seemingly problematic, vague and fluid relationship between religion and modernity (Katzenstein 2006). For the most part, this relationship has been interrogated within 'national' boundaries. Postsecularist discourse has neglected, as Camilleri notes, 'the rise of identity politics of which the resurgence of religion is but one striking manifestation, and the limits of modernity that spell the slow but probably irreversible demise of the grand narrative associated with the Modern project' (Camilleri 2012: 1030). The slowness of its demise, however, does not necessarily diminish modernity's appeal for all, especially to those seeking emancipation from material want, alternative horizons of connectivity and belonging, or escape from 'ascriptive' identities.

Islam and the postsecular

Is postsecularity merely a signpost for Europe's anxiety and response to Islam's unavoidable presence in its midst, a Europe unable or unwilling to absorb Muslim alterity either in the public sphere or social relationality? These questions are easy to pose against received binaries and discriminations between the traditional and the modern, the religious and the secular, or totality and particularity. However, as Casanova notes, '[s]elf-definitions of modernity are tautological insofar as secular differentiation is precisely what defines a society as modern' (Casanova 2006: 20). In mainstream analyses of Islam, naturalized common sense readily displaces complex answers. Furthermore, in a politically charged climate of civilizational divergence (Huntington 1996), cognitive certainty furnishes defences against ontological insecurity; the greater the paranoia, the greater the need to lean on the familiar and the known: in this case, Islam, the familiar Other manifesting its true disposition, except only now visible across the full spectrum of the international. In this context, the difficulty of forging alternative thinking spaces becomes readily apparent. Can the 'postsecular turn' unfreeze common sense?

Although postsecularity draws no territorial boundaries, in relation to Islam it helps comprehend European anxieties and responses about an unassimilable Other. Islam's assumed position within the broader culture of 'misrepresentation, disadvantage, and discrimination' (Ansari 2002: 4) makes postsecularity a potential source for generating a new cultural code of inclusion. Recent proposals to establish this code (Habermas 2006), however, tend to reproduce cultural hierarchies embedded in strategies of translation. A principal flaw of several extant dialogical approaches is their inherent propensity to reduce the problem of difference to language, stressing the need for translating incommensurable speech. The problem lies deeper. It is not merely one of language, even of metaphysical incompatibility, which are certainly important, but more crucially, one of recognizing the heterogeneity of immanence/transcendence complexes in different cultural settings. In other words, postsecularity can offer more fruitful avenues of engagement if its proponents appreciate not only the limits of rationality, but also the multiplicity of attempts to reconcile rival claims of immanence and transcendence. The limits of postsecularity, nonetheless, become acutely visible not necessarily in attempts to impose stringent criteria for including religious speech and subjectivities attached to that speech, but in reinforcing the otherness of Islam. Cultural and civic forms of citizenship sought by postsecular thinkers do not overcome the problem of difference (Inayatullah and Blaney 2004). Rather, the unassimilable otherness of Islam and the (new) requirements of inclusion both reveal and disguise the cultural makeup of postsecular theorizing.

The obvious challenges postsecularity faces in reference to Islam are the effects of the 'secular' point of departure intrinsic to these conceptions. The new cultural code promised by the postsecular is contingent upon specific readings of the career of secularity. To be of general value, the new cultural code cannot merely reproduce *particular* temporalities inhabiting the world of secularity, but recognize suppressed heterodox religious desires subsumed under the 'deprivatization of religion' (Casanova 1994: especially chap. 8), a universal temporal reference can impede appreciation of other forms of negotiations between religiosity and secularity. Extant conceptions of secularity, secularization or secularism inevitably find their originary impetus in Protestant Christian settlements negotiated *within* European cultural spaces and *within* specific histories (Asad 2003). In this context, Taylor's magisterial opus, *A Secular Age*, remains remarkably, albeit self-consciously, Eurocentric. The universalization of secularity, akin to notions of modernity's global diffusion, comes at the price of marginalizing alternative histories and sites (Trouillot 1995). Postsecular theorizing appears to reproduce this social imaginary.

To the extent that conceptions of 'the religious' or 'the secular' are fluid and unevenly distributed across time and locale, the advent of postsecularity can only be partial and arbitrary; its meanings heterodox and malleable. As Calhoun notes, '[t]he "sharp binary of secularism and religion" obscures (a) the important ways in which religious people engage this-worldly, temporal life; (b) the important senses in which religion is established as a category not so much from within as from "secular" perspectives like that of the state; and (c) the ways in which there may be a secular orientation to the sacred or transcendent' Calhoun (2010: 35).

Acknowledgement of other temporalities does not mean a recycling of relativist notions in which the non-European (read Islamic) cultural zones have preserved their religious essence, uncontaminated by processes of flux, change or transformation of social and life-worlds – a view basic to orientalist mappings – but to concede heterogeneity and plasticity of cultural programmes in which 'the religious' intermingles with the 'secular', on the one hand, and to recognize alternative temporalities, on the other. In that sequence, the conception of religion itself needs denaturalization (Asad 2003). As Waardenburg notes in reference to Islam:

> The word 'Islam' itself is used in very different senses: by scholars (Islamicists with different approaches) as a subject of study, or a 'symbol' for their concrete subject of inquiry; by Muslims who, as Fazlur Rahman points out, may have different orientations as to what they consider to be religiously normative, to them; and in ordinary language in the West (with different evaluations and appreciations of what is felt to be 'foreign' to the West).
>
> *(Waardenburg 1997: 199)*

Postsecularity opens up new spaces for recognizing suppressed religious vernaculars within Western modernity as a condition of possibility to be attentive to alternative cultural programmes, including their religious idiom. Yet, it cannot serve as a blanket concession to the immutability of religious sentiment, but help recognize its unsettled character here and elsewhere. Reflexive postsecularity would show an awareness of cultural particularism inhabiting its own universe.

Despite the postsecular promise, the historical baggage of secularity is carried into postsecular frames of understanding with the penchant to replicate an image of an overdetermined Islamic faith unwilling to yield to sociological dynamics. For Casanova, 'the core component of the theory of secularization was the conceptualization of societal modernization as a process of functional differentiation and emancipation of the secular spheres – primarily the modern state, the capitalist market economy, and modern science – from the religious sphere, and the concomitant differentiation and specialization of religion within its own newly found religious sphere' (Casanova 2006: 12–13). On this image, the 'religious' lurking behind the sign of Islam resists modernity and defies modernity's inherent immanentist force – an unyielding transcendent faith remarkably impervious to attritions of time. This image not only confounds recognition of fluidity and flux, but disregards Islamic heterogeneity and the plurality of discourses that inform social or political practice (Al-Azmeh 1996). The postsecular promise to allow recognition of a largely variable nexus between the secular and the religious characterized by multiplicity easily succumbs to established secular modes of capture. The secular gaze resists supersession. Unwittingly, perhaps, postsecularity recycles the confining perspective of orientalism. The acknowledgement of the durability of religious sentiment appended to Islam has a familiar ring to it, its antipathy to modernity.

Rupture and displacement

The language of postsecularity captures the durability of religion in IR with recognition of the enduring presence of faith in politics. However, can the post-secular also acknowledge the ontological dislocation in the character of religion itself under conditions of late modernity? Can it avoid an exceptional stance relative to Islam, exempting it from the force of immanentist imaginings, horizons or practice? Secularization claims or those of the privatization of religion are easier to discard in the face of 'living' Islam. From Weber (Salvatore 1996) to Gellner to Lewis to Tibi, Islamic exceptionalism ensured the supposed absence of secularity in Muslim doctrine, consciousness, politics or lived practice. The narrative of unity of all spheres militated against the separation of faith and the mundane. Muslim self-conception also allowed no worldly intrusions to disrupt the primacy of faith; politics could never untie God from the polity; social practice in the ICZs indelibly coloured by the experience of the Holy. Similarly, however, tacit knowledge of Islamic alterity taints postsecularity in a variety of both known and unexpected forms. This is an instance of what Charles Taylor calls, 'block thinking' which 'fuses a varied reality into one indissoluble unity, and in two ways. First, different manifestations of Islamic piety are seen as alternative ways of expressing the same core meaning. Second, all Muslims are then seen as endorsing those core meanings (Taylor 2007b). Sensitivity to alterity ends up freezing it in time.

The transformed character of Islam, however, presents more pain than consolation. Postsecular theorizing readily acknowledges the transformation of public, cognitive and private spheres in the West (Taylor 2007a), yet this logic languishes on the 'Islamic' cultural shores: the ICZs remain unaffected, seeking refuge in transcendental dreams and commitments. As noted, this establishment perspective makes postsecularity largely irrelevant to Islam, since presumably the problem of secularity never breached the impregnable walls of religiosity in Islam's vast, albeit unchanging, universe. An alternative to this recognized notion is the implicit distinction between modernization and secularization. Disjuncture between the two is likely to disrupt established narratives long naturalized in hegemonic frames. A disturbing question emerges: if Islam is *modernizing but not secularizing*, how does the post-secular turn simultaneously avoid post- or reflexive orientalist mappings or the relativizing scheme of 'multiple modernities'?

This totalizing view of Islam allows no distinctions between, for example, 'official' and 'popular' forms of Islam. The 'official' religion, as Waardenburg notes, 'is that of true Tawhid, and although Islam has no "official" organization of its own, throughout Islamic history this Tawhid has been upheld by all religious scholars in opposition to the popular religion of shirk' (Waardenburg 1997: 318). By contrast, 'popular' Islam expresses the heterogeneity of everyday religious practice, open-ended and fluid (Waardenburg 1997: 318).

Similarly, the ideal of Islam and its practice, as with any other faith, not only diverge, but inescapably face immanent rationalities; materialist civilization is unavoidable. Yet, what cultural resources become available and how they are in turn shaped by this encounter is not pre-ordained. Above all, this confrontation is *political*, which can often metamorphize into existential struggles.

> A sharp distinction should be made between 'normative' Islam and 'actual' Islam. Normative Islam consists of the prescriptions, norms, and values that are recognized as divine guidance by the whole community. These are taken from the basic normative texts, mostly with what is held to be normative interpretation. Actual Islam comprises all those forms and movements, practices and ideas that in fact have existed in the many Muslim communities in different times and places, and that have been considered to be 'Islamic and subsequently legitimate and valid'.
>
> *(Waardenburg 1997: 199)*

To escape Eurocentricity, the postsecular must furnish an apparatus to recognize other struggles, and more to the point, Islamic subjectivities that are forged by those struggles (Mavelli 2012).

The major problem, however, is the overdetermined character of Islamic alterity, an otherness accessible only in *religious* terms, marginalizing the wider sociological and political context in which the force of immanence confronts Islamic understandings of transcendence. This problem is compounded with the assumption of a singular (Protestant) narrative of salvation equally distributed across the monotheistic field. A simpler way out of this conundrum is the adoption of frames produced by 'multiple modernities' (Eisenstadt 2000).

Linked to the 'multiple modernities' option, the postsecular presents greater possibilities to escape the risk of over-determination. No longer attached to the equation, West=modernity in standard civilizational narratives, the potential for an 'Islamic' modernity is conceded. However, this promising option tends to conflate logical and historical categories. The former continues to derive its constitutive elements from the European experience, which conditions the trajectory of its travel elsewhere. A more fundamental problem persists: a failure to appreciate 'connected histories' and entanglements across civilizations in the making of the 'modern'. 'Contrary to what "area studies" implicitly presumes, a good part of the dynamic in early modern history was provided by the interface between the local and regional (which we may call the "micro"-level), and the supra-regional, at times even global (what we may term the "macro"-level)' (Subrahmanyam 1997: 745). Although addressing 'early modern Eurasia', Subrahmanyam's general point about connectivity applies with unequivocal force to entanglements between Islam and Europe. Denying connectivity and entanglement, monadic 'alternative' modernity programmes seek realization in more or less spatially bound containers. The potential for cross-contamination, mutual borrowing, caricature or mimicry can be sacrificed in favour of alternative pathways towards the same destination. This problem becomes more pronounced in mappings of the international.

The location of the ICZs within a Westphalian order poses specific challenges for postsecularist theorizing. Notwithstanding several extant readings of the existence of a global *Ummah* (a worldwide community of believers), Muslims negotiate their social world principally within state boundaries subject to the operations of *raison d'être*. This does not limit Muslim horizons which may have a tendency to spill over, but *conditions* forms of cultural life, citizenship and political community. Although considerably enfeebled by global connectivity, the Westphalian order enjoys considerable fidelity amongst political elites in the ICZs. Hence, a distinction needs to be drawn between the idiom of politics in the ICZs, and its substance. The former often betrays compulsions of religiosity, not the latter.

Paradoxically, demands for aligning political practice to doctrinal principles in much of the ICZs confirms the actual chasm separating political and civil society. The exceptional cases of religiously coded politics (Iran or Saudi Arabia) confirm the rule: *political* struggles shape the content of religious practice. The so-called 'return' of religion is invariably subordinated to the dictates of the state. A further distinction between statist and non-statist Islam illuminates the dilemmas facing the ICZs. Statist Islam solidifies legitimating processes by the political classes. Wedded to the narrative of national sovereignty, statist Islam enjoys the stability of the Westphalian order. This version of Islam feeds nicely into imperial constellations of power. By contrast, non-statist Islam is inherently tied to transnational narratives of a borderless Islamic community. This postnational vision of Islam presents mixed challenges for organizing political life. Postsecularity must speak to both variants.

To reiterate, postsecularity offers new horizons for reimagining the international. Cognizant of the limits of secular reason in structuring dialogue with religious others, postsecular sensitivity can allow circumvention of hubris drawn from stories of progress, the Great Divergence (Huntington 1996; Pomeranz 2000), or self-affirming tales of European exceptionalism (McNeill 1963; Ferguson 2011). It is, however, uncertain how postsecular sentiment can forge new horizons of post-Westphalian relations unaffected by narrower interpretations of 'community' or the 'cosmopolis'. Can the appeal of the postsecular to the ICZs also lead to a real, not nominal, discovery of civilizational others?

To release new vernaculars of engagement effectively, postsecularity must find an alternative idiom of interpreting the assumed stubbornness of Islam to secular modernity. This exercise rests upon recognition of the *relative autonomy* of political practice detached from religious attachments. Neither secular nor religious, recognition of the *political* can portend new orders of interpretation. Implicit in this process is a rejection of the totalizing nature of Islam, not only in contemporary but historical terms. The presence of differentiated spheres, albeit conditioned by Islamicity, presents an important signpost. Presence of differentiated spheres (Zubaida 2003) renounces the fictionalized totality of Islam, offering instead alternative sites for understanding the kernel of the Islamic 'reformation'. Calhoun's remarks also seem relevant: 'Europe's trajectory was state churches followed by militant *laïcité* ... In fact, postcolonial societies around the world have given rise to most of the regimes of religious pluralism and religious tolerance' (Calhoun 2010: 42). Gellner also presents a provocative reading of the Islamic reformation:

> The great reformation which has overtaken the Muslim world in the last hundred years or so and which the West has noticed barely, if at all, has been the displacement of folk superstition, particularly the previously widespread practice of saint worship, by a more 'proper', scholarly, not to say scholastic, puritanical, scripturalist version of the faith. The high culture which had ever coexisted with a folk low culture, but had never been able to dominate it properly, has at last achieved a victory, thanks to modern condition.
>
> *(Gellner 1990: 320)*

Both law and politics yield alternative constructions of the social order in relation to faith. In this context, an alternative perspective would rest ultimately upon rethinking modernity's relation to historicism. The received timeline of modernity inescapably shadows the career of the Protestant settlement. On a postsecular reading as well, this timeline erects a universal reference. The task, paradoxically, is to produce a more *secular* history of modernity in which Christian retrenchments against the force of secularism would no longer sanction authorizations of authority.

In brief, the postsecular must come to terms with rival, if mutually connected, forms of Islamic encounters with modernity: a more homogenized Islam at odds with an 'open Islam'. According to Casanova, the Islamic tradition has experienced 'an unprecedented process of pluralization and fragmentation of religious authority' (Casanova 2006: 29). However, Casanova does not take into account processes that have given scripturalist and puritanical variants of Islam greater visibility and force. The apparent democratization of interpretation has not guaranteed that a more 'open' Islam would be accorded greater legitimacy. The potential for a more homogenized Islam to emerge in contexts of mass media dissemination is unaccounted for in Casanova's otherwise rich account. 'The destabilization of religious authority does not offer any insurance against a more puritanical version of the Faith to inspire the multitude under conditions of cultural or economic dislocation in much of the ICZs' (Casanova 2001: 1059). This classification is well established, but usually drawn within culturalist readings of Islamic history (Gellner 1981). Stressing the *political*, this distinction would, instead, capture struggles within the ICZs over the nature of the social and political order. Inescapably, the real political contestation is *not* between the secular and the religious in these zones, but political struggles linked to battles over the *religious* itself. Mavelli (2012) shows how the 'secularist-Islamist polarisation' has been defied in the recent struggle in Egypt.

An 'open' Islam suggests an ecumenical faith responsive to internal heterogeneity and difference. Paradoxically, it is in its 'traditional' forms that an 'openness' has been enacted, recognizing historical continuities, diverse patterns and multiple temporalities. By contrast, a 'closed' Islam is the end result of ruptures in Islamic history and memory, exacerbated by the dismantling of traditional religious institutions both under colonial and globalized modernity. Separated from the certainties of locality and place, and under pressures of generalized exchange, infirm secondary attachments, urbanization and 'cultural schizophrenia', a more homogenized faith has engendered illusions of ontological security. Modernity does not expand the discursive space of religion, but narrows it. Often, politics masquerades as piety. It is not the assumed success, but 'failure of political Islam' (Roy 1994) whose exhaustion assumes puritanical variants of religion and its pathologies, including nihilistic violence (Pasha 2012).

The deterritorialized character of Islamic imaginaries (Roy 2004) is not peculiar to this faith; it has been representative of all world religions refusing bounded walls sanctioned by political authority. However, the temporal context of deterritorialization is remarkably different now, relative to earlier historical epochs. The speed, acceleration and scope of global connectivity produced by flows of information, ideas, symbols, objects and people (Appadurai 1996) are linked to a globalized political economy producing distanciation between identity and territory. In this larger context, the diminutive capacity of the postcolonial state does not produce localism or tribalism, as generally believed, but translocal commitments. Globalized forms of Islamic intersubjectivity assume more 'modular' forms. Reshaped by global flows, both politics and piety require postnational modes of recognition and address. Exportable forms of a homogenized Islam can circulate more easily than those 'traditional' variants interwoven into local structures. The more homogenized the faith, the greater is its capacity to transcend 'borders'. The notion of 'borders', however, is increasingly weak to comprehend global connectivities. Perhaps a more accurate description of processes of religious deterritorialization is to acknowledge spatio-temporal dislocation.

Displacements in Islamic identities are products of global processes of connectivity, producing ruptures in the social and life-worlds of Muslims. These ruptures show an uncanny resemblance to fractures experienced in the past. In a 'postnational' context, however, deterritorialization increasingly severs the nexus between community (ascriptive or imagined) and location. While the political elites in the ICZs recite eulogies on behalf of post-Westphalian sovereignty, the state in much of the Islamic world appears increasingly fragile. It is unable to regulate the effects of globalizing currents, provision distributive justice or generate domestic security, except to rely on large-scale repression against potentially restless populations. Conversely, dependence upon managerial forms of governance to align 'national' economies to the globe offers a favoured passage out of persistent crises. Clearly, ruptures and displacements do not produce singular trajectories. As the 'Arab Spring' and its immediate aftermath highlighted, the 'religious' question is not the most pivotal one in the politics of the ICZs. Protest and 'revolution' in globalizing times may not herald ideological dreamworlds. Rather, the ordinariness of cries for justice in a world with few certainties may simply reveal the pervasiveness of the crisis that afflicts the ICZs. It is obviously too early to ascertain the contours of politics in the ICZs (or elsewhere) in the wake of the Arab Spring. A key point, though, is apparently the sudden disappearance of 'religion' in the analysis. Less noticeable is the mutation within religion itself, not secularization; religion finding new modes of instantiation.

'Open' and 'closed' Islams are ideal-typical images of the two principal forms noticeable in capturing the terrain in which the postsecular confronts the ICZs. In actuality, there is considerable plurality in both the discursive and non-discursive realms of religiosity. The discursive field ranges from redemptive to rejectionist mappings of the Muslim predicament. On the other side of the equation, the non-discursive arena is saturated with social, class and gender divisions, each with its own political effects. What is less ambiguous, however, is the ascendancy of more puritanical answers to the supposed crisis in Islamic identity: an apparent disillusionment marked by weakened conviction in evolutionary utopias. The extreme expression of this state of dystopia is the spectacle of nihilistic violence, more as certitude of apolitical powerlessness, than politics. Without the ability to materialize alternative futures, a refracted world of internal fracture stages its pathologies in self-defeating attempts to seek coherence or meaning. Neither coherence nor meaning is easily available, especially to a variant of faith that subverts any possibility of dialogue or tolerance.

Although the exteriority of fracture is not uniform, it is the extreme variant that typically appears as the public face of Islam. The postsecular may provide a countervailing tendency in deploying more heterodox modes of capture. Freed from secularist prejudice, the Islamic world can become more recognizable in its heterogeneity. Yet, in order to achieve that aim, the postsecular has to release itself from orientalism or cultural relativism. This would entail not just reflexivity towards religious plurality, or recognition of universality in particularized otherness, but a shift from the endogenous to the international plane. A key aspect of that shift is an appreciation of the wider global context in which seemingly local processes materialize. The forms of 'postsecular' politics in the ICZs are inseparable from globality, its processes, dimensions and effects.

Conclusion

Postsecularity casts its shadow upon the intricate relation between religion and politics in IR, principally in its successful dismantling of the hegemony of the secularization story. Yet, the forms postsecularity assumes are heterodox and recursive. A meta-narrative of postsecularity is clearly fraught with more ellipses and silences than discrete moments of its unfolding in time. Within the context of Islamic political practice, historical and contemporary registers are opened up. Recognition of both the heterogeneity of the ICZs and the discourses that inform that practice presents a first step towards an appreciation of the transformed nature of the secular-religious nexus.

'Provincializing' postsecularity (Chakrabarty 2000), therefore, offers more promise than merely its embrace as a universal template for global distribution. At a minimum, this exercise entails baring the cultural assumptions embedded in the postsecular critique of secular reason. Concretely, this would mean de-Christianizing postsecularity, while profiting from the cosmopolitan aspects of Christianity (Žižek 2000, 2001, 2003).

On the other hand, greater engagement with internal dialogical processes in the ICZs can help curtail the monological character of postsecular reason. These are only preliminary steps in a long journey, but necessary to avoid the fateful career of postsecularity's forerunner. Indeed, a more ambitious undertaking would involve engagement with other cultural zones, their subjectivities and cosmological imaginings. In a sense, stepping outside the worlds of monotheism could furnish even more fruitful avenues to comprehend fully the limiting horizons of the postsecular.

This chapter cautions against celebratory receptions of the 'postsecular' in IR with reference to the ICZs. Without delineating processes that will allow the postsecular to produce more expansive terms of religious inclusion in the global public sphere, it could end up consolidating older barriers, or simply erecting new ones. The repudiation of secularization theory clearly releases discussions of the relation between Islam and modernity. The universal 'Western' reference of modernity, essentially an *ethos of secularity*, can be discarded in favour of more generous understanding of modernity – a spatio-temporal horizon combining the religious and the secular. Similarly, the confining framework of secularization can be replaced with less hegemonic modalities of engaging with Islamic subjectivities. However, the postsecular is a global condition of possibility only in a very general sense: it remains chiefly a European problem and problematic. Hence, it still remains unclear how the postsecular will bear upon political practice in the wake of turbulent times gripping the ICZs.

The international serves as the limit of political modernity. Only in relation to the international can particular political forms emerge. The international is also the container of political modernity. The organizing principle of political modernity is sovereignty – which congeals the essence of the settlement between the sacred and the secular. The postsecular is recognition of the exhaustion of that settlement; sovereignty can no longer operate within national containers. Both the secular and the sacred must attach themselves to forms that transcend the nation-state. However, the struggle over the character of the nation-state must first play out (Chatterjee 1998); this assumes heterodox forms. The 'return' of religion is only a condition of possibility for the postsecular. Rather, the 'postsecular' is better conceived as the undoing of the sacred/secular settlement within political modernity without a discernible alternative. The sacred/secular settlement in Islam precedes Protestantism, but under colonialism, that settlement is undone with the emergent divergence between state and society. On balance, the state gravitates toward the secular; society embraces the sacred (initially in the private realm); in the postcolonial era, society seeks to redefine the 'secular' state in its own image. In some instances, the state pre-empts society by adopting the language of the sacred. The secular international constrains this transition by unleashing a war against the sacred, paradoxically sacralizing the international. The secular international is never totally secular; it reflects the hegemony of the Protestant Westphalian settlement. Political Islam, and its varied manifestations, is, therefore, not anti-modern, but a rejection of that Protestant settlement.

PART II
Challenge and response

5

GLOBALIZATION AND CULTURAL CONFLICTS

The ascendancy of market fundamentalism on a world scale and Islamic 'religious resurgence' appear to follow opposite structural trajectories informed by competing logics of openness and closure. Throughout this chapter, the term 'resurgence' is used in place of the politically charged language of 'fundamentalism'. Resurgence underlines the *political* nature of Islamic social movements seeking to restructure state and civil society, not simply conform to some 'fundamentals'. Fundamentalism also carries an implicit liberal preference of relegating religion to the private realm.

On this popular construction, unabashedly drawn from earlier modernization claims, globalization is future-directed, promising a brave new world of freedom and wealth, of porous boundaries and inclusiveness. Fulfilling the evolutionary, teleological promise of progress and the Enlightenment, globalization underscores the last phase of the unfinished project of modernity (Beck 2000), an irreversible march towards a universal civilization, the worldwide embrace of liberal economic and political rationality (Fukuyama 1992), and the emergence of a 'flat' world (Friedman 2005). By contrast, Islamic resurgence is backward looking, a retrograde ideological obstacle to emancipatory movement, more in the nature of a social pathology than a self-subsistent social phenomenon (Lewis 2001), a reaction to Western modernity and its global diffusion (Lewis 1976). Globalization takes on the appearance of market fundamentalism. As Seabrook (2001) puts it:

> The industrialized world has for 200 years subjected its own peoples to a long and persistent development that has taken a single direction: the extirpation of all previous ways of answering need and its supersession by the market. It is no wonder that we invest in the market with a veneration bordering on idolatry, and see it as vehicle of salvation, arbiter of destiny and embodiment of morality. Not for the first time, human beings make a cult of that which is destroying them, even as the wealth accumulates around us, and the

iconography of luxury and ease bid us assent to the endless expropriations to which our daily life is witness.

On the other side of the equation, echoing orientalist cartographies (Said 1978) and familiar tradition–modern dichotomies (Parsons 1951; Eisenstadt 1966), the hegemonic view takes Islamic religious resurgence as a repudiation of modernity. With pervasive appeal in the corridors of global power and policy, establishment thinking sees it as a rejection of cosmopolitan impulses unleashed by time-space compression and increased social interconnectedness. On the other hand, it merely regards it as a moralizing lament against the rationalizing force of capitalism and individualism.

Accordingly, Islamic resurgence is seen fixated on the past, an atavistic residue of a dying civilization, yielding bigotry and barriers (Lewis 2001, 2002). Against the liberating force of West-centred globalization (Friedman 2005), social movements inspired by Islam reveal the stubbornness of traditional culture (Tibi 1990). Ascriptive attachments of faith and family, tribe and community collide with volitional drives for individual selfhood and autonomy. Hence, conventional wisdom views globalization and Islamic resurgence as completely contrary phenomena. If, indeed, there is a nexus between the two, it can only replicate a universal-particular hierarchy and a stimulus-response modality. In the first instance, globalization represents a universal and universalizing phenomenon; Islamic resurgence manifests the distempers of particularism and exclusivity. In the second instance, there is a recognizable temporal sequence – first globalization, *then* resurgence, mirroring active (Westernizing) and passive (Islamic) cognitive and experiential registers. Globalization congeals flow and fluidity (Appadurai 1996; Castells 1996), Islamic resurgence stasis and rigidity (Lewis 2002). Merely reactive, the latter can only respond, not initiate; 'outside' modernity, Islam-inspired social movements lack agency or originality (Lewis 1976, 2001, 2002).

An integral part of hegemonic consciousness, these representations circulate as common sense, fully backed by the institutional power of global capital in the public domain. For Gramsci, common sense covers the 'diffuse, uncoordinated features of a general form of thought common to a particular period and a particular popular environment' (Gramsci 1971: 330n). 'Common sense' sees neoliberal globalization and religious resurgence to reside in separate worlds, unbridgeable and incommensurate.

If Islamic resurgence is considered as a variant of worldwide religious resurgence (Marty and Appleby 1991), a wider process of global desecularization (Berger 1999), or a challenge to teleological understanding of historical movement (Beyer 1992), contemporaneous with globalizing modernity, and in fact the latter's instantiation, then these claims can potentially raise serious disquiet and tension in hegemonic thinking. However, in an environment of binary opposites, a global state of emergency, and renewed orientalist mapping of the world, the Islamic cultural zones assume a naturalized otherness (see Chapter 1), removed from the general flow of history, politics or political economy. The term 'Islamic cultural zones' (ICZs), as noted, connotes the plurality of the institutional and cultural experience of Muslims rejecting essentialist readings of Islam as a totalizing, monolithic entity. The particularity of these areas metamorphizes into particularism, uniqueness and 'repellent otherness' (Al-Azmeh 1996). While the distinction between the *different* and the *exceptional* is an important one, in a geo-cultural context of friend and enemy (Schmitt [1932] 1996), Islamic specificity appears as deviance from the global norm.

Mapping Islamic resurgence

Islamic resurgence is an undeniable fact (Esposito 1983; Ayubi 1991; Roy 1994). In generic (and minimal) terms, it is characterized by: (1) an increased assertiveness of Islam in the public and private domains; (2) self-consciousness of Muslims *qua* Muslims combined with a certain self-assuredness in their *Islamic* identity within a diverse field of multiple identities drawn from religion, nationalism or ethnicity; (3) attempts to restructure the moral code and conduct in a secularizing world, especially with regard to the question of gender and sexual relations, on the one hand, and assumed corrosion of the moral code under conditions of materialism, on the other; (4) politicization of Islam and the Islamization of politics, reflected in increasing participation by Islam-inspired social agents in political discourse and institutions, including political parties, universities, think-tanks and, in some instances, outside established channels of government and governance; (5) self-help and reliance on Islamicist non-state organizations and associations for economic and social welfare; and (6) reshaping of the terms of political and social discourse in light of assumed religious principles, among others. The relative mix of these elements is varied across regions, localities and nations, from Jakarta to Algiers – virtually all corners of Muslim heartlands and peripheries, including the majority non-Muslim cultural zones. Moreover, within these cultural spaces there are degrees of commitment to the faith; Islamic resurgence though ubiquitous is not necessarily the most significant phenomenon in the social and life-worlds of Muslims. The crucial distinction between *Islam as culture* and *Islam as politics* can help dispel over-categorization of social reality in the ICZs, a by-product of religion. The first speaks to the wider social milieu, offering no political projects but the assurance of commonality or familiarity. By contrast, the second aims to enter the public and private worlds of Muslims to restructure links to authority and power, morality, and social conduct. Collapsing the two, as in orientalist constructions of Islam, yields a totalized and totalizing view with few analytical spaces to grasp the complex relation between globalization and Islamic resurgence.

Islamic resurgence is linked principally to processes within civil society, but its primary aim is to restructure the state. The failure of secular nationalism has dramatically shifted the political discourse towards the question of cultural assertion. With neoliberal globalization downsizing the welfare (not coercive) functions of the state, civil society has become an arena of contesting the cultural form of globalization and providing an alternative resource for material sustenance. Islamic social movements are, therefore, both avenues of mobilization against perceived cultural corrosion as well as the provider of last resort in an environment of diminished or failed welfare state capacity. With the state receding from its historic Keynesian (and developmental) role, the task now falls upon Muslim schools, clinics and other self-help associations. A close nexus links state retrenchment and its delegitimation in the public domain. Islamic resurgence, on this premise, is not simply a crusading moral order to construct a City of God, but a discursive framework and movement to build or rebuild communities abandoned by the neoliberal state. The assumed appeal of Islamic institutions among the *lumpen* and middle-class sectors of the population is largely based on their amphibious character as reservoirs of cultural cohesion against materialism and providers increasingly of scarce public goods in a climate of atomistic contentment and social apathy. Those with diminished power and material capacity are most likely to gravitate to Islamic resurgence. Islamicists tend to emerge from the peripheral sectors of political economy, but increasingly, sectors of the vernacular elites.

Islamic resurgence is a highly differentiated, heterodox and contradictory phenomenon. Islamicists demonstrate ambivalence towards modernity, generally embracing its technical-instrumental side, but rejecting its cultural forms. In the arena of politics, for instance, the aspiration to exercise power in the service of social or moral purpose is easily entertained, but the institutional implications of modern political subjectivity receive, at best, a lukewarm reception. In part, this ambivalence emanates from the tortured historical experience of political subordination vis-à-vis the West, the duality of liberal colonial institutions in the subordinated zones producing subjects rather than citizens, and the unending neo-colonial dispensation in the post-colonial period. It is important to place Islamic resurgence within an historical context to avoid hasty inferences regarding its character and goals.

Cultural or class conflict?

Conventional wisdom tends to see not only a basic cleavage between Islam and the West (Huntington 1993), and as a corollary, a battle between Islam and modernity (assuming the natural affinity between modernity and the West), but cultural conflicts *within* the ICZs in isomorphic terms. As Huntington notes:

> The fault lines between civilizations are replacing the political and ideological boundaries of the Cold War as the flash points of crisis and bloodshed. The Cold War began when the Iron Curtain divided Europe politically and ideologically. As then ideological division of Europe has disappeared, the cultural division of Europe between Western Christianity, on the one hand, and Orthodox Christianity and Islam has remerged.
>
> *(Huntington 1993: 29–30)*

From this perspective, the fault line in the world of Islam is between traditionalists and modernists, between those who reject Westernization (and modernity) and the 'reformers' seeking to embrace post-Enlightenment West-centred progress. The binary, Manichean world separating the savage and the civilized reappears, now disguised in the language of globalization, particularly in its neoliberal variant. Huntington's (1993, 1996) cultural cartography sums up this uncomplicated view, and by extension the nature of cultural conflict. The possibility of entanglement between Islam and the West/modernity (see Introduction) or 'intertwined histories' (Said 1993) is not seriously entertained to allow a more complex picture of historical trends. Rather, the surgical economy of irreconcilable difference is summoned to afford analysis, but also to rationalize attitude and policy towards Islam and its diverse cultural instantiations. Alternatively, as subsequent discussion will show, the imbrication of Islam and modernity/West/globalization renders binary classifications and analyses problematic.

Within the broader context of a transformed post-Cold War world order, leading public intellectuals with strong links to Western hegemony either celebrated the triumph of Western liberalism marking the 'end of history' (Fukuyama 1992), permitting no room for alternative projects to structure society, or cautioned that the end of ideological and political conflict had ushered in a more protracted 'clash of civilizations', principally between the West and Islam (Huntington 1993, 1996). 'For the relevant future, there will be no universal civilization', warned Huntington (1993: 49); the driving force in history is likely to be cultural conflict. The implicit battle between globalization and resurgence in both triumphalist and alarmist accounts is not hard to detect, informed by a universal–particular distinction. Given the normative hierarchy of civilizations, an understanding of cultural conflicts is already transparent, premised on the assumption of a totalizing Islam feeding the ICZs against a liberal West. This hegemonic image presents an assumed clash between Islam and the West as more pivotal than conflicts *within* the ICZs.

In the post-9/11 Manichean climate of the saved and the damned especially, despite nominal gesturing towards recognition of heterogeneity within Islam, complex cultural dynamics have readily succumbed to orderly classifications. Islamic resurgence appears uniform, indistinguishable from militancy, rage or terrorism (Lewis 1976, 2002). The twin pillars of market fundamentalism and secularism provide the promised frontier; any deviance from pathways leading up to that destination is condemned as heresy. Consequently, the demonization of any recognizably self-subsistent Islamic current untamed by capitalist rationality or secular leanings appears as a sinister global presence. The drive to secularize the Muslim world through public diplomacy or conquest becomes explicable on this view.

A favourite corollary to hegemonic mappings of the nexus between globalization and Islamic resurgence is an allusion to political contingencies, either the Arab defeat in 1967 and the 1973 oil crisis (Lubeck 2000), or the decline of communism (Mazrui 1991). On this reading, Islamic social movements are *responses* to dramatic events. Stressing the changing regional or global environment in the ICZs, these claims situate the rise of political Islam to shifts in the political field. Absent in these accounts, however, is an *extended* historical understanding of globalizing processes working within both the ICZs, and providing the wider context of their constitution. A complex phenomenon is typically reduced to structural changes in the global political economy during the 1970s (Cox 1987), or the new international division of labour (Mittelman 1996), or the advent of the cyber revolution (Castells 1996). Instead, an historical mapping of globalization would decidedly capture neoliberal globalization only as a more recent 'moment' of an otherwise extended process. A serious reappraisal of globalization as an extended historical process implicating inter-civilizational exchange, cultural borrowing and the agonizing experience of domination/subordination takes inquiry in different directions. As an *integral* part of historical processes of globalization or increased social connectedness on a global scale (Held et al. 1999), the relation between globalization and Islamic resurgence acquires a different trajectory and substance. The two phenomena appear contemporaneous on a single temporal scale and distempers in the ICZs materialize fault lines within historical structures. Neoliberal globalization has *deepened* extant socio-economic, political and cultural fractures. A key implication here is the repudiation of the traditional–modern dichotomy. The analytical task then is one of deciphering *internal* movement and connectivity, not correlation. In this sense, cultural conflicts within the ICZs mirror the polarizing logic of globalization; social agents within the ICZs embody that logic.

In recent years, a variety of sociological approaches to understanding Islamic resurgence have also added to the fast growing cottage industry of Islamic Studies, particularly those that take 'political' Islam as a geopolitical threat requiring policing and surveillance. More sober, mostly pre-9/11, accounts identify important determinants of Islamic resurgence in varied settings: demographic changes and the swelling *lumpen* populations (Richards and Waterbury 1996), urbanization and changes in social interaction (Ayubi 1991), and general economic malaise (Roy 1994). Unlike accounts that privilege the global over the local, analyses premised on contingent factors tend to over-specify rupture at the expense of continuity and transcendence. These lacunae are largely filled by scholars, who find in Islamic resurgence a search for 'alternative' modernity (Göle 2000), a realization of identity politics. Islamic resurgence in these 'alternative' formulations is treated in non-essentialized terms recognizing variance and contingency. However, the quest for authenticity and cultural autonomy captured in 'alternative modernities' appears *particularistic*, not as a *particular* feature of generalized modernity. Missing in this formulation also is an appreciation of co-construction of modernity. Rather, the West continues to serve as the norm against which 'alternative' (non-Western) variants are assessed.

The failure to recognize co-construction and contemporariness produces a dualistic model of cultural conflicts sparked by globalization in the ICZs, best expressed in treating Islamic resurgence as a reaction. According to Lubeck, for instance, 'Islamic movements have now largely displaced secular nationalist and leftist movements as the *primary mobilizing force of resistance* against real and imagined Western political, economic and cultural domination' (Lubeck 2000: 149, emphasis added). To reiterate, the recurrent image of Islamic *resurgence as resistance* fails to recognize the mutually constitutive nature of globalization and religious resurgence. Though a considerably more charitable view than the established traditional–modern frame, the characterization of resurgence either as resistance or a reaction is ahistorical and reductionist. The notion of Islamic resurgence challenging West-centred globalization, or as a struggle against the corrosive effects of 'savage capitalism', fails to consider the historical wellsprings of Islamic social movements (Butterworth 1992; Keddie 1994, 1998). It also fails to recognize their multiple forms, antecedents and aims. Resistance to globalization is but *one* expression among many, though this expression appears hegemonic.

On balance, Islamic social movements are inwardly directed, seeking to transform state and civil society within the ICZs, notwithstanding the rhetorical content of their discourses (Esposito 1983). In other instances, resistance to globalization becomes indistinguishable from struggle against an 'unjust' political and social order. Upon closer scrutiny, the terms of Islamic political discourse share 'functional equivalence' with familiar terms drawn from the Western experience. The context may be different, but they typically address questions of legitimate authority, the ends of government, the balance between acquisition and social cohesion or the relation between private acts and public consequences. Summary repudiation of Islamic discourses obfuscates the experiential and ideational dynamics of alternative settings and, therefore, misguides an appraisal of deeper motivations undergirding social action.

Despite demographic and sociological variance in local conditions, in all the ICZs class tensions show elective affinities with cultural contestation between globalizing elites and the bulging ranks of the disenfranchised. However, this contestation is often mistaken as a struggle between reformers and traditionalists (or in the present vocabulary between reformers and extremists). Given the traditional–modern frame of reference, cultural conflict appears autonomous, divorced from questions of power/powerlessness or domination/subordination. The intrinsically class dimension of this conflict recedes from the analytical field of vision. Conversely, the struggle between modernizers and traditionalists (or 'extremists') is presented without an accounting of overlapping discursive and non-discursive elements. Intersubjective commonalities usually blunt the intensity of cultural and class conflict. Given shared historical memories, symbols and lived experience, conflict can be mitigated, but not always. As the Algerian civil war during the 1990s demonstrated, for instance, a breakdown of the discursive and cultural fields is also possible. On the other hand, the ICZs typically appear as monolithic entities, especially those designated as 'sponsors of terrorism' by hegemonic Western powers, Iran until recently being a case in point. These states presumably harbour rabidly anti-Western fervour, entertain few internal fractures except those drawn by a traditional/modern vector. Totalizing views such as this can lend credence to the thesis of a 'clash of civilizations' (Huntington 1993; 1996), legitimizing policies of destabilization and 'regime change'. Consequently, Western anxieties subordinate an understanding of the role of Islam in generating the terms of political discourse in the ICZs.

Antecedents

From an ideal-typical Islamic civilizational perspective, the current phase of globalization is superimposed on earlier Christian-Muslim encounters and subsequent

European ascendance. In the first instance, opposing civilizations drawn from a common monotheistic tradition faced each other, discovering commonality and difference in their respective cosmologies and social order. The inter-civilizational encounter contained misgiving and respect, recognition and denial, complex motives separating two communities of faith, conscience and political power. Commerce and cultural exchange influenced the encounter. Both eastern and western Christendom acknowledged Islam as a superior civilization for over five centuries. During the eighth and twelfth centuries, the Islamic civilization demonstrated unprecedented achievement in philosophy and science, literature and the arts.

The second great encounter between Islam and the West occurred in a radically transformed political environment with an increasing sense of Muslim weakness in the face of rising Western military, technological, economic and political might (Keddie 1994, 1998). Consequently, new pressures conditioned the fabric of Muslim social life, producing Muslim self-doubt and subsequent humiliation. The colonization of large areas of Muslim empires through direct, mediated or indirect control undermined Muslim self-confidence and collective identity. During this phase, confrontation, reterritorialization and consolidation of fixed attitudes of cultural particularism replaced inter-civilizational dialogue. A key impact of colonialism was not only the break-up of Muslim empires, but the introduction of identities informed by nationalism. The post-colonial period witnessed a growing wedge between secular-nationalist leadership in the ICZs and the vast majority of *Muslim* masses, whose faith remained important to them, particularly in the face of alienating political and social processes.

The main sources of Islamic resurgence lie at the fault line between the different forms of political and cultural identity imported to the ICZs. However, there is also considerable overlap and fusion between the social agents located at the interstices of fractured identities. A binary classification of fractures in the ICZs evades the complexity of living Islam. Hence, the struggle for decolonization contained elements of nationalist fervour, religious identity and cultural autonomy. The picture of a bifurcated post-colonial world of 'Westernizing' reformers and traditionalists also misguides analysis. Overlapping identities, 'religious' and 'secular', political and non-political, characterize the social field in the ICZs. Any thick description would show the presence of heterogeneity, not hybridity. The latter deflects analysis given the prior assumption of 'purity', but hybrids also cannot mutate. Drawn from natural sciences, 'hybridity' misguides understanding of social processes, especially their reflexive character.

Western domination produced two distinct temporal structures in the Islamic world, one linked to the past, the other denying the past. Under globalizing conditions, an externally driven modernization project sought to erase the Muslim past. Initiated first by secular modernists in the opening phase of the post-colonial era, this largely failed project has now acquired a very new character, compromising 'national' autonomy in favour of a transnational order of global capitalism. Despite historical constrictions, the spirit of decolonization minimally ensured respect for cultural autonomy and independence, albeit of an 'imagined' kind under nationalism, subordinating internal differentiation. The zealousness to the aims of modernization under a secular-nationalist banner reflected the constriction of nationalism in complex cultural environments. Secular-nationalism failed to articulate deeper cultural moorings of subordinated and colonized populations or to realize the false promise of economic development. Rather the post-colonial state in ICZs appeared even more intrusive than its colonial predecessor, yet inadequate in delivering material progress. The suppressed temporal structure of cultural meaning and identity has managed to rework post-colonial institutions simultaneously repudiating secular nationalism and its more aggressive neoliberal successor.

Falk's (1993) distinction between two variants of globalization offers a useful point of entry into an account of the contradictory dimensions of the neoliberal 'phase' of globalization. 'Globalization-from-above' mirrors 'the collaboration between leading states and the main agents of capital formation' (Falk 1993: 39). A key aspect of this type of globalization is a ceaseless quest for accumulation driven by a culture of consumption. The principal agents in this process are transnational capital and transnational political elites. Homogenizing in scope and content, neoliberal globalization equates material culture with civilization, making consumption the centrepiece of human self-expression. Ensconced in this framework is the implicit recognition of exchange as the ordering principle of social life and atomistic self-seeking a natural human tendency. Social action designed to pursue alternative ends appears irrational or savage. Affinities drawn from non-material principles become fetters to progress and prosperity. Hence, 'globalization-from-above' seeks to remove social limits to the logic of unfettered consumption placed by the state or community. Paradoxically, proponents of neoliberal globalization deny historicity to its claims, preferring a naturalized view of the societal phenomenon. The cultural underpinnings of this project seem opaque.

By contrast, 'globalization-from-below' addresses the corrosive elements of neoliberal globalization, including a collapse of community, individual autonomy, social capacity, an ecological crisis and cultural coherence. The self-organization of 'global civil society' imbued with a new consciousness seeks to reverse these negative trends, contesting cultural, social and ecological breakdown. 'Globalization-from-below' is a cry of the disinherited, a call for reversing the onslaught of neoliberalism on society and nature, and resistance to its predatory logic. Global social movements of various hues – human rights, feminism, labour, peace, the environment – seek a common twofold end: to tame neoliberal globalization and envision an alternative social order. On this terrain, religious social movements are a part of 'globalization-from-below'.

Revisiting cultural conflict

To reduce Islamic social movements to the *effects* of globalization, however, misreads its instantiation in the ICZs in both form and content. As noted, in its neoliberal variant, globalization tends to deepen the fractures and tensions between state and civil society, on the one hand, and between various strata of society within the

ICZs. On this alternative reading, the divide between state and civil society is not simply a product of neoliberal globalization but a structural legacy of colonial and post-colonial arrangements within political economy; the state increasingly diverging from civil society in areas of legitimacy, political orientation and cultural policy. Recent statist attempts congealed in 'Islamization' drives to bridge the divide have either come too late or lacked substance. They have merely exposed the political fragility of state managers in the face of a revolution of rising frustrations in the context of faltering accumulation and legitimation process, on the one hand, and demands for religious assertion within a wider process of cultural decolonization, on the other.

The chasm between privilege and misery, domination and powerlessness takes on the appearance of cultural conflicts. Recognizable distinctions can be drawn from the degree of proximity to state power and capital; spatial apartheid and forms of internal othering; lifestyle and patterns of consumption; degrees of Westernization and access to global symbolic and cultural capital, often congealed in foreign (usually English) language proficiency; and varied scales of religious commitment in quotidian practices encompassing public or private realms. The hold of globalizing elites over political and economic power has only increased with the advent of neoliberal dispensation. In virtually all the ICZs, the lines between plenty and want are visible on the spatial landscape with new lines of distinction between the few 'gated' communities guarded by private security personnel and the masses without adequate access to material sustenance. However, a psychological chasm has also grown between the privileged and the dispossessed with the intensification of atomistic self-seeking, the decline in state welfare and a diminutive culture of sharing. Distinct patterns of consumption and lifestyle further this divide, enhancing the process of 'internal othering' or the stereotypical negative attribution of 'the poor' – the undeserving, indolent or unclean – by the rich, or conversely of 'the rich' as immoral, Westernized and unkind by the poor. The picture is obviously complicated, but 'internal othering' combines class with cultural distinctions, widening the gulf between the haves and the have-nots. In this wider framework, unequal access to 'global' culture (foreign language proficiency, products or travel) plays an equally divisive role. The form of access can usually translate life chances into guarantees of a 'good life' or relegation to a lifetime of unending struggle without discernible improvement. Neoliberal globalization has fostered these varied distinctions, sharpening the historical partition between the privileged and the under-privileged. Hence, Islamic movements do not lie *outside* globalization, but within its polarizing cultural (not merely economic) logic, seeking to redress social wrongs within a religiously inspired ethical order. The temptation to separate an economic logic (neoliberal globalization) from a cultural logic (religious resurgence) mischaracterizes the mutuality and complexity of the societal makeup of globalization processes.

Cultural contestation within the ICZs also defies assumed patterns including, for instance, the alignment of Islamic assertiveness to 'traditional' sectors of society. The apparent concentration of self-proclaimed Islamicists in the urban sectors of Muslim society, modern institutions of state and civil society (including the bureaucracy, universities and schools), and technical and scientific competence seems paradoxical. However, the source of this 'paradox' lies both in the flawed equation of modernity and the West (and by default the designation of Islamicists as anti- or pre-modern), as well as the anticipation of an isomorphic link between religiosity and tradition. To the degree that living Islam in the ICZs is modern, not traditional, the assumed anomalies suggested in extant analyses (for instance, Lubeck 2000) evaporate.

The suggestion that living Islam is *modern* denotes an important corrective to established readings of Islamic resurgence within a traditional–modern frame. There is no discernible outside to global modernity. As previously suggested, the idea of co-construction eliminates the fiction of an untouched traditional zone in the ICZs. This is not to propose the obverse fiction of homogeneity and uniformity now produced by modernity, but the difficulty of sustaining the notion of duality, a traditional–modern bifurcation. Clearly, modernity materializes unevenly in institutional, ideational and experiential terms, but it can radically redraw the social and political landscape.

An uneven pattern is reflected in the emergence of the (modern) nation-state, the principle of sovereignty and the ubiquitous presence of exchange as the ordering arrangement for material provisioning. These elements are not unchallenged, especially in subordinated environments, including the ICZs. Alternative commitments to religious community, ethnic or tribal affiliation or pan-national awareness dilute the potential hold of nationalism or diminish the state's monopoly over the symbolic economy. The (secular) principle of sovereignty has also encountered strain and challenge from an alternative understanding of (divine) sovereignty, often placed in contention with claims for legitimate authority and governance. Cries for a City of God disguise real demands for justice and fairness. Lacking in actually existing polities, these ideals congeal perhaps a displacement of sentiments against illegitimate government. Modernity bears a local stamp, conditioned by available material and symbolic resources.

Yet, the arrival of capitalist exchange has radically transformed the system of needs, expanded and transformed the social division of labour, redirected social provisioning from 'subsistence' to 'exchange', and produced conditions for the emergence of new subjectivities and sentiments. Erstwhile family structures have changed under new conditions of work and the balance between labour and leisure. Despite compulsory indictment of materialism in the discourse of the Islamicists (see Esposito 1983), the pervasiveness of capitalist exchange remains undeniable and irreversible. The modern world has profoundly conditioned the social and life-worlds of Muslims. Perhaps a decoupling of the institutional structure of modernity from Westernization permits a less opaque picture of the ICZs.

Conclusion

The sources of Islamic resurgence run deep, but under globalizing conditions, the character of Islamic resurgence acquires a distinctive tenor. Neoliberal globalization makes fractures within Muslim society appear as a cultural contestation between tradition and modernity or between Islam and the West. Islamic resurgence is both a moment of, and a reaction to, neoliberal globalization, but is not reducible to its imposing presence and impact. Highly heterodox in its social and political makeup, Islamic resurgence congeals multiple currents conditioned by local conditions. Resurgence is neither new nor a monolithic phenomenon. There are historical antecedents to Muslim self-assertion. Furthermore, resurgence scarcely exhausts the spatial or symbolic spheres of Islamic cultures and civilization. It is simply one expression, albeit a significant one. The political idiom of Islamic resurgence often attracts notice. Political Islam is not the sole realization of Islamic resurgence, the latter ranging from quietist attempts to redefine Muslim social and life-worlds to seeking political power within established institutions of party, civil society and the state to militancy that typically operates outside the zone of politics.

The unifying thread in Islamic resurgence is a sense of rupture in the social and life-world of Muslims traceable to the collapse of Muslim empires in the eighteenth and nineteenth centuries and the consolidation of Western power. Muslim society has been in a state of reconstitution and self-examination, a process exacerbated by a growing internal cultural conflict over questions of legitimacy, identity and an ideal Islamic political community. In this historical trajectory, several social movements lie, bearing reformist, revivalist, or funda-mentalist (or scripturalist) proclivities. Often these movements supplied symbolic and material resources to anti-colonial movements, only to be abandoned by the nationalists in the post-colonial era.

Alternatively, the assumed paradox between globalization and Islamic resurgence embodies the materialization of a clash of civilizations between large liberal and illiberal cultural entities seeking domination, a spatial contestation reminiscent of imperial rivalry and civilizational conflict. This cultural cartography takes essentialized difference as the marker and arbiter of international relations in the post-Cold War era. Missing in extant analyses is an appreciation of the *modernity* of Islamic resurgence as a here-and-now social phenomenon, the divisive cultural logic of globalization, and the decoupling of identity and territory that provides Islamism its transnational appeal despite the nationalization of religion in the ICZs.

Since 9/11 Islamic resurgence appears coterminous with global terrorism, a view naturalized in the Western media and mainstream scholarship. Conversely, in apologetic accounts the militant tendency within political Islam is readily rebuked as Western hubris. Neither view is sustainable. Despite popular representations, the violent expression within Islamic resurgence remains in the margins of both faith and politics although, in the symbolic economy of domination/subordination, it has acquired an exaggerated presence. Militant Islam overlaps with nihilism, the death of politics; it is an acknowledgement of the impossibility of producing alternatives within the received worlds of modernity or the West. The anti-Western or anti-modern garb it adorns disguises how patently 'Western' and 'modern' militant Islam is both in embracing a rationalized vision of governmentality and abandoning divine interlocution in human affairs in favour of technical materiality of Western civilization. The world it seeks is neither the City of God nor a City of Man, but the destruction of all that exists. To the extent that a death wish inspires militant Islam, it stands in the centre of modernist currents that have punctuated counter-Enlightenment musings on nihilism and civilizational death. It also speaks to the weakness, indeed the impossibility, of creating a City of God, not strength within the cultural or civilizational boundaries of Islam.

6

FATE OF DEMOCRACY

Introduction

The rise of Islamic activism worldwide, including the appearance of illiberal politics in Islamic cultural zones (ICZs), is usually seen as a reaction to globalizing modernization. Based on the assumption of an elective affinity between Western cultural assets and liberal democracy, most analysts neglect to see globalization, particularly, in its predatory form, as a constitutive condition of Islamism. Accentuating the cultural divide within ICZs, predatory globalization strives to constrict political space for democratic expression. The growing disconnect between an already fractured political community and an increasingly illegitimate state provides Islamicists with the opening to capture key institutions in civil society or to create alternative avenues of communal identity, participation and civic action. Prospects for building a liberal democratic order hinge mainly on a resolution of the internal dialectic within the ICZs. The unstoppable march of predatory globalization, however, appears unlikely to yield either the political space or the historical time to bridge the deep chasm within ICZs.

The enduring otherness of Islam has long ensured recurrent mockery of its culture and people in Western scholarship and the popular media, with orientalist truisms of inherent Muslim abnormality and excess regularly colouring examinations of the faith, including understandings of the seemingly tortured career of democracy in the ICZs. Predictably, the reputed failure of Muslims to negotiate modernity and modernization has become a constant motif of representation. Apologetics about Islam, on the other hand, generally express a persistent defensiveness characteristic of the intellectual and political subjection of the Muslim community, an acquiescence to the dominant terms of the discourse, which authorize democratic ideals and their realization as cultural idiom. Accepting these terms, the Western political experience, notably in its institutional form, becomes the universal currency for worldwide circulation, as the current discourse on global democracy suggests. Between ridicule and apologia lies limited analytical space to assess the nature of democracy in ICZs, further circumscribed by the current international climate. The putative turmoil in several ICZs has only deepened the divide separating analysis from caricature; it confirms the general image of Islam as a religion of rage, an illiberal, anti-modern culture. Given the recent disfigured climate, an informed understanding of the liberal democratic project in ICZs is an obvious challenge.

Orientalist constructions of Islam and the totalizing logic of predatory globalization (Falk 1999) take the resurgence of Islam in the political and personal spheres of Muslim social life as an anti-modern phenomenon. The focus on the 'predatory' aspects of globalization include, but are not confined to, the 'cumulative effects' of neoliberalism and attendant political choices on human well-being, which are basically negative (Falk 1999: 2).

Hegemonic accounts reduce cultural processes in Islamic societies to a revolt against the West or challenges to a universal civilization. Assuming a basic cleavage between a globalizing project and forms of politics that are encoded in a religious idiom, these perspectives reproduce an irreconcilable breach between universalistic claims of the rise of a global society and particularistic forms of political and cultural expression. Suppressed in these accounts is the possibility that social processes in ICZs are not simply about transitions to (Western) modernity but the workings of complex inner dynamics now complicated by globalization. With this leaning, the purpose of this chapter is to recognize the current phase of Islamism (or the increasing assertion of Islamic idiom into political practice) as both an articulation of internal processes in ICZs and as a constitutive element of neoliberal globalization (Pasha 2000; Pasha and Samatar 1996), not simply a reaction to its predatory instincts.

Globalization and democracy

Neoliberals see the movement toward global democratization as both cause and consequence of globalization. Free association of capital and labour intensifies and extends worldwide social connectedness. Open markets and the unfettered spirit of enterprise, in turn, pave the way for democratic politics as institution and practice. Economic globalization, global democracy and a global commercial culture are closely intertwined. The expansion of the market opens up political spaces. Liberal democracy (synonymous with procedural democracy) facilitates and nurtures the human capacity to realize its natural economic instincts. A global commercial culture shatters barriers of difference and identity (Holton 2000). In this context, neoliberal globalization and liberal democracy are mutually constitutive and reinforcing. Clearly, the density of both globalization and liberalism as complex constructs is subordinated to a self-evident logic: neither the contradictory nor the contested nature of these phenomena are examined. On one hand, liberalism is emptied of its core content, namely, its emphasis on socially self-determined citizenship. On the other hand, neoliberals reduce globalization to homogenization, not recognizing increasing global relatedness as the recognition of heterogeneity and cultural difference.

Rather than facilitate, predatory globalization threatens liberal democracy in multiple ways. The liberal democratic project as theory and historical experience once premised on the nation(al)-state – a well-marked, territorially distinct political community – is in deep trouble. On questions of political membership, participation, accountability and legitimacy, the nation-state once effectively served as the principal locus and agency of mobilization and authorization. Both procedural and substantive notions of democracy have hinged on varied concatenations of state-society relations secured within an imagined, but spatially designated, political community. With a rearticulation in the nature of power, authority and governance afforded by new divisions of labour between capital and the state locally and globally, the dimensions of the liberal democratic state are severely tested. More directly, neoliberal globalization, with its emphasis on diminished state intervention in political economy, except in matters of surveillance and security, facilitates governance, not government. Cross-border flows of people and commodities are difficult to tame, resulting in reduced state capacity to perform its political, not simply functional, role. What is the imagined political community of neoliberal globalization? A tentative answer to this difficult question lies in appreciating the subordination of politics to technical rationality inherent in neoliberalism.

It would be a mistake, however, to neglect new forms of social connectedness on a global scale, often occasioned by the expansion of the global market, but not limited to its logic. Alternative forms of cross-national and cross-cultural interaction may also be entirely consistent with an awareness of human diversity and dignity, a consciousness about the borderless nature of ecological problems, and respect for the rights of the weak and the dispossessed. Some claims of cosmopolitan democracy, therefore, are not without merit, particularly those that recognize the diminishing relevance of notions of nationally articulated popular sovereignty, but also arguments that draw our attention to the indivisibility of global political action and mobilization given time-space compression of social processes. Yet these putative forms of social connectedness are confined mainly to the more prosperous, the affluent and the better-organized sectors of the global political economy. The parallel structures these new modalities of social relatedness produce are incapable of incorporating the vast majority of the powerless, politically unrepresented or under-represented quasi-citizens of the world. In the absence of the state that is unable to exercise sovereignty over its own community, a general crisis of representation becomes a distinct possibility.

The contention between predatory globalization and democracy is accentuated within political economy. Once the common purpose is substantially relegated to the exchange principle under a neoliberal order, redefining the role of the state, reliance on private enterprise substitutes the ideal 'ethical' state. In addition, in countries where the state, despite its own predatory instincts, has supervised welfare, neoliberal globalization can spell calamity by inverting the public-private societal equation. With the state becoming the custodian of global private, not societal, interests and civil society (the realm of private association) given the responsibility to shoulder collective projects, including development and welfare, powerful interests dominate civil society. Liberal democracy, under conditions of inequality, without available redress for the powerless, is not a very sustainable project. Despite often-cited contradictions, Keynesian compromises underscored the necessity of redress to legitimate both democracy and capitalism. The effects of revisions in the Keynesian compact are clearly more pronounced in the marginal regions of the global political economy.

A major effect of predatory globalization most directly relevant to ICZs is the growing detachment of the nation from the state. If dominant parts of the state collude with global economic forces to stay afloat, the nation must drift and lose cohesion, common purpose and solidarity. Though this scenario is too dramatic to have factual significance, the growing power of global capital and its institutional com-plementarity in unaccountable international agencies portends the sign of the times. Once political content empties, democracy assumes a mere symbolic, procedural or formal character. This is not to suggest the collapse of liberalism entirely but its radical rearticulation under conditions of flux.

Against the backdrop of predatory globalization, the prospects for building and sustaining liberal democracy in ICZs assumes a tenuous character. To examine this question, however, a short detour on the relation between Islam and democracy in received wisdom seems appropriate.

Democracy and Islam

Despite ritualistic and polite qualification, the pervasive scholarly sentiment suggests a basic divergence between democracy and Islam. Democracy is ultimately a Western ideal-type; spatial and cultural distance weaken its resemblance to the original (Lewis 1993; Abootalebi 1995). 'Liberal democracy', writes Lewis (1993: 93), 'however far it may have traveled, is in its origins a product of the West ... No such system has originated in any other cultural tradition; it remains to be seen whether such a system, transplanted and adapted in another culture, can long survive'.

By implication, Westernization (not merely modernization) alone can provide the prerequisites for building a universal civilization in which democratic polities can thrive and realize the promise of liberal enlightenment. According to this modernist claim, some cultures are obviously incompatible with democratic senti-ment; their destiny is glued to particularistic political expression. The inclusion of the ICZs as favourite undifferentiated others inhabiting this fixed universe naturally follows.

Muslim society of all shades and hues can only fulfil its consecrated fate as broker of anti-modern passion, illiberal politics and religious fervour. Despite the lure of global democracy, the ICZs cannot generate projects of either state or civil society bearing the signature of liberalism: Islamism is sheer continuation of the endless, if sometimes modulated, drama of oriental despotism. Moreover, in the context of globalization, it is an open rebellion against the latest phase of modernity.

An initial step toward approaching an alternative reading of the relation between Islam and democracy, especially in the context of global consciousness of societal processes worldwide, perhaps, is to appreciate the possibility that 'democratic' ideals do exist in ICZs; these (alternative) ideals may not be so readily accessible or even recognizable (Moten 1997). Both the historical site of their inception and the form in which democratic aspirations are articulated can elude examination informed by culturalist assumptions (Zartman 1992). Cultural beliefs and institutional inheritances remain crucial determinants of politics, including democracy (Clague et al. 2001). In addition, to the degree liberal democracy is equated with particular cultural endowments and orientations, the future of this relation is already determined: arrested political development remains the only probable trajectory for ICZs, released only by externally induced compulsions and opportunities. Advanced modernization or globalization thus can only herald new opportunities to permit an unfreezing of domestic societal processes in ICZs; alternatives to neoliberal globalization are mere acts of resistance. This logic, smuggled from doctrines of political modernization, undergirds much of the recent thinking among neoliberal globalists on building democracy in the ex-colonial world, including the ICZs.

A corollary to the empiricism that typically accompanies common sense, neoliberal triumphalism fortifies its claims by assembling cases that provide obvious antithesis to liberal democracy in its varied social and cultural forms. An absence of procedural democracy in many parts of the West's periphery thus lends credence to an array of oft-repeated lines declaring the implausibility of democracy without cultural pre-requisites. In the present era, however, not Marx but Keynes now stands between democracy and development. Welfare, equity, redistribution or ecological justice, not class conflict, allegedly obstruct the inevitable passage to the brave new world of neoliberal globalization. The fate of ICZs is not too difficult to ascertain within this circumscribed horizon.

As argued in the previous chapters, the official story of incompatibility has familiar sequential parts, beginning with an essentialized view of Islamic culture and civilization, leading to the current phenomenon of militant rage serving as a proxy for the entire civilization. In its abbreviated version, this narrative locates the failure of political liberalism to the totalizing structure of Muslim cosmology and political theory, an unchanged fixture of irrational unwillingness toward recognizing and separating ecclesiastic spheres from the more mundane (Kramer 1993; Lewis 1993). The inseparability of religion and politics in Islam foretells the political fate of its believers. Unable to secure an autonomous realm for building politics and citizenship, Muslims are forever condemned to the purgatory of rendering everything to God that ought to belong to God *and* Caesar. The subsequent historical episodes in Islamic history replay this theme in varied guises: the recognition of a *de facto* separation between religion and politics (Lapidus 1975) is repeatedly subordinated to the over-arching precepts of conformity to the central belief. Despite the appearance of multiple political forms through the centuries in diverse settings (hence the usage of 'cultural zones' after 'Islamic' in this volume), the incompatibility thesis has survived, giving contemporary incarnations of a totalizing religion the status of a utopia (Addi 1992).

On this view, the political language of Islam is possessed by the ghosts of failed past attempts. The inseparable cannot be separated. The absence of a true political reformation, in part, is explained in this way. Informed and sympathetic scholars are not too far behind authentically orientalist observers of ICZs to deliver the familiar message. Islam brooks no separation between the faith and politics, not even in the face of expediency, colonial onslaughts or recent externally induced challenges, the argument goes. Extrapolating from this account, globalization further closes the opening to separate religion and politics, as Islam and its culture become renewed sites and agency of resistance against modernity. In a total reversal in the argument, neoliberal globalists now find ICZs impenetrable to globalization's enlightening mission, given Islam's notorious rigidity in the face of change.

A so-called 'paradox of democracy' in the ICZs buttresses the incompatibility thesis. While embracing the procedural accoutrements of Western-style democracy, Islamicists on this reading are opposed to the vision of an open society. Clearly, the range of illiberal politics in ICZs is elastic, including an attitude of exclusionary politics, a disregard for the values of tolerance and respect for political difference, and a programme for amending the rules of democratic politics. Depriving uncertain believers of equal participation by curtailing voting rights is a clear example of illiberal politics. The climate of intolerance can be both implicit and explicit as the political platforms of Islamicists suggest, especially on questions of women's rights and minority status. In the face of illiberal pronouncements by Islamicists themselves, the arrival of democracy in ICZs prefaces its demise in the hands of those who deny its liberal promise. Allowing Islamicists the benefits of liberal democracy thus invites political suicide. However, blocking Islamicists from participation in the formalized political process equally undermines and delegitimizes the essence of the liberal project itself. This proposed paradox serves as a regular staple to rationalize repression of Islamicists in ICZs, notably Egypt, with nominal commitments to democracy.

The central inference drawn from the conventional perspective takes Islamism as a form of cultural resistance to globalization or, more poignantly, a repudiation of the basic civilizational principles of enlightenment thought and operation. Hence, the prospect of democracy in the ICZs in the context of globalization is likely to repeat the history of the original mismatch between modernity and Islam. Although some recent diagnoses of democracy's ailing health in the ICZs bend toward more sociologically oriented explanations, the claim of culturally dependent social pathology of ICZs endures; Durkheimian anomie becomes yet another layer above extant neo-patrimonial state structures.

Predatory globalization introduces new challenges for democratic construction. The older question of compatibility between Islam and modernity is resurrected with globalization – once modernization, now globalization. Nevertheless, a focus on the internal character of social formations in the ICZs must precede discussion of globalization's impact on democracy. The actually existing world of Islam, it will become clear, is more fractured politically than conventional readings permit.

A fractured political community

Shifting the focus away from an essentialized perspective on Islamic politics entails a recognition of the heterogeneity of ICZs but also their heterodox character internally. To suggest the class nature of ICZs is to rehearse the obvious. Perhaps more relevant for present purposes is the awareness of a cultural divide drawn by access to the accoutrements of a West-centred modernity (especially European languages) and its relative or partial denial to the vast majority. The division, by no means absolute, is not between Westernizing moderates and Islamic militants per se but between centres of privilege and the marginalized periphery structured and stabilized by access to global cultural capital, in addition to a monopoly of control by elites over material wealth. The cultural manifestation of social distinction disguises the materiality of its institution, however. Hence, Islamicists are better recognized more as repositories of subaltern sensibilities, not irrational opponents of modernity or modernization. The cumulative effect, nonetheless, of past inheritances and contemporary societal dynamics is the growing fragmentation of the imagined Muslim nation, fractured by a practical breakdown in the dialogue between its various cultural parts; the weakening of the state in the ICZs heightens 'national' disintegration.

Acknowledging the existence of alternative expressions of the democratic ideal in ICZs also entails a recognition of the national context in which the new Islamists' social movements operate. However, the nation is an increasingly fractured political community. The calls for democratic participation by Islamists in the idiom of religion, not liberalism, underscore the rift within ICZs. The question, then, is not of whether Islam and democracy are compatible but one of recognizing the process of building a new social order drawn from alternative conceptions of the common good, including the character of political identity. Islam provides ample intellectual resources to articulate alternative visions (Lapidus 1992) but, like other religions, is equally susceptible to 'absolutism and hierarchy as well as foundations for liberty and equality' (Esposito and Voll 1996: 7) and, as Esposito and Voll (1996) suggested, a ready source for provisioning ideas of equality and legitimate opposition.

Islamism seeks a reconstitution of state and civil society in ICZs. Moreover, it is the form and context in which reconstitution must occur that conditions its relation to democratic principles and practice; there is no inevitability built into the social process. One useful site for analysing processes of reconstitution lies in the contrasting views on the state and civil society (Zubaida 1992) in ICZs. Islamicists propound several alternative conceptions of civil society, ranging from civil society's equation with a realm of voluntary association, informal networks or the market. Similarly, they see the state in ethical, instrumental or structural terms. Despite variance in the language, parallel (Islamic) concepts suggest the vitality of political discourse. Given the official marginalization of the Islamic discourse in most ICZs, however, informed understandings of state–civil society relations are subordinated to simplified prose. The growing dependency of politics on the popular media further drowns serious conversation.

Another layer in a complex and evolving political process in ICZs is decolonization (Sayyid 1997), especially at the cognitive level: the awareness of the possibility of alternatives to West-centred worlds. The emphasis on Islam is not coincidental but contingent on the indigenization of ideological production and circulation in Muslim civil society. However, in the context of mass and social media, the indigenization of knowledge may not be supportive of inclusionary politics. The circulation of popular opinion without careful reflection or scrutiny may even hamper efforts to fight prejudice, especially in areas of gender equality and the rights of minorities. Celebrations of the nativization of knowledge, therefore, must be read as cautious tales pregnant with unexpected twists and plots.

Despite these disclaimers, the demand for democratization, albeit of an Islamic variant, embodies struggles for empowerment of the many against secular-nationalist elites. These struggles are quite diverse in character. Esposito and Voll (1996) provided a useful typology of Islamicist movements, which continues to have considerable analytical purchase. First, some movements highlight the successful assumption of political power by Islamicists: Iran, through a revolution against secular modernization, and the Sudan, with the development of an Islamic movement and its takeover of the state, provide obvious examples. Then there are movements centred around political parties willing to operate with recognized rules of the game. The cases of the Jamaat-i-Islami in Pakistan, on one hand, and the Angkatan Belia Islam Malaysia, on the other, offer good examples. Finally, there are movements that stand in severe contention to state structures, operating largely outside legal channels. The Islamicist movements in Syria, Morocco, Algeria and Egypt, with many variations among them, illustrate the third kind (Esposito and Voll 1996). Under globalizing conditions, new movements may also be originating, while established ones experience fresh challenges.

Three elements in the social production of Islamism are relevant here: (1) the generally inhospitable climate and attitude of secular-nationalist elites toward Islamicists in general; (2) the breakdown of an internal dialogue between different sectors of society; and (3) the *lumpen* nature of the Islamic intellectual discourse(s) in ICZs. All three elements contribute to illiberal politics. In the first instance, Islamicists, who generally come from the more marginal sectors of society, are often perceived as the internal other in ICZs, except in national contexts where they have concentrated political power. The marginal sectors here are defined not simply in economic terms but by a complex process of social layering involving access to cultural capital. Access to Western modernity, despite the shallowness of its articulation, is invariably a basis of privilege and mobility in ICZs. It is against culturally articulated distinction and inequality that marginality becomes recognizable. The presumed resentment of Islamicists directed at Westernizing elites is not a repudiation of modernity per se, as the rhetoric often suggests, but an expression of protest in deeply divided social formations (Deeb 1992). Often, repression of Islamicists is rationalized based on their presumed backwardness or potential menace to the legality of state structures and policy. Calls for equity, fairness or redistribution once couched in an unfamiliar (Islamicist) idiom immediately invite suspicion and draconian policing. Without openings in the political process, the extremists in Islamicist movements can often prevail in justifying their own exclusionary version of politics.

The breakdown of the internal dialogue also reflects the cultural divergence within ICZs, now exacerbated by the resurgence of sectarian conflicts. Even the vocabulary and syntax of communication deployed by secular nationalists and Islamicists, to simplify a very complex picture, appear incommensurable. Globalization contributes to the growing chasm, acknowledging only those who are conversant with the West-centred forms of expression while ignoring those who speak in vernaculars that are more indigenous. However, the original source of this breakdown is not globalization but a legacy of political and social schizophrenia injected into the cultural fabric of ICZs by colonialism; then by post-colonial secular-nationalist state managers guided by the mythology of modernist progress, economic planning and social engineering; and now by predatory globalization. The crisis of political representation in most ICZs is a logical outcome of the divergence within Muslim society, reflected in the cultural gulf that separates the powerful from the subaltern.

Finally, the nature of the Islamicist discourse in most ICZs increasingly reveals a *lumpen* intellectual character. The decline in major centres of intellectual activity in most ICZs, especially the alienation of contemporary discourses from rich currents in Islamic thought, have helped foster political, not philosophical, Islam: an unwavering reliance on formulaic logic in dealing with complex issues, supplemented by linear solutions (Butterworth 1992). Intellectuals better skilled in the art of manipulating the mass and social media can now enjoy the widest audience. Once the principal vehicle in struggles for decolonization, print capitalism alongside the new media serves the tyranny of common sense. The Islamicists are no strangers to the technical and instrumental aspects of either print capitalism or the telecommunications revolution. Islamicists are moderns, but without the baggage of secularism. Artful use of the new instrumentality of communication especially helps Islamicists bypass formal political channels imposed and closely guarded by secular nationalists. In either case, the result is the oversimplification of social inquiry and a deterioration in reflexive habits of analysis. Against this backdrop, perhaps, the rise in the capacity of Islamicists to influence the nature of the discourses in ICZs, often disproportionate to their relative size, becomes more comprehensible.

The fractured nature of political community in the ICZs and pressures of neoliberal globalization combine forces to nurture new forms of exclusionary politics. Globalization theorists recognize Islamism mainly as a reaction to neoliberal globalization. Instead, the attempt to see globalization and Islamism as mutually constitutive avoids the perils of binary constructions of contradictory phenomena. On this alternative reading, the rise of exclusionary politics globally, especially in ICZs, becomes more fathomable.

Conclusion

Premised on a logic of inevitability, predatory globalization provides both the context and the pretext for bolstering religious activism in ICZs at two levels. First, it weakens state capacity for secular nationalists to provide basic social and economic services to a demographically expanding and restless population. Entertaining neo-liberal prescriptions for chronic ills further draws state managers in the ICZs into global processes over which they exercise diminishing influence. Embracing neo-liberalism also means acknowledging the hegemony of global market rationality, its largely homogenized cultural enunciation, liberal institutionalism, and incorporation into a worldwide vortex of social connectedness via telecommunications and the global media. These structural arrangements further polarize the social formation in ICZs, deepening both the economic crisis and the crisis of representation.

On the other side of the equation, political alienation of state managers from their populace becomes the impetus for wider and more elaborate forms of repression and authoritarianism, shrinking an already limited space for political expression and pushing Islamicists further into the clasp of extremism. A source of solace and succour, but also legitimation, religion readily supplies the pretext for the extremist turn in ICZs, as secular legality increasingly correlates statist neglect and malfeasance. This is not a propitious context either to build or consolidate a liberal democratic project; the (alternative) ideal of Islamic democracy in several ICZs seems infinitely more attractive to Muslims under these conditions. Yet this alternative assumes a more rejectionist, and often illiberal, profile given its marginalization within a globalizing context – spurned, mocked and attacked as a symbol of barbarity or social pathology. Standing outside the preferred world of homogenized cultural space drawn by neoliberal globalization, the complexity of this alternative ideal is compromised by its appearance solely as a grotesque stain on a universal civilization. The growing militancy and rage of some zealous converts to this (alternative) Islamic ideal only validates the lunacy of their project or, in religiously charged prose, the evil that animates random acts of savagery.

7

LEADERSHIP IN CHALLENGING TIMES

Introduction

Hegemonic, orientalist frames of capture and understanding present Islamic models of restructuring social and cultural life as pathologies of alterity or as failures on the part of those living in the Islamic cultural zones (ICZs) to fully absorb modernity and its cognitive attributes. Such 'zones' include large regions that may span more than one nation, as well as areas within particular nations. The term refers to those parts of the world, particularly in urban centres, where Islamic culture is most prevalent, such as across much of the Middle East and North Africa. In orientalist discourse, this tends to render specific forms of political contestation that emanate from such Islamic cultural areas over ethics and questions of justice and dignity as mere representations of a 'clash of civilizations' on a world scale. Silenced in received hegemonic narratives is the deeply political nature of struggles over justice within such zones – to redesign political economy, reshape political community and place ethical constraints on market fundamentalism. In essence, these struggles exemplify efforts to reimagine legitimate governance, responsibility and leadership. To be sure, global leadership provides the wider context of these struggles. This chapter interprets some contemporary political struggles in such zones against the backdrop of Islamic conceptions of justice as a commentary on the global political economy, focusing particularly on the ethico-political assumptions of 'disciplinary neoliberalism'. The principal aim here is twofold: (1) to reinterpret Islamic ethics – encoded in cultural or religious idiom – as *both* a critique of, and an alternative to, the hegemonic settlement under globalizing conditions; and (2) to draw out the implications of the Islamic critique and alternative for reimagining global leadership.

Critiques of 'disciplinary neoliberalism' (Gill 1995) have assumed heterodox forms. In some cases, they are encoded in the language of environmentalism, indigeneity, authenticity or religious resurgence. In others, they depend on the political language of resistance to globalization. However, in all instances, critiques meld moral and political disquiet. This disquiet is impregnated *in* and *through* political struggles. Critique exemplifies these struggles. The moral tenor residing in critique tends to disguise the contested nature of social existence and its growing incorporation into globalization. In this vein, *local* instantiations of critique are rarely localized; they have the potential to reveal the contours of an increasingly globalized social reality and its discontents (Mittelman 2000).

This chapter explores an Islamic critique of the present global political constella-tion as a moral discourse with the potential to offer lineaments of future political alternatives to the world order. Specifically, it reinterprets some latent aspects of political Islam, or Islamism – the self-conscious project of *Islamicizing* politics in the areas of Islamic culture – principally as a challenge to the established social and political order in both its local and global manifestations. Departing from the con-ventional script, in which the proposed vision of Islamicists is captured as a general negation of modernity (in its manifold permutations), as a 'return' to the past (Lewis 2003), or as mere resistance to globalization (Barber 1996), this intervention is motivated by the intuition that the language deployed by Islamicists masks key elements of the intrinsically moral and political nature of their critique of the status quo – a critique germinated by the emergence of the 'global modern'. Political Islam here is taken as an internally contested phenomenon, one with many tendencies and contradictions. The received emphasis on violence, or calls for the establishment of an 'Islamic state' or *Ummah* (Islamic community) by Islamicists, divert attention away from the general disquiet afflicting Islamic social reality – a condition that finds the vast majority of Muslims in situations of dire economic, political and cultural stress, massive social inequality, subordination to structures of wealth and power, and with a generalized sense of betrayal by all brands of Muslim political and secular intellectual elites. This sense is heightened within the context of the 'global modern' – the 'spatial extension of modernity' and 'the production of an immanent cognitive and social field that has no outside' (Pasha 2010: 177, note 3).

The 'global modern' limits the horizon of political projects, but it also provides resources for realizing heterodox visions. The field it produces offers 'a condition of possibility for both politicization and de-politicization'; more significantly, 'this field shapes both projects of mimicry and escape'. Mimicry takes 'the form of development and modernization'. By contrast, 'projects of escape struggle to articulate cosmopolitan dreams or dystopias' (Pasha 2010: 177). Two key features of the 'global modern' are particularly important here to help appreciate the hidden transcripts of the political vision proposed by Islamicists: an acute awareness of *global* Muslim connectivity across boundaries, and the conviction that human action is necessary to alter the destiny of the Islamic community (Roy 2004). The latter – itself a modern sensibility – rejects an attitude of acquiescence to an assumed unjust social order. Within the frame of the 'global modern', therefore, Islamicists, who themselves are products of its uneven enactment in terms of power hierarchies, have reinterpreted alternative Islamic notions of justice, equality, human dignity and fairness. These alternatives do not derive merely from Islamic exegesis, but from an active, if elastic, interpretation of the religious texts within the context of Western hegemony and its specific articulation in the ICZs. The content of these alternatives betrays the imprint of a very heterodox mix of influences, including Islamic eschatology, the West's own internal dissent, captured in critiques of technology, capitalism, secularity and possessive individualism, and Southern discourses in other non-Islamic areas of the ex-colonial world. This heterodox mix gives the discourses of political Islam a modern and global texture; it also obfuscates the ethical substance of the Islamic message. These discourses would not come to be, and especially not in their present form, without the global connectivity produced by flows of capital, people, and cultural products and images.

Paradoxically, though, the ethical and moral vision embedded in discourses of political Islam inverts the original message of Islam as a *moral* community in favour of an ideal of a *political* community, enshrined in the idea of an Islamic state. This radical departure shifts the philosophical terrain of Islam away from transcendence towards an immanentist vision. A principal facet of this departure reworks an essentially secular notion of sovereignty into Islam, with the Islamic state, *not* community, emerging as the focal point of initiating projects of change and transformation. The embrace of political power to necessitate social action redefines obligation not as an act of individual responsibility but as a transaction administered by a watchful and heavily intrusive state. With the ascendancy of political power to unprecedented heights of salience within the new cosmological design, political Islam allows Islam's latent ethical impulses to be compromised. Instrumentality replaces ethics. The goal of building an Islamic community is used to rationalize all the means necessary to attain it.

The recent sustained infusion of *piety* into the regions of Islamic culture, in matters as diverse as the nature of dress, public speech, everyday ethics pertaining to visible expressions of devoutness, such as mosque attendance, permissive and prohibited exchanges between members of the opposite sex, attitudes towards work and leisure, and relations within the family under the aegis of political Islam, translates into a growing *politicization of civil society*. Making these matters questions of existential import rather than simply personal preferences significantly alters the social ethos of Islamic society. The boundaries of political Islam have now become more extended, especially against the backdrop of a general retrenchment of the post-colonial secular state. Nevertheless, civil society provides political Islam with its most potent vehicle to wage a 'war of position' against 'decadent' social forces, including the state. Cultural divisions within Islamic civil societies provide fortuitous conditions to introduce alternative (Islamic) terms of discourse into social and political communication. These terms of discourse distort the ethical content of an alternative Islamic vision in highly ambivalent and contradictory ways. However, the difficult task is to recover the distinctive features of an Islamic alternative that is increasingly subordinated to the aims of political Islam and its representation in public consciousness.

This chapter is therefore developed in three stages. In the first, the prevailing difficulty of recognizing ethical currents within Islamicist discourses *as legitimate formulations of alternative conceptions of world order* is located more broadly within the cognitive field produced by orientalism and its variants. This difficulty is also widespread in dominant versions of international relations scholarship, particularly its assumptions regarding sovereignty, identity and political obligation. The second section probes the fiction of a monolithic Islamicist heuristic. Closer scrutiny reveals that considerable heterodoxy marks political and intellectual commitments in various Islamic political discourses. Despite the apparent overlap and synergy, the different discourses allow access to the complexity of political practice *within* Islamism. Although these political discourses – without exception – seek to diagnose the illness afflicting Islamic state and society in local contexts, they propose divergent remedies. To reiterate, no singular *Islamic* critique is readily accessible. There is considerable divergence between and among the discourses under discussion (Moaddel and Talattof 2000).

Nevertheless, there are common threads binding these discourses, including adherence to a single text, remonstrations for justice drawn from Islamic history, the affinity of a common and shared faith, the experience of both triumph and decline in terms of their civilizations and, above all, an Islamic intersubjectivity transcending spatial and cultural barriers. Furthermore, in the context of West-centred globalization, the psychic, emotional and political aspects of perceived Muslim subordination to the West supply abundant resources for producing both the appearance and reality of a transnational Islamic consciousness. However, the important thing to stress is the presence of major fractures and fissures within Islamic society, drawn from a variety of factors including class, gender, ethnicity, sectarian affiliation, region, language and access to cultural capital linked to West-centred globalization.

The final part of the chapter draws out some general inferences from the previous discussion concerning the present global crisis and the crisis of global leadership. Needless to say, the examination here of a very complex theme is highly compressed and mostly indicative. Only a detailed and thorough investigation can yield a more nuanced picture.

Perilous orthodoxy

Despite repeated assaults on orientalist structures of knowledge production and representation (Said 1978; Michael 1988), analyses of Islam remain firmly ensconced in binary classifications. The most salient is the traditional–modern divide, used both to distinguish Islam from the West and to capture internal tensions within Islam. In the first instance, the parsimony of this classification guarantees Islam's location outside the modern. 'Hard' orientalism confers fixity to familiar attributes of tradition, including unchanging cognitive and behavioural features of Islamic society. These pertain to various facets of social and political life, but allow little variation across space and time. The basic aim, it appears, is to grant Islam an alterity unbridgeable from either the West or modernity: *Islam is placed outside time.* 'Soft' orientalism, pronounced in theories of modernization and development, leaves open the possibility of change and transformation. However, religion and culture continue to reproduce 'obstacles', which can be removed only through secularization, political and societal modernization, and, above all, individuation. Such obstacles are assumed to be inherent to the ICZs.

The harder and softer versions of orientalism share common sentiment not only about political Islam but about Islam in general, as a retrograde phenomenon, hostile to modernity. Their major difference lies in their respective characterizations as to whether Islam is or is not a totalizing faith. In the former instance, *all* variants of Islam are *totalizing*, since this monotheistic faith brooks no separation between mosque and state. Right from the time of its origins, the argument suggests, Islam has collapsed social spheres. In the West, these have been highly differentiated since the advent of the Reformation. Having experienced no similar shift in its religious temper, hard orientalists (Crone 1980; Lewis 2003; Pipes 1983) essentialize Islam, notwithstanding their unrelenting scrutiny of its past. This sentiment is not shared by soft orientalists (Binder 1988; Tibi 1998; Voll 1982), who display an awareness of differentiated spheres. However, soft orientalists also succumb to a binary logic in which only two principal possibilities materialize: traditional and modern Islam. Soft orientalists are also resistant to the notion of temporal coevalness between Islam and the West. The 'modern' in Islam is still lagging behind, aspiring to catch up with the West. A significant implication of this characterization is the refusal to recognize the 'global modern' as *the* condition of possibility for Islamic political movements of all kinds. This refusal also extends to the historical fact of the mutual constitution of Islam and the West. Either the idea of Western exceptionalism or that of Islamic exceptionalism (see Chapter 1) ensures that two worlds exist independently of one another. The recognition of mutual constitution, by contrast, can help dispel both essentialism and the prevailing 'common sense' of timeless Western superiority. It can also afford an awareness of the historicity of social orders, whether past or present.

A corollary of orientalist sentiment relative to Islam is the easy circulation of the nexus between Islam and violence (Venkatraman 2007). This sentiment is pervasive in the global cultural economy – the worldwide circulation of signs and symbols. Often, the self-characterization and acts of certain Islamic groups endorse the nexus between Islam and violence, either in the excesses of anti-Western rhetoric or in indiscriminate terrorism directed against innocent civilians, and now increasingly against fellow Muslims *within* the ICZs. More recently, the self-destructive cycle of violence has colonized the international public sphere. The intellectual and political aims of different variants of Islam are easily subordinated to a blurred cartography produced by these events, making it virtually impossible to separate resistance to occupation from 'terror'. The heterodox interpretations of the concept of jihad (Bassiouni 2007) are reduced to a single register: that of holy war. Complexity is compromised: the self-evident nature of the nexus between religion and violence serves as a general template to evaluate and assess all forms of Muslim political and social action. However, within the grossly asymmetrical discursive economy of representation, some clues can be found to this query. To the point, the aim of deciphering alternative conceptions of justice or meaningful societal existence is now easily eclipsed by received representations equating *all* of Islam with terrorism. Receding into the background are deep ethical codes associated with the 'venture' of Islam (Hodgson 1974), specifically positive principles of equality and justice, individual responsibility and obligation, honour, dignity and respect, tolerance and hospitality, balance or harmony in social and political temperament, and decency and humility. On the other hand, negative principles also provide constraints on avarice, self-centredness, political ambition, social exploitation and any discrimination based on ascriptive ties. In this regard, the design of leadership proposed in both scriptural and lay Islamic literature merits attention. The second section of the chapter addresses some key elements of this question.

Similar problems of apprehending Islam ensue in the dominant narratives of international relations (IR). A specific difficulty attending understandings of Islamic discourses on the *international* front, including Islamic meditations on the shape of global leadership, is the existence, as with orientalism, of established, albeit implicit, frames of capture in IR. These understandings typically derive from particular conceptions of politics (Beyer 1994), of the separation of religion and politics, or of the convergence between faith and political action in Islam. These conceptions reproduce assumptions of a Westphalian settlement instantiated in narratives of sovereignty, citizenship, right and obligation, the centrepiece of which is the evacuation of religion from interstate relations (Hurd 2007) or the severance of religious rationalities from the logic of (secular) power. Sovereignty, on this view, adopts the life process of immanence, subordinating claims of transcendence in an increasingly disenchanted universe of human agency and its fragilities. Modern citizenship refuses shared commitments to God and state in favour of the latter. Infused with political agency, but also what Adam Smith (1981 [1776]) refers to as that 'certain propensity in human nature' – the 'propensity to truck, barter and exchange' – the modern subject seeks fulfilment on earthly ground. Political obligation takes on the character of singularity, jealously guarding loyalty to sovereign authority against competition from other sources. Alternative notions of ordering social life or locating human purpose within different hierarchical schemes appear unnatural, pre-modern, atavistic or archaic. Above all, the modularity of the Westphalian settlement serves as a template to perceive relations between political communities across space. Viewed as 'anarchy' (Waltz 1979) or 'anarchical society' (Bull 1977), the terrain of the international takes embrace of the logic of sovereignty or the 'standard of civilization' (Gong 1984) as the only viable models for international relations. In order to function as legitimate members of the world community, non-Western states have to conform to these models. Lost in this hegemonic narrative is the deeply religious character of the Westphalian settlement, including the more profound presence of religiosity in seemingly secular social domains in the West. On this alternative reading, the supposed clash between a 'secular' West and Islam requires re-examination.

Most non-Western states do actually participate in a (post-)Westphalian international community. However, their culturally coded concerns, in engagement with the hegemonic structures of the world system, rarely receive the acknowledgement they deserve; *their* understandings and subjectivities, which inform international relations, remain marginal. Clearly, this is not the case with the political elites in the ICZs. Westphalia – either as utopia or reality – presents no problems for them. The real problem is elsewhere: with the multitude, or those without power or representation. Compromised by their own elites, the multitude seek counter-avenues of political articulation. Their alternative mappings of ethics, justice, equality, dignity and fairness remain residual to the hegemonic scheme, in which their 'national' elites willingly participate in order to secure power, wealth, privilege and longevity. Typically, the concerns of the Muslim multitude appear in the guise of grievance or critique of the existing world order. However, embedded in Islamic discourses are not merely a critique of the world but the lineaments of alternative worlds. The religious idiom of these discourses tends to mask the intensity of critique, as it becomes susceptible to dismissal within an economy of secular language.

Alternatives, cast in the language of globalization or cosmopolitanism, provide fruitful avenues for escaping the strictures of Westphalia, but offer no determinate pathways to comprehend the 'return of religion' in world politics. Cosmopolitan impulses take religious sentiment as a latest form of particularism – one that would eventually succumb to the power of universalism embedded in cosmopolitan dream-worlds (Bhagwati 2004). Globalization theorists, on the other hand, recognize the return of religion principally as a form of resistance to the homogenizing force of West-centred globalization. In the case of Islam, as noted, this problem is compounded in virtually all extant narratives by the durable presence of orientalist structures of understanding (Said 1978), built upon the historical fault lines of relations between Christendom and Islam (Daniel 1960), or Western imperial encroachment into the Muslim heartland, notably in the nineteenth and twentieth centuries (Sayeed 1994). Indirectly, these historically textured understandings impinge upon not taking alternative conceptions of sovereignty, statecraft or governance as legitimate; they invariably appear as relativistic counterpoints to a universal meta-narrative. Specifically, the notions of overlapping sovereignties or concentric circles of obligation cannot seek materialization as viable alternatives.

The notion of overlapping sovereignties in several Islamic juridical texts recognizes not just the claims of God but those of Caesar as well, based on determinate principles. Although God's sovereignty is recognized as absolute, Islamic jurists have long made a distinction between the non-negotiable domain of faith and worldly affairs, including political matters. The idea of limited government in Islam remains an ideal, wholly violated by secular dispensations of national autocrats in all the ICZs. Similarly, the notion of concentric circles of obligations, drawn from Islamic thought, lays out different sets of principles to regulate alternative spheres of human activity: the family, the community, the state and the world community. In each sphere, different rights and obligations operate. This image challenges the misleading view that there is no appreciation for differentiated spheres in Islam.

Islamic discourses and the crisis of leadership

Islamic commentaries of all shades share the impression that the Islamic world is plagued by a perennial, multidimensional crisis of leadership. This crisis is visible on multiple registers, including the pervasiveness of authoritarian rule in the regions of Islamic culture, the absence of political legitimacy, diminished and declining state capacity and, most significantly, political corruption, reflected in the use of state apparatuses to advance private material interests. The state, on this view, does not represent the public interest; it serves only to help consolidate and promote vested interests without recourse to legal, judicial or political accountability. From the standpoint of Islamic political discourses, the fault lies in the nature of secular political authority divorced from Islamic norms and principles. The origins of this state of affairs lie in the collapse of the Caliphate under colonial and imperial domination, the substitution of comprador secular elites for Islamic authority and the effacement of piety from governance. Produced over an extended historical period, especially during the fateful centuries of European colonization of Islamic lands, the crisis of leadership is intertwined with the character of the world order. Without the active sponsorship of hegemonic Western powers, Islamicists maintain, the Islamic predicament would be inconceivable.

However, disagreement exists whether the primary source of the crisis of leadership is internal to the Islamic political ethos, even to Islam itself (as hard orientalists such as Daniel Pipes would suggest), or a derivative of the subordinate position of Islamic states within the world order (a view increasingly promoted by Islamicists). In either case, Muslim leadership is seen as the Achilles heel of Islamic civilization. Within this broader frame, complex questions arise linked to the evolution of political authority in the ICZs: the persistent problem of political succession in Islamic history; the absence of a unified religious authority in Islam (unlike Catholicism), with the ever-present danger of dissension and instability; the excessive reliance of political rule on the military (Crone 1980) standing above society; and the endless cycle of 'barbarian' invasions threatening settled Islamic social life.

Political analysis and moral critique go hand in hand, often indistinguishable in popular Islamic consciousness (Davis and Robinson 2006). Moral critique provides sustenance and support for politics encoded in religious idiom. Politics presents the potential to realize moral values. A distinctive quality of political Islam is its readiness to collapse political and moral critique. Without recognizing this quality, the appeal of political Islam is unrecognizable. At the same time, Islamicists represent, perhaps, the *only* viable opposition to extant political regimes in most Muslim-majority countries. Bernard Lewis (1991: 7, emphasis added) sums up this historically produced sentiment:

> For many, probably most, Muslims, Islam is still the most acceptable, *indeed in times of crisis the only acceptable*, basis for authority. Political domination can be maintained for a while by mere force, but not indefinitely, not over large areas or for long periods. For this there has to be some legitimacy in government,

and for this purpose, for Muslims, is most effectively accomplished when the ruling authority derives its legitimacy from Islam rather than from merely nationalist, patriotic, or even dynastic claims – still less from such Western notions as national or popular sovereignty.

As noted, Islamic discourses provide both critique and alternatives to the existing social and political order. These discourses also offer meditations on the global order as a necessary complement to an engagement with the wider political field. Both are sustained by reference to the other. The distinguishing mark of political Islam is the seamless unity of critiques of internal political and social orders *and* critiques of the global order (one that buttresses the internal order). In this sense, current Islamic discourses conjoin (domestic) politics and international politics.

Wide varieties of discourses paint the intellectual and political landscapes of the ICZs with diverse genealogies, commitments and aims. The historical contexts of the origins, constitution and maturation of each discourse are complex and multi-faceted. Any attempt to render them into neat taxonomies, therefore, runs the risk of negating context and the salience of temporality. There is the other, all-important, aspect of an overlapping Islamic discursive field drawn from history, culture and belief. However, the effort to identify the principal currents presents the value of locating the *distinct* character of each discourse. Against that recognition and caveat, five separate discourses become identifiable, each centred on a key theme: redemption, rejection, reformation, revolution and reconciliation.

The discourse of *redemption* is embedded in the recognition of *internal* moral failing. Islamic decline after a millennium of civilizational glory is traceable in this instance to the inability of Muslim elites and subjects to adhere to the pure message of Islam. One part of this narrative finds fault with dissension, corruption and a generalized incapacity to reconcile Islam's moral message with conduct. In this discourse, the advance of Western modernity in the institutional straightjacket of colonial dispensation appears as a second-order cause of Islam's retrenchment. The theme of redemption feeds all discourses, moral and political. In essence, it seeks the rebuilding of the old Islamic city (a generic urban form prior to the ninth century that reflected and reinforced Islamic religious and social principles), or else erecting a new city over the ruins of the unsavoury political order found today in the ICZs. There is an obvious ambivalence in the politics of redemption, towards the West and modernity alike. To the degree that the diagnosis of decline lies *within*, the West serves the dual role of an unwelcome intruder, but it is also largely irrelevant to restoration from within. The relation between Islam and modernity in this discourse is more complex: the latter is instantiated in the ICZs only in its malevolent forms, but becomes unavoidable – a condition of possibility for Islamic alternatives. As with several other discourses, redemptive politics can also assume militant tendencies (Deeb 1992).

Rejectionist currents in the ICZs take Islam to be self-subsistent, as a total system. These currents are premised on the assumption that all practical answers for ordering society, polities and human conduct are already well defined in the

Islamic canon, notably in the *Qur'an*. No accommodation with things non-Islamic is necessary in order to build an Islamic community. As with the discourse of redemption, the rejectionist tendency can appear in both non-violent and violent forms. In the former instance, it assumes the form of Islamic *piety*: the regulation of human conduct, with an emphasis on the interior aspects of individual behaviour but also on social conduct. Pietism often presents itself as an apolitical social movement, divorced from the pressures of political agendas or juridical matters (*fiqh*). A notable example of such tendency is the Tablighi Jamaat (Society for Spreading Faith), a major global religious movement. However, rejectionist currents can also take dystopian forms, which are prominent in the directionless tendency towards violence, terrorism and nihilism (Pasha 2010). This tendency appears to present the external face of Islamic politics in the global imaginary.

The theme of *reformation* departs radically from its Christian predecessor. Aspects of the latter are intrinsic to the modernity now engulfing the world, including Islam. Relations between piety and the work ethic or religious rationalization for the acquisition of wealth are found in all transcendental faiths, including Islam. However, to the degree that salvation escapes Islamic cosmology, playing virtually no role in structuring human conduct in the Islamic *Weltanschauung*, there are no fundamental contradictions in Islam between the pursuit of earthly happiness and rewards in the hereafter. Islam neither commands asceticism nor makes eternal life contingent upon earthly existence. It requires that, in *all* spheres of human activity, Muslims conduct their affairs in ways that live up to the ethical standards prescribed in the *Qur'an*, or the practice of the Prophet (*Sunnah*) or the Islamic ethos of goodness and decency. The source of Islamic reformation currents lies in attempts to reconcile the *Qur'an* and the *Sunnah* with the changing social reality facing Muslim society (Hashmi 2002). In the context of modernity, therefore, reformist movements have offered highly innovative schemata for interpreting the sacred texts in view of the radically altered conditions. These elaborate efforts are based on the assumption that continuity and change both constitute an essential part of projects to preserve and advance the Islamic faith (Voll 1982).

The most compelling case for the success of political Islam is offered by the triumph of the Islamic revolution in Iran, a predominantly Shi'a country, but an example for the entire Islamic community. It shows to millions of Muslims the possibility of establishing an Islamic state and society, through a very rapid revolutionary transformation – or 'war of manoeuvre', in the Gramscian sense. The discourse of *revolution* in Iran presents the most obvious synthesis of a moral and political critique of the *ancien régime*, on the one hand, and a critique of an 'imperialist' world order presided over by the 'Great Satan' (the United States) on the other. At the core of both aspects of the discourse is an unrelenting repudiation of the 'Westoxification' of Iranian society and morals. Needless to say, the internal contradictions and ambivalences of embracing political power as the agent of transformation in the direction of a presumed Islamic future are becoming more pronounced as the regime faces the compulsions of world politics. What remains significant about the Iranian case, despite its Shi'a identity, is that Islamicists no longer see the establishment of an Islamic political and social order as an impossibility.

Ironically, the discourse of *reconciliation* originates from the same cultural zone that produced the first Islamic revolution in modern history: Iran. Perhaps the self-confidence generated by the Iranian Revolution allowed this to happen. A former president of the Islamic Republic of Iran, Mohammad Khatami, has articulated this discourse as a 'dialogue among civilizations' (Khatami 2000). Eschewing a 'clash of civilizations' (Huntington 1996), Khatami locates his proposal within an ethical perspective: 'The paradigm of dialogue among civilizations requires that we give up the will for power and instead appeal to the will of empathy and compassion.' Khatami (2000) outlines two principal ways to realize his proposal:

> First, actual instances of the interaction and interpenetration of cultures and civilizations with each other, resulting from a variety of factors, present one mode in which this dialogue takes place. This mode is clearly involuntary and optional and occurs in an unpremeditated fashion, driven primarily by vagaries of social events, geographical situation and historical contingency.
>
> Secondly, alternatively, dialogue among civilizations could also mean a deliberate dialogue among representative members of various civilizations such as scholars, artists and philosophers from disparate civilizational domains. In this latter sense, dialogue entails a deliberate act based upon premeditated indulgence and does not rise and fall at the mercy of historical and geographical contingency.

Repudiating 'the Cartesian–Faustian narrative of Western civilization', Khatami underlines the need to 'listen to other narratives proposed by other human cultural domains' with regard to the relation between humans and nature and among civilizations. The message of reconciliation embedded in Khatami's proposal offers a substantive blueprint to reimagine the philosophical contours of a more humane world order. Combining Khatami's vision with an Islamic conception of global leadership can yield new intellectual resources to challenge the confining strictures of both orientalism and global market fundamentalism. Ultimately, these resources are contingent upon a remapping of the philosophical design underpinning the existing order.

What are some of the more durable elements of an Islamic conception of political leadership? In its elemental form, leadership in Islam is viewed both as guardianship (*wilayah*), but also as trust between human beings, suggesting moral responsibility as a core value. According to the *Qur'an*, human beings are regarded as God's representatives or vicegerents on earth (Al-An'am 6:165):

> He has given you the earth for your heritage and exalted some of you in rank above others, so that He might prove you with His gifts. Swift is your Lord in retribution; yet is He forgiving and merciful.

Those in rank above others have a duty to abide by their moral obligation to create an environment in which Islamic piety can be fully realized. In exchange for their successful discharge of that foremost duty, Muslims have an obligation to obey. There is a complex network of rights and obligations binding the ruler and the ruled (Marlow 1997). In no case is the ruler or the ruled granted absolute licence. Authority and obedience are interwoven (Mottahedeh 2001). The ruler must have qualifications to lead, and must enjoy the confidence of the community. Any failure to produce the conditions that allow Muslims to meet their primary obligations to God renders the ruler illegitimate. In situations 'when the individual's religious duty as a Muslim and his political duty as a subject come into conflict, it is the individual's duty as a Muslim that must prevail' (Lewis 1991: 69).

Contrary to the expectation that the Islamic political ethos can generate only autocratic or charismatic leadership, lacking the correlates of modernity, two key elements of an Islamic conception militate against received orientalist wisdom: the notions of *shura* (consultation or deliberation) and *ihtisab* (accountability). Both notions underline the processual nature of leadership. In the first instance, deliberation is essential in the selection of leaders. In all vital affairs, leaders are expected to seek the counsel and advice of the Islamic community, especially its intellectuals and legal experts. The notion of accountability, in the second instance, places severe checks on arbitrary or capricious rule. Limited government is the essence of an Islamic conception of relations between rulers and ruled. However, the difficulty that emerges in both instances is the potential for abuse. To guard against this eventuality, the concept of *ad'l* (justice) plays a pivotal role in the Islamic scheme. As Lewis (1991: 70) notes:

> The notion of justice becomes central to Muslim discussions of the duties owed by the ruler on the one hand to God, on the other to his subjects. While definitions of justice vary from period to period, from country to country, from school to school, even from jurist to jurist, the basic principle remains that justice is the touchstone of the good ruler. It is the counterpart of obedience, the converse of tyranny (*zulm*).

The main sources of the principles of Islamic leadership derive from the *Qur'an*, from the sayings and conduct of the Prophet, the example of the Rightly Guided Caliphs and other pious individuals in Islamic society. However, the *Qur'an* provides the original basis for leadership principles. In Muslim belief, the *Qur'an* is an eternal text with universal validity. It spans the totality of social and personal conduct, including relations between the leaders and the led. Since the times of the Prophet Muhammad, this view has offered the ideal-type against which to evaluate subsequent political performance. In the Shi'a tradition, in the absence of the Imam, leadership or guardianship belongs to selfless and righteous legal experts.

Concentrated on the notion of guardianship, the Islamic conception of leadership rests principally on the aspiration of establishing boundaries for permissive action. Human conduct, especially the conduct of those in authority, is circumscribed by ethical principles: respect for life and dignity in all its spiritual, biological and artistic forms. A second constraint emanates from the demand for respecting cultural and religious diversity. There is no compulsion in Islam, as the *Qur'an* enjoins. A third limit arises from the awareness that sovereignty belongs only to God. This makes absolute sovereignty, both of the state and of the individual, forms of *shirk* (heresy). Finally, within established boundaries, material pursuits such as wealth creation are fully endorsed, but they must all conform to the survival and sustainability of the human species. Material life cannot be its own end. The task of the leader is to ensure that these limits are observed. Self-observance is the first step in this regard. No leader is immune from the application of those vital principles. However, the gulf between received theory and current practice remains wide and unbridgeable. This is the major source of much of the perceived turmoil in the areas of Islamic culture.

The growing divergence between subaltern forces and dominant elites in the ICZs rests principally on a crisis of legitimation engulfing state and society. To be certain, subalternity here is seen as a condition of *both* economic *and* cultural subordination in the face of West-centred globalization, neoliberal rationality and secular governance. Despite the rhetoric of Islamization, the vast majority of Muslim elites are largely alienated from the social temper of the multitude. Elites are drawn to the globalizing logic of neoliberal governance, ensuring their own longevity. Political repression is readily applied to address social and political protest.

Against the hegemonic current, the Islamic impulse becomes more explicable. Despite its heterodoxy, this impulse seeks alternatives to disciplinary neoliberalism in the form of ethical governance based on Islamic principles. A key element of ethical governance is the reconfiguration of notions of sovereignty and the liberal regime of rights. In the first instance, subordination to some higher authority places constraints on the power of the state, offering protection to citizens. The liberal regime of rights is seen as a frail substitute for social and political obligations to community. In terms of global governance, the implications of these principles are significant.

An Islamic receptivity to the question of global governance imposes strict limits on the drive towards self-seeking and institutions designed to realize self-seeking as an organizing principle of social existence. Global institutions cannot merely represent private authority; they need to balance societal needs with the compulsions of wealth creation. Equally salient is the balance between nature and society. Limits to self-aggrandizement can produce the conditions for such a balance. Second, an appreciation of the value of human diversity – including cultural diversity – is a repudiation of the drive towards homogenization. Multiple forms of life (as Khatami might suggest) require protection, not singularity.

Greater representation in global institutions from a variety of cultural zones is but an initial step towards a recognition of the diversity and multiplicity of political and social desires. A more critical element towards reshaping the contours of governance is an awareness of a civilizational crisis – a compound of multiple crises – demanding a paradigm shift. Islamic notions of permissive social action, self-regulation and cultural embeddedness offer one among many alternatives to rethink global governance. However, ultimately, alternatives emerge only in and through political struggles. Tragically, the forms some struggles have assumed in the ICZs – often inspired by nihilistic violence or instrumental reason – not only are self-defeating but also have the potential to obviate other alternatives. The ethical content of reconstituting the world often recedes into the background. However, despite these challenges, the significance of the Islamic alternative cannot be negated, since it is inextricably tied to ordinary aspirations to build better lives in accordance with received principles and to reconcile very difficult life choices with faith.

Conclusion

The present conjuncture of global crises raises critical questions concerning the limits and possibilities of structural change and transformations in world order. These limits and possibilities are inextricably tied to the form of global leadership; the latter gives the world order the agency and mechanism to connect its different parts. The limits of the current global political constellation are marked by a growing tendency of both governance and surveillance to escape traditional patterns of political representation. The latent tension between politics and administration is augmented in the shift from a liberal form of representative governance to governance without either representation or accountability. It is also underlined by a widening gulf between the compulsions of managing the global political economy and the compulsions that reflect societal needs at local and national levels. In the second instance, the present conjuncture has brought to the surface wider concerns about the need for humane global governance, greater social justice and social/ecological sustainability. New avenues to rethink the global political economy and its precarious reliance on neoliberal rationality are now urgently sought in multiple geographical and cultural sites. Nonetheless, there is also an apparent disjuncture between discourses on justice, equality and fairness in different cultural zones of the global South and the self-rationalizing claims to universal appeal of disciplinary neoliberalism.

The ideological predilection in reigning circles of the global political economy to silence alternatives to disciplinary neoliberalism has assumed two principal forms: depoliticization and delegitimation. Both are closely linked, as they mutually reinforce each other. Depoliticization typically rests on the strategy of marginalizing dissent through co-optation or repression. Delegitimation draws its sustenance from control over discursive fields of producing and circulating knowledge and information. Intellectual challenges to the hegemony of global neoliberalism are often presented as romantic utopias, as impractical or as merely unnatural. Hence, the ascendancy of liberal market fundamentalism is seen as the triumph of reason, materialized in the emergence of a 'flat world' (Friedman 2005), 'the end of history' (Fukuyama 1992) or West-centred globalization (Bhagwati 2004). On this view, alternative conceptions of world order lack the vitality of reason, practicality or intellectual merit to serve as viable paradigms. Not only is this sentiment prevalent in the upper tiers of global governance (the World Trade Organization, G8 or Davos) but it travels liberally among 'national' elites – those wedded to securing privilege and plenty through positive engagement with, or service to, the structures of global authority, both public and private (Cutler et al. 1999). Challenges to the hegemony of neoliberal discourse, therefore, are met with disdain and active opposition at local and global levels alike.

Aspects of the Islamic ethical vision briefly outlined in the preceding pages offer the kernel of an alternative template. Part of the success of neoliberal hegemony has been the foreclosure of different modes of thought, particularly those that originate in the global South. With the recent crisis of global neoliberalism, possibilities for entertaining alternative conceptions appear both real and attractive. However, the difficulty lies in aligning new philosophical schemes with political leadership committed to meaningful change. Engagement with elements of thinking originating from the Islamic world may constitute part of the journey.

PART III

Beyond Western IR

8

CRITICAL IR AND ISLAM

The neo-Gramscian turn has offered a major theoretical and methodological challenge to the conventional wisdom surrounding issues of power and world order (Cox 1987), structure and agency (Bieler and Morton 2001b), and global transformations (Gill 1993), displacing understandings that once appeared firmly established and canonized in the field of international relations (IR). Developed principally by Robert Cox (1981, 1983, 1987), with significant contributions by scholars on both sides of the Atlantic (Gill and Law 1988; Gill 1990, 1993; Augelli and Murphy 1988; Murphy 1994; Van der Pijl 1998; Rupert 1995; Robinson 1996; among others), the neo-Gramscian framework represents one of the more innovative contributions to a discipline long embedded in the self-same verities of behaviouralism, positivism and neo-realism (Morton 2003a, 2003b). Exploring the materialist underpinnings of state structures (Bieler and Morton 2001a; Germain and Kenny 1998), recognizing variations in state-civil society complexes (Cox 1987), and showing possibilities of newer forms of political agency (Gill 2000), neo-Gramscians destabilize conventional neo-realist orthodoxy.

Neo-Gramscian scholarship in IR is varied (Bieler and Morton 2001a; Germain and Kenny 1998). A distinction can be made between those who elect to separate Gramsci's metatheoretical commitments from his conceptual and methodological uses (Augelli and Murphy 1988; Murphy 1998), and others who seem to avoid such separation (Rupert 1995). However, they all share scepticism of problem solving or the discovery of scientific laws as the hallmark of theoretical practice (Cox 1983).

Drawn from the richer terrain of Italian political thought exemplified in the works of Machiavelli, Vico, Croce and above all Antonio Gramsci (Cox 1983; for background see Bellamy 1990; Bellamy and Schecter 1993; Fontana 1993; Femia 1981; Finocchiaro 1988; Adamson 1980), neo-Gramscian IR recognizes the changeability of social forms, tempered by historicism (Falk 1997) and an awareness of 'the concrete and the conjunctural' (Kalyvas 1998: 344; see also Buttigieg 1986b). Neo-Gramscians reject formulaic soundings on national compulsions and interests pervasive in the core hermeneutic circles of the IR community in favour of a differentiated character of historical blocs and changing configurations of power. On this view, the fixity of the social and political worlds dissolves (Cox 1987; Gill 1993; Morton 1999; Bieler and Morton 2003).

Antinomies and silence

Despite producing a self-subsistent alternative mapping of the social and political worlds, however, neo-Gramscians have not been entirely successful in avoiding the constrictions of *Western* IR, especially with regard to the uneasy presence/absence of cultural otherness in IR theory (Inayatullah and Blaney 2004; Jahn 2000). Furthermore, as with conventional wisdom, neo-Gramscians reproduce, perhaps inadvertently, either assumptions of *liberal neutrality* or *cultural thickness* in relation to the 'peripheral' zones of the global political economy. Together, these tendencies produce a variant that can be likened to 'soft orientalism'. In the first instance, cultural difference is not much of an impediment to the establishment of (West-centred) global hegemony. In the second instance, otherness becomes the principal source of counter-hegemonic movements or resistance to a globalizing economy and its homogenizing cultural accoutrements (Robinson 1998; Rupert 2000, 2003). These contradictory uses of culture are also noticeable in claims about the 'clash of globalizations' (Gill 2002).

This chapter links the neo-Gramscian treatment of culture to the limits of *Western* IR in general. To illustrate the problem, the discussion takes as its point of departure the apparent consolidation of a natural attitude (Benhabib 2002) toward Islam in the wake of dramatic recent events (see Introduction). On this view, established narratives rooted in the Manichean idiom of civilized-savage distinctions have returned to endorse pervasive popular opinion (Euben 2002a). Political power helps unify fragmented popular consciousness, deploying it for its own ends. The cultural boundaries of an increasingly porous West are being fortified, a form of 'enclavization' (Shapiro 1999), sealing off the 'body politic' from assumed menacing threats of radical Islam to liberal Western polities. This cultural mood embodies deep historical prejudices that now circulate as common sense (Gramsci 1971, 1992, 1994, 1996). One source of this common sense is the enduring legacy of entangled relations between the worlds of Islam and the West, at once mutually constitutive and conflictual (Daniel 1960), but also overburdened by changing configurations of power (Said 1978; Asad 1993; Arjomand 2004).

The appropriation of Islam in IR reveals the general problem of difference and Islam's assumed resistance to an easy assimilation into a universalized modernity (Davutoglu 1994). The familiar strategy to subsume historical and living forms of otherness as the pre-history of modernity (Fabian 1983) is readily subverted in the face of Islam's nagging presence, neither inside nor outside modernity. The alternative strategy to annihilate the radical otherness of Islam produces a vicious cycle

(Benhabib 2002). It reproduces the conditions for Islam's insistence on difference, and especially on an occidental reading, an incommensurable difference (Euben 1999). The quest for reconciliation of one/many worlds, or universality/particularity (Walker 1988) seems increasingly feeble. Neither assimilation nor annihilation promises a resolution.

Thomas Butko (2004) proposes a 'Gramscian' analysis of 'political Islam' to avoid these avenues of resolution. Through an exegetical comparison of Gramsci with key 'modern' Islamic intellectuals (Syed Qutb, Abu al-'Ala Mawdudi and Ayatollah Khomeini), he sees Islamic movements as a genuine 'counter-hegemonic' force. Despite some curious parallels between the Marxian thinker and the organic intellectuals of political Islam, Butko's analysis ends up conflating dominance with hegemony. To be certain, the Muslim Middle East is characterized by an absence, *not* presence, of hegemony, which may be the core basis of movements seeking an Islamic alternative. In Butko's own reading of the Muslim Middle East, the masses do not 'accept the morality, the customs, and the institutionalised rules of behaviour disseminated throughout society as absolute truths that cannot or should not be questioned' (Butko 2004: 43), a central dimension of hegemony. Butko also fails to distinguish between shades of movements in what is referred here as the Islamic cultural zones (ICZs), as well as the different strategies of 'war of position' with 'war of manoeuvre'. His repeated use of 'hegemon' mischaracterizes the dense nature of a conception of hegemony.

In the IR field, neo-Gramscians do not make the question of otherness their principal object of analysis. In some cases (Augelli and Murphy 1988, 1993), they help decipher subaltern claims on a hegemonic system 'crusading against alternatives' (Augelli and Murphy 1988: 138), reading the limits of Third World political action from the empathetic perspective of the Third World itself. In other cases, they examine the effects of Western (mainly American) hegemony on the Third World (Robinson 1996). Any form of demonization of others would escape the neo-Gramscian critical project. Yet to the degree that neo-Gramscians share the cultural space of *Western* IR, they unconsciously reproduce binary constructions, mostly congealed in a rather neutral and opaque centre–periphery model with its own cultural baggage of notions of development reflected in differential (core or peripheral) economic capacity.

Culture or cultures?

The real problem emerges in the neo-Gramscian understanding of transnational hegemony, culture and resistance. First, the tendency amongst neo-Gramscians to over-emphasize the *consensual* aspects of hegemony, and (perhaps inadvertently) to downplay the *coercive* foundations of contemporary IR practice, becomes apparent. This tendency rests upon the mixed appropriation of culture. Initially, 'culture' is seen in rather *thin* terms despite a *diffusionist* core–periphery model of cultural transmission, which subsequently exposes that model's latent economism.

Hegemony, to modify Ortner, 'is often treated as something that arrives, like a ship, from outside the society in question' (Ortner, in Crehan 2002: 50). Although neo-Gramscians eschew a tradition/modernity duality, the transnationalist neo-Gramscians (Robinson 1998), with the notable exception of Davies (1999) and Morton (2003c), do not theorize cultural reception. How do peripheral societies *actively* transform hegemonic effects? In the neo-Gramscian formulation, passivity rules the cultural worlds of the subalterns as they readily succumb to global hegemony. Only in 'resistance', informed by an essentialist culture, can agency materialize.

Second, neo-Gramscians tend to overlook the salience of *otherness* in the constitution of (domestic) hegemony. Although domestic hegemony has been secured by 'anti-communism and the politics of productivity' (Augelli and Murphy 1988: 140), this is not an extended historical perspective on the constitution of (Western) hegemony, a project implicating cultural practices, distinctions and demarcations over a considerably longer phase in human history (Wolf 1982). Hegemony is seen as a projection of domestic hegemony on a transnational scale. The recognition of the distinction between friend and enemy à la Carl Schmitt (1996), or an appreciation of how otherness *outside* shapes hegemony *inside*, does not interest the neo-Gramscians. On a Schmittian view, an inversion of the relationship between domestic and transnational hegemony can be an important collective to the diffusionist assumptions underpinning the neo-Gramscian worldview.

The indispensability of the periphery's *difference* in the consolidation of the core's (cultural) *identity* can help bring to the surface the pivotal role of antagonisms in international relations (Mouffe 1999). This is not to essentialize either difference or antagonism (Huntington 1993), but to acknowledge the banality of a conception of politics without a meaningful notion of otherness (Tully 1995). The distinction between friend and enemy 'is a reminder of the inexorable and ineradicable nature of conflicts, which no overall, comprehensive ideological worldview will ever succeed in removing from social relations. The political will never be hegemonic' (Kalyvas 1998: 368). To assume otherwise is to lend authenticity to claims of sameness and conformity (Tully 1995), and to misperceive the bestial nature of power (Buci-Glucksmann 1980; Showstack 1987). Coercion remains a constitutive basis of consent, though it cannot sustain effective rule without adorning a more benign form. The neo-Gramscian privileging of consent disguises the nature of coercion, manipulation, chicanery, disguise and concealment, which never escaped Gramsci's field of vision.

Third, an unstated assumption underpinning the neo-Gramscian framework is the idea of homogenized cultural space (Chatterjee 1988) on a global scale, drawn from the domestic analogy. This assumption allows neo-Gramscians to erase the distinctiveness of non-Western cultural regions in sketching out the spatial terrain of hegemony. Hegemony moves vertically and horizontally from the North to the South.

Transnational hegemony or diffusion?

The neo-Gramscian historical trajectory for the emergence and consolidation of hegemony follows a familiar Anglo-American pathway inscribed in the IR canon.

This pathway includes the origination of the modern world order with Westphalia and subsequent consolidation of two liberal-imperial hegemonies (Pax Britannica and Pax Americana), punctuated by balance of power, mercantilism, the crisis of liberalism, and the constitution of 'hyper-liberalism' after the Second World War (Cox 1987; Gill and Law 1988; Gill 1993; Arrighi 1993), superseded by globalization (Robinson 1998). Neo-Gramscian historical trajectory situates Anglo-American hegemony at the centre of analysis. There is nothing parochial about a renewed subscription to this late post-Westphalian temporal mapping. What remains uncertain, though, is the importance of non-Western regions to the historical *formation* of capitalist hegemony. These regions are not merely peripheral and subordinate to the constitution of hegemony in an historical sense, but appear marginal and external to the theory itself. Paradoxically, the initial neo-Gramscian silence over the integral role of the non-West in the consolidation of hegemony is subsequently broken. These regions are smuggled back into analysis as the principal site of counter-hegemonic struggles in the era of globalization (Robinson 1996; Augelli and Murphy 1993; Rupert 2000; Gill 2002; Rupert 2003). Their challenge, though, is to an order *already constituted*. The centrality of Islam in the formation of modernity, stressed previously, is occluded.

This temporal mapping reveals a *presentist* bias, with an inherent proclivity to deny the *dynamic* and *interactive* aspects of hegemonic consolidation. Without invoking the untidy legacy of primitive accumulation on a world scale, the neo-Gramscian theorization of hegemony does not fully integrate *chains of elective affinities* between historical processes in core and peripheral regions either before or during periods of hegemonic consolidation. The initial conditions for the establishment of hegemony are seen as patently *internal* to the core. Hegemony then becomes a process of *diffusion* from North to South.

Another source of paradox is the neo-Gramscian aim to escape the domestic analogy by simultaneously relaxing 'national' categories as they appear beyond the state and to depend upon 'national' processes to concretize hegemonic consolidation. Hegemony is not strictly the product of *national* state–civil society complexes, but the congealment of material practices, ideas and institutions in *transnational* space, autonomous and bearing no isomorphic relation to those complexes (Robinson 1998). Yet, national processes are indispensable to hegemony's global march. Without securing the spatial confines of national space, transnational or 'global' hegemony is unimaginable. 'A world hegemonic order can be founded only by a country in which social harmony has been or is being achieved', Cox explicitly posits. 'The expansive energies released by a social hegemony-in-formation *move outward onto the world scale* at the same time as they consolidate their strengths at home' (Cox 1987: 149, emphasis added).

Ironically, the diffusionist thrust in the neo-Gramscian formulation, unlike cognate diffusionist thinking in modernization theories of an earlier scholarly generation (Pye 1963), is based on a *thin* understanding of culture, a slightly modified variant of the idea of culture of the economic determinists despite compulsory references to Gramsci and deployment of the notion of intersubjectivity in social theory

(Taylor 1976). Gramsci's sustained battle with economic determinism continues to serve as a preamble for the neo-Gramscians, but the import of his analysis is bid farewell as soon as culture reaches the analytical shores of the international. Inside the nation-state, culture enjoys thickness; outside it gets diluted. One illustration of this dual performativity is the relative ease with which hegemonic transmission across 'national' boundaries is made possible by a fungible and exportable global culture (Robinson 1998). This is not the culture of meanings and interpretations, but an empty container of shallow signifiers, instantly recognizable without attachment to indigenous structures of feeling (Williams 1977). What is the *cultural* content of transnational hegemony? Culture appears principally as ideology. If, indeed, there is a *thick* conception of culture, it only materializes as counter-hegemonic resistance, native, local and particularistic. Thick culture returns but only to record a protest. The unencumbered culture of soft orientalism confronts the encumbered culture of hard orientalism.

Unlike Gramsci's understanding of culture as a complex ensemble of materialist, symbolic and interpretative practices – as common sense and good sense, aesthetics and literature, theatre and poetry, high and low brow (Gramsci 1992, 1996) – neo-Gramscians offer a nominalist and formal view of culture: culture as intersubjectivity but intersubjectivity restricted to the domain of dominant ideology (Cox 1987). Though neo-Gramscians self-consciously repudiate the equation of hegemony with ideological practices, trying to preserve, as in Cox's case, Gramsci's Crocean and neo-Hegelian intellectual lineages, transnational hegemony assumes easily the form of *dominant ideological practices* of core ruling classes on a transnational scale, imbued with the accoutrements of a commoditized global culture. The richness of differentiation collapses into the parsimony of homogenization.

Hegemony or dominance?

Cox's observation that hegemony 'means dominance of a particular kind where the dominant state creates an order based ideologically on a broad measure of consent' initially opens up an alternative avenue of investigation. Yet *ideology* continues to maintain its grip on the Coxian formulation. Translated in transnational space, hegemony rarely engages with culture or *cultures* either as singular or heterodox materialization in a meaningful sense, limited to the domain of 'mutual interests' and 'ideological perspectives' (Cox 1987: 7).

'Later' Cox (2000) eschews the productionist bias and moves to an entirely new discursive field overriding neo-Gramscian understandings of transnational hegemony, all but abandoning the parsimony of his earlier historical materialist leanings in favour of an open-ended engagement with civilizational concerns. This is a major (and welcome) adjustment to his earlier commitments. It remains an open question, however, how other worlds enter and reframe Cox's fundamental understanding of global hegemony in 'later' Cox. Recognition of a 'plural world' and its multiple intersubjectivities does not resolve the analytical conundrums of neo-Gramscian thinking on 'transnational hegemony'. Without fully appreciating the coercive nature of power in the so-called 'periphery', and the mutually constitutive nature of inside/outside, appreciation of a plural world appears more nominal than real.

Rupert tries to resolve the problem partially by stressing the need to understand the 'mutually constitutive relations of governance/resistance' in the making of global politics (Rupert 2003: 181). However, he fails to identify the processes that allow 'resistance' to reshape hegemony beyond its obvious oppositional instantiation, as for example in Zapatista claims for cultural autonomy (Rupert 2003: 194–195; but see Morton 2002). In part, Rupert is unable to overcome the paradox inherent with the neo-Gramscian enterprise of theorizing global capitalism, simultaneously as a reified totality in the core and as a non-reified particularity in the Third World. Without resolving this problem, the formation of a 'counter-hegemonic bloc' (Rupert 2000, 2003) faces an insurmountable theoretical hurdle in addition to the lived (cultural) diversity of its constituents.

In the strictly neo-Gramscian mode in his magnum opus, *Production, Power and World Order*, however, Cox essentially tells a *Western* story of late modernity. The non-West remains a silent spectator, marginal both historically, but also analytically. To the point, the mutual interactions between the West and the rest (including especially the Islamic world) are largely absent from an account devoted to what is essentially a more subtle reading of imperialism, its genesis and evolution. The question is not merely of silencing the effects of the periphery on the core, but recognition of the *indivisibility, not juxtaposition*, of the core and periphery. The trajectory of societal development in Europe is largely insulated from other worlds. Although Cox recognizes that 'the liberal state and the liberal world order emerged together, taking shape through the establishment of bourgeois hegemony in Britain and of British hegemony in the world economy' (Cox 1987: 123), he avoids the historical burden of exploring the mutual constitution of core and periphery. That burden is restricted to an investigation of development in the core. The post-colonial unease regarding comparative, not 'connected histories' (Subrahmanyam 1997) or what Said calls 'intertwined histories' (Said 1993), is a spectre that would haunt the neo-Gramscians. The notion of connected histories renders the two-stage model of hegemony (first 'national' then 'transnational', first European or American, then the non-Western world), highly problematic. Conversely, a largely Anglo-American historical lens enfeebles the notion of 'transnational' or 'global' hegemony if that notion empties out the 'transnational' and 'global' of much of the spatial world outside of the West. Why call it hegemony?

Cox provides a densely structured account of class struggles that produced the hegemonic order in Britain, especially regarding the diffusion of conflict (Cox 1987: 138). However, a similar commitment to dynamic processes is missing when the international appears, how peripheral struggles reframe hegemony or annul it, how culture complicates things. At most, a theory of compliance is summoned (Cox 1987: 146). Cox's cartography of the spatial terrain of hegemony helps fully explain the theoretical dilemma: 'Hegemony, though firmly established at the center of the world order, wears thin at its peripheries' (Cox 1987: 150).

What are the transnational *political* processes then that shape hegemony? On a Gramscian interrogation, what are the transnational *cultural* processes that produce hegemony? On one hand, the 'transnational' in the neo-Gramscian formulation is an amalgam of distinct national fragments. On the other hand, the 'transnational' stands above the interstate system, but in political and cultural terms, it embodies a very thin layer. Hegemony works primarily through states, although their form may be quite diverse (Cox 1987: 218).

States remain pivotal to transnational hegemony. Transformations of historical structures of world order must rely on changing configurations of the dominant states accompanied by 'uneven development of productive forces leading to a new distribution of productive powers among social formations', the rise of new historical blocs in social formations as well as new production structures of accumulation (Cox 1987: 209). Recognizing the separation of politics from economics, the hegemonic order circumscribes state form and is hospitable only to structures that agree with the hegemonic order. The centrality of states to hegemony complicates the relative autonomy of the transnational sphere. To the point, the character of the state in the Third World, in Cox's (1987: 230–244) own reading, affirms its non-hegemonic character, a case of dominance without hegemony (Guha 1997).

To recapitulate, the absence of hegemony in those vast zones of the world makes transnational or global hegemony problematic. There are two principal ways to overcome the problem. First, transnational hegemony can be seen as a mixture of hegemony *and* dominance: hegemony in the core, dominance in the peripheral zones of the global political economy. Clearly, this is the neo-Gramscian intent, which is subverted by more ambitious claims of the coming of a 'global culture' (Robinson 1998). The other option is to reframe global hegemony as an inter-state project in which dominant classes collaborate. However, this formulation, which is closer to the textual utterances of the neo-Gramscians, contradicts statements on the *transnational* character of hegemony. In actuality, the analysis suggests the absence of transnational hegemony given basic cleavages between subordinate groups in core and peripheral zones.

The *interstate* nature of transnational hegemony is borne out by Cox's examination of the internationalization of the state. Internationalization of the state is characterized by 'a process of interstate consensus formation regarding the needs or requirements of the world economy that takes place within a common ideological framework (i.e. common criteria of interpretation of economic events and goals anchored in the idea of an open economy)' (Cox 1987: 254). However, Cox recognizes the contrast between the core and the periphery in that 'a stricter regime than that applying to advanced capitalist countries has been enforced on Third World countries ... Third World elites do not participate with the same effective status as top-level elites in the formation of the consensus' (Cox 1987: 260). Cox is also quite aware of the incidence of violence as a stubborn feature of parts of the world system:

> Militarism is a symptom of the regression of global economy on which the world economic order has rested. The more that military force has to be increased and the more it is actually employed, the less the world order rests

on consent and the less it is hegemonic. *Economic benefits appear to flow less from the operation of universal laws of the market that is the basic article of faith of liberalism and more from power positions backed by force.*

(Cox 1987: 289, emphasis added)

The difficulty of producing transnational hegemony is also borne out by Cox's recognition of resistance in the periphery. 'The internationalizing of the Third World state is more openly induced by external pressures than the internationalizing of the advanced capitalist state is and thus provokes more awareness and resentment' (Cox 1987: 265). Why the need for external pressures? Cox's answer sums up the nature of the problem and the latent orientalism in neo-Gramscian international cultural cartography:

Hegemony was more secure at the center of the world system, less secure in its peripheries ... While caesarism secured the passive acquiescence of Third World societies in a global hegemony centred in the advanced capitalist countries, counter-hegemonic movements in other Third World countries constituted open and active challenges to global hegemony. Corresponding to this differentiation in hegemonic intensity between core and periphery of the world system, class struggles were muted by corporatist structures in the core but more open and self-conscious in peripheral areas.

(Cox 1987: 266–227)

Robinson's (1998: 562) discussion of transnational hegemony demonstrates even more intensely the analytical conundrum. His bold plea 'to study transnational social structure', in place of 'national' social structures, assumes the redundancy of the 'nation-state' system. Yet, the emergent transnational networks 'operate both "over" and "under" the nation-state system and undermine its institutional logic and any rationality in conceiving of social structure in national terms' (Robinson 1998: 567). The demand for a new vision for Robinson is necessitated by globalization, which 'denotes a transition from the linkage of national societies predicated on a *world economy* to an emergent transnational or *global society* predicated on a global economy' (Robinson 1998: 563). The introduction of 'global society' is not gratuitous, but an important plank of Robinson's theory of transnational hegemony. Although he fully recognizes the non-economic aspects of globalization, he remains wedded to an unyielding economic determinism. In the first and last instance, economic forces are in the driver's seat:

Economic globalization brings with it the material basis for the emergence of a singular global society, marked by the transnationalization of civil society and political processes, the global integration of social life, and a 'global culture'. In this view, nations are no longer linked externally to a broader system but internally to a singular global social formation.

(Robinson 1998: 563–564)

Robinson is fully cognizant of 'mutually reinforcing economic, political, and cultural forms' of a 'new global social structure of accumulation', but culture consists mainly of consumerism and individualism, 'diffused globally through mass communications and advertising' (Robinson 1998: 588). Under globalization – 'the central dynamic of our epoch' – 'developed and underdeveloped populations (have) no nationally defined geographic identity' (Robinson 1998: 581, 578). Transnational capital 'brings with it the transnationalization of classes in general' (Robinson 1998: 581). This formulation of globalization cannot escape the legacy of economic determinism:

> A full capitalist global society would mean the integration of all national markets into a single market and the division of labour and the disappearance of all national affiliations of capital. These economic tendencies are already under-way. *What is [sic] lagging behind are the political and institutional concomitants – the globalization of the entire superstructure of legal, political, and other national institutions, and the transnationalization of social consciousness and cultural patterns.*
>
> (Robinson 1998: 581, emphasis added)

Robinson's lag theory of social movement is fully evidenced in the transnationalization of the state which is 'lagging behind the globalization of production' (Robinson 1998: 585). Supranational economic institutions are considerably more developed than their political and cultural counterparts (Robinson 1998: 586). To the extent that a base-superstructure model is awkwardly placed to recognize the richness and autonomy of difference, it should come as no surprise that the neo-Gramscian formulation of transnational hegemony necessitates and employs a *thin* notion of culture. The irony is the competing requirement for a notion of *thick* culture to bestow counter-hegemonic substance and political meaning.

Neo-Gramscians fail to recognize the autonomy of the political, which is *the* instantiation of the cultural. Unlike Gramsci, who saw the political 'as a distinct realm of human experience and as an independent domain of investigation with its own internal laws' (Kalyvas 1998: 344; also see Laclau and Mouffe 1985), neo-Gramscians tend to subsume the political with the economic. The political appears as an appendage to transnational processes of the workings of capitalism on a world scale. In developing their theory of transnational hegemony, 'questions about the constitution of legitimate authority especially have been sidelined in favour of worries about other things' (Walker 2002: 7). Efforts to analyse the new global constitutionalism (Gill 2002) have injected an important corrective to the prevailing, albeit diluted, economic determinism, but it clings to a notion of politics not fully recognizing its self-subsistent character. Invariably, the political remains trapped in a logic not of its own making.

Davies (1999), Morton (2003c) and Bieler and Morton (2001a) offer disclaimers to a self-subsistent transnational logic divorced from local context and texture. Proposing a non-deterministic understanding of culture, they recognize the particularity of culture and its relative autonomy, as well as the contradictory nature of intellectuals as 'critical substitutes of civil society' and/or perpetuators of the social order (Morton 2003c: 28). Morton uses a Gramscian framework to analyse the tensions between national and cosmopolitan cultural impulses in Mexico, but also shows the complex nexus between the realms of 'pure art' and 'pure politics'. Davies recognizes both the political agency of (Chilean) intellectuals and the international context of programmes of social transformation without reducing one to the other. By analysing various forces conditioning national politics and intellectuals operating transnationally, or with both national and transnational resources at their disposal, the national–transnational divide is obviated. The focus on communication theory and its creative reception, furthermore, injects agency into the notion of transnational hegemony (Davies 1999). Similarly, Bieler and Morton (2003) address the relative autonomy of the state, showing sensitivity to the autonomous realm of the political, not reducing it to the economic, nor trading the transnational for the national.

Conclusion

The neo-Gramscian appropriation of culture generally fails to match Gramsci's acute awareness of culture's relative autonomy from material production, peripherality, its real and symbolic materialization, and the limits of proletarian hegemony (or its neo-Gramscian counterpart, counter-hegemony). Neither Gramsci's critique of economic determinism nor his astute understanding of the role of intellectuals affords a greater analytical resource for IR than his sensitivity to the *relation between subordination and forms of political life*. Ironically, the theoretical marginalization of the periphery in the neo-Gramscian framework ends up peripheralizing culture. Furthermore, strategies to foment a new (integrated) order under conditions of subalternity generate real hurdles to overcome the historical legacy of structural deprivation. Gramsci's location within the West's economic and political periphery sensitized him to Italy's cultural division between 'particularly the developing north and the underdeveloped south, and the educated classes and the unschooled masses' (Bellamy, in Gramsci 1994: x, xi). On a Gramscian reading, global tensions between a West-centred liberal order and its assumed antithesis in much of the Third World (particularly the Islamic world), becomes explicable not simply in material terms, nor as a cultural clash, but as the cumulative effect of a culturally partitioned world of privilege and unity, want and fragmentation. The subalternity of the ICZs is not only tied to global political economy but also the global cultural economy in which questions of representation and agency occupy centre stage.

The neo-Gramscian preoccupation with global hegemonic consolidation, which is primarily a process of extending hegemony from the core to the periphery, expunges the cultural question raised by the nagging presence of conflicting intersubjectivities of dominant and subaltern social forces on a world scale. Yet, neo-Gramscians are quick to embrace the cultural question as it clings to notions of resistance. Gramsci's recognition of the mixed heritage of native culture (Gramsci 1994; Buttigieg 1986a), its cultural richness and docility, tradition and the fetters it places on collective societal action, or embeddedness and its concomitant denial of certain forms of agency, contradicts the celebratory tone and content of many self-avowed neo-Gramscian accounts of counter-hegemonic struggles in the Third World. Neo-Gramscians do not fully appreciate the Gramscian necessity of the acquisition of 'self-knowledge and with it self-mastery' (Bellamy in Gramsci 1994: 9–10) to lend proletarian (counter-)hegemony the (alternative) character of transcendence. The lure of resistance against global capitalism or globalization, without the additional burden of seeking 'the attainment of a higher awareness, through which we can come to understand our value and place in history, our proper function in life, our rights and duties' (Bellamy in Gramsci 1994: xvi), merely endorses a 'soft' orientalism. Yet, it is equally important to avoid the latent (Western) teleology in the Gramscian formulation. One possibility is to recognize political struggles, especially in the ICZs, not as resistance to globalization, but constitutive of the contradictory processes of an unequal world in which particular forms of cultural expression appear illegitimate.

On a Gramscian reading, the incorporation of many non-Western zones into the global political economy has subordinated them politically, economically and culturally. As Gramsci recognized, structures of 'patronage and compromise between elites and clienteles' (Bellamy, in Gramsci 1994: xii) can produce both insurmountable obstacles to social reform and unorthodox forms of political expression. The virtual disenfranchisement of many cultural zones in global politics is not coincidentally linked to political nihilism on the global plane. In this reading, the exacerbation of culturally and religiously coded conflict becomes less opaque. Equally pertinent in this context are Gramsci's analysis of fascism and his acute recognition of the dual face of power (Gramsci 1971; Fontana 1993). Centaur's beastly side is not simply a theoretical, but a real possibility in a world increasingly drawn towards a Manichean logic in the centres of global power. The difficulty of acknowledging the persistent and significant presence of violence as the political grammar of capitalist modernity, especially in the peripheral zones, gives the neo-Gramscian theory of transnational hegemony the character of a benign, mostly apolitical, project. Gramsci's constant disquiet over the Southern question (Bellamy and Schecter 1993; Brennan 1988–89) provides an effective riposte to the diffusionist proclivities of the neo-Gramscians.

An important implication of the dual deployment of culture in the neo-Gramscian framework is to circumscribe the theoretical possibility to recognize the nature of hegemonic and peripheral fractures in the ICZs (see Introduction). This would entail questioning both the notion that homogenizing force of West-centred globalization brooks no resistance as well as challenging the idea of an essentialized (unchanging and monolithic) Islam standing firm against assimilation. As mentioned, in the first instance, the culturally textured world of Islam appears simply as an atavistic residue of an unfinished modernity. In the second instance, an undifferentiated faith successfully launches counter-hegemonic struggles. Absent in this framework is the *transformed* and *transformative* nature of both hegemony and the ICZs. This alternative reading repudiates the one-dimensional picture of homogenization. Politics refracts culture in fundamental ways. The insistence on relative cultural fixity to authenticate counter-hegemony faces the burden of differentiation and fissure. To recognize sites of resistance, therefore, entails more than recognizing difference. It rests on an appreciation of the possibility of tensions within otherness and attempted resolutions that can no longer remain insulated from the wider worlds inhabiting otherness.

9

POSTORIENTALISM AND CIVILIZATIONAL DISCOURSE

[Injury has been done] to every nation which has been dominated by others and treated harshly. The same thing can be seen clearly in all those persons who are subjected to the will of others and who do not enjoy full control of their lives.

(Ibn Khaldun 1950: 61)

Every culture thrives on establishing difference from others, and pursues this establishment of savage difference with particular energy in situations of serious external conflict or internal flux and uncertainty.

(Al-Azmeh 1993: 164)

The 'return' of civilizational analysis in international relations (IR) presents contradictory messages about the state of the contemporary world. In the first instance, it affirms the arrival of a globalized *modern* community. In the second instance, it stresses the durability of unbridgeable differences between and among distinctive forms of cultural life underpinning political association. Some observers have received civilizational analysis with considerable scepticism. As Bruce Mazlish puts it:

Civilization is one of those great Stonehenge figures looming over our mental landscape. Like its adjacent figure, culture, it is one of the major concepts invented and constructed in the eighteenth century and subsequently elaborated in the course of the development of the social sciences. In the new millennium, it has become a fetish. In the new time-space we have entered, it should not only be 'deconstructed' but taken down.

(Mazlish 2004: 160–61)

The recognition of globalized modernity (Featherstone et al. 1995) and its consolidation as a civilization in its own right (Eisenstadt 2001) overcomes conventional claims of elective affinities between Western cultural uniqueness and the rise of a materialist civilization. The core of modernity is the crystallization and development of mode or modes of interpretation of the world, or of a distinct social imaginaire, indeed of the ontological vision, of a distinct cultural programme, combined with the development of a set or sets of new institutional formations – the central core of both being an unprecedented 'openness' and uncertainty (Eisenstadt 2001: 320).

With capitalism flourishing in vastly heterodox terrains, allowing varied mixtures of economic purpose and cultural orientation, the thesis of Western exceptionalism has been undermined. The potential and possibility of self-expanding growth and material achievement in non-Western contexts, particularly in Asia, undermine the notion that 'modern' or 'industrial' ways of life are somehow uniquely the province of Western sensibility and culture. However, the question of correlates attending liberal political and social formations and their putative absence in non-Western worlds remains. There is a long lineage, however, on both the left and right sides of the political spectrum of this sentiment (Moore 1966; Anderson 1974a, 1974b). What promised a significant departure from hegemonic claims of Western uniqueness now appears in a refurbished narrative, claims of its exceptional *political* achievement, captured in the negative language of 'failed states' and the emergence of 'a string of shabby tyrannies' in the Islamic world (Lewis 2002). The presumed inability of several non-Western states to fulfil the minimum requirements of statehood, including the provision of security, internal cohesion, peace and economic viability, appears to reinforce the thesis that these political entities do not share Western cultural assets. The latter would encompass political culture, habits of citizenship, and the achievement principle reminiscent of modernization claims. With regard to the Islamic cultural zones (ICZs), in particular, the democratic deficit apparently reflects cultural rigidity drawn from a religiously coded social order.

The assertion of incommensurable civilizational difference seems self-evident. By lifting civilizational analysis from the academic periphery to the centre and according an implicit parity to rival civilizational complexes, however, Huntington's 'clash of civilizations' thesis has revived the study of civilizations. The revival of civilizational talk, especially in view of its political uses, poses intriguing questions about the indivisible nexus between IR and the world it seeks to interrogate.

Huntington trades the offensiveness of erstwhile morphological categories with civilizations. Yet, the sweeping rhetorical strategies in his account with warnings of a coming global war, with particular reference to Islam's radical difference vis-à-vis the West, have also brought intellectual closure. The process of opening up spaces within a conversation on civilizations, therefore, is an enormous challenge, especially given the relative ease with which civilizational analysis has been absorbed into new hegemonic claims of defending universal Western values against atavistic forces of irrationality. The term 'universal Western values' that authorizes a particular *weltanschauung* to represent humanity paradoxically combines appeals to universality with particularistic conceit. A clear example of this paradox saturates former British Prime Minister Tony Blair's address to the World Affairs Council in Los Angeles on 2 August 2006:

> [T]his struggle is one about values. Our values are worth fighting for. They represent humanity's progress throughout the ages and at each point we had to fight for them and defend them. As a new age beckons, it is time to fight for them again.
>
> *(Blair 2006)*

Challenging the above paradox, this chapter revisits the nexus between orientalist essentialism and hegemony in search for a more inclusive conversation on civilizations. It hopes to offer the lineaments of an agonistic reading of the constitutive politics of civilizational identity, with particular emphasis on the ICZs. Acknowledging the plurality of religious and cultural expression in different spaces/times with a relatively fluid and changeable Islam, this chapter also shows the difficulty of releasing civilizational analysis from the grip of received imaginaries that circulate as common sense. Furthermore, recognizing the problematic global location of Islamic cultural expression and its relational status to the symbolic economy of IR, the task here is to further the 'dialogue among civilizations', albeit on a non-essentialist register.

The return of civilizational analysis sharply reveals how cultural essentialism can be effectively mobilized to consolidate hegemony. Essentialism and hegemony are mutually constitutive. In the post-Cold War climate, civilizational talk has principally congealed disciplinary strategies of consolidation. In this vein, popular pronouncements on civilization, such as the 'end of history' (Fukuyama 1989, 1992), or 'the clash of civilizations' (Huntington 1993, 1996), have offered common sense simplifiers to demarcate presumed cultural borders. Observed from their dominant geo-epistemological site, these civilizational claims are fundamentally political technologies of hegemonic consolidation. Essentialist accounts show an inextricable nexus between knowledge claims and their authorization within discrete spatial and cultural boundaries. As Sabine (1937: preface) notes, 'theories of politics are themselves a part of politics … they do not refer to an external reality but are produced as a normal part of the social milieu in which politics itself has its being'. Despite their appeal for universalism, as with Tony Blair's hubristic remarks, these claims bear the imprint of hegemonic locales and mentalities. These accounts respond to new constellations of power, legitimizing hegemony, either in the name of civilizing purpose or civilizational insecurity. In both cases, civilizational analysis of the Huntington variety help secure the boundaries of 'Western' identity. Marrying elements of hubris (Connolly 1998) and disquiet (Coker 1998), civilizational analysis associated with Huntington and those who follow his lead (Gismondi 2004) encodes hegemonic thinking. An alternative formulation reads recent civilizational analysis as a series of ambivalent commentaries on the difficulty of securing hegemony in an increasingly porous world; triumphalism may actually hide worries about the curve of imperial power, as Wallerstein (2006) notes. Worries of hegemonic decline now reappear, but adopt the supremacist language of empire (Ferguson 2003; Nye 2002, 2004).

Cultural essentialism supplies the apparatus for hegemonic projects. Civilizational analysis from other (non-Western) geo-epistemological sites, however, depicts a different portrait of the times. In general, the discourse on crisis metamorphizes as a return to civilizational analysis. Combining nostalgia with aspirations of renewal in the ICZs, for instance, civilizational analysis congeals weakness. The language of crisis symbolizes shades of powerlessness in the face of (Western) hegemony. The longing for glorious times, frustration to reverse the order of things, remonstrations for spiritual awakening or the death of futures belong to this genre. On the other hand, the language of crisis, as in Spengler's (1922) case, can signal deep historical pessimism, limits to civilizational progress, and the possibility of decline.

Alternatively, the language of civilization can also serve as a pragmatic survival strategy to negotiate (Western) power. In this context, the 'dialogue among civilizations' proposed by former Iranian President Khatami (Khatami 2000; Akhavi 2003) combines cultural self-confidence with pragmatism. The idea of dialogue offers a forceful counterpoint to the alarmist language of a 'clash of civilizations', but also shows the constrictions of Western modernity, albeit in a dialogical spirit. Unlike orientalist readings of Muslim negative 'responses' based on Islamic exceptionalism (Lewis 2002), dialogical modes of engagement with the West are advanced. Implicit to this alternative formulation is an embrace of an *Islamic* variant of modernity. If Lewis is the ideal-typical proponent of Islamic exceptionalism, the belief of Muslim deficiency to reconcile modernity with Islam, Khatami places Islamic civilization within universal history. Khatami seeks to protect cultural autonomy in a runaway world of homogenization, and in this sense amplifies dialogical voices providing alternatives to hegemonic thinking (Dallmayr 1996; Mushakoji 1996). As subsequent discussion shows, the conditions for dialogue reside not merely in new global power constellations, but in non-essentialist modes of cultural recognition. The former would entail the emergence of multiple civilizational centres, each respecting agonistic modes of cultural belonging. The latter would substitute particularity for radical alterity, the appreciation of commonality as a ground for difference, but also recognition of difference as a condition to forge commonality.

The strategy of unfreezing orientalist essentialism also requires avenues to deconstruct the fixity in occidental accounts and their reliance on notions of permanence and homogeneity. In this regard, the distinction between the West's changeable self-construction (Jackson 1990) and a relatively fixed negative portrait in the non-West (Buruma and Margalit 2004) can be useful. In the latter portrait, the West is depicted as a static, monolithic other, a soulless monster bent upon colonizing the social and life-worlds of humanity (Buruma and Margalit 2004). Non-Western occidentalism, however, comes in various guises, not simply as anti-Western rage, as Buruma and Margalit propose. Other forms include both negative and positive images, including the West as a 'counterdiscourse', a critique of domestic exclusionary structures of authority or presumably moribund cultural practices (Chen 1992), or as an escape from the 'cage of nature' (Maruyama [1952] 1974). On the positive register, the West represents a zone of liberation from non-Western cultural and political strictures. Finally, occidentalism provides a rationale and an apology for jumping on the fast-track train of economic globalization, the promised land of economic opportunity, wealth and freedom (Bhagwati 2004). The uses of the West are diverse and malleable.

Anti-essentialist civilizational analysis also acknowledges the effects of power and its reproduction in different historical settings. These effects and mechanisms tend to replenish essentialism, which in turn can abet hegemony. In times of emergency, which typically engender sovereign claims over boundaries and 'truth', fixed 'us/them' classifications can return. Essentialist typologies help the reinforcement of cultural and political boundaries. The fate of post-Saidian (Said 1978, 1993) critique in the current global climate can be read on these terms.

To contextualize, postorientalist constructions in the shadow of Said's (1978) brilliant deconstruction of orientalism have yielded multiple and wide openings linking hegemony and understanding. In the wider cultural field, orientalism was deeply scarred by the reflexive turn in the social and human sciences (Bonnell and Hunt 1999). A paradigmatic instance in this context was the growing self-scrutiny in anthropological accounts of otherness and feminist critiques of orientalism (Yeğenoğlu 1998). Recognition of scholarly complicity in empire making (Asad 1973), appreciation of power hierarchies between knower and known (Derrida 1976), the implausibility of Cartesian framing in ethnographic work (Clifford 1988) and recognition of the pervasive scope of Eurocentrism in knowledge production (Said 1978; Wolf 1982) were some of the major aspects of the so-called reflexive turn. Presumably, the reflexive turn would produce new frames of understanding Otherness, especially the ICZs.

However, post-Saidian critique undervalued the elasticity of orientalist strategies of survival, resistance and *reconquista*. In part, the problem has rested with post-orientalist critique itself, deflecting analysis away from politics to culture; shifting Said's focus on orientalism as ultimately a *political* vision of reality (Said 1978), an unending process of struggle, to a lifeless frame in the service of power. More importantly, orientalist modes of (mis)recognition have benefited from unforeseen historical events and their psychic effects on negotiating Otherness, especially Islamic alterity. The consolidation of essentialist stereotyping of Islam and Muslims as common sense (Gramsci 1971) underscores the salience of the politics of knowledge production and the inextricable nexus between discourse and politics. It also underscores the need to shun notions of linear progress and the fiction of cumulative knowledge. Cultural fields are susceptible to political contestation. In turn, politics can mobilize deeper affective resources from established wellsprings of understanding, including classificatory schemes, prejudice and bias, to produce new enclosures.

Politics and civilizational analysis

A striking feature of mainstream civilizational thinking in world affairs is its unambiguous *political* tenor. Confirming Western liberal triumph over its known illiberal rivals (Fukuyama 1989, 1992) or forecasting the coming dark season of an inevitable Western 'clash' with Islamic otherness (Huntington 1993, 1996), the popular currency of civilization gestures toward the character of asymmetrical global power, both material and symbolic. Yet, this gesture is fraught with ambiguities and pitfalls. In Fukuyama's case, 'the end of history' appears as a curtain call of a directionless West, robbed of its (missionary) purpose, as explicitly observed by Coker (1998). Huntington's supplication for an 'enclavized' West (Shapiro 1999) misreads globalizing tendencies in the homeland and abroad, endangering the principal object he wishes to secure. In either case, hidden or revealed transcripts of power invade the representational field, either fully transparent or not entirely hidden from the cognitive field. Civilizational analysis, despite appearing distant from power, is chained to the Western story of modernity (McNeill 1963). Hence, Ibn Khaldun (1332–1406) appears as a residual figure in extant civilizational discussion, largely outside the purview of *relevant* theoretical speculation – usually cited, but rarely interrogated to supply meaningful insight (see Chapter 10). Civilizational analysis has a rich historical source in Ibn Khaldun's magisterial opus on the philosophy of history (*Kitab al-ibar*), centuries before 19th- or 20th-century discoveries of this important heuristic. The fixation of Western IR with insular narratives of the 'civilizing process' shows a consistent refusal to go beyond the musings of Kant or Hegel and their contemporary disciples.

Hence, extant civilizational thinking principally engages *the modern*, an outcome of European exceptionalism (Arnason 2001; Eisenstadt 2001; Elias 1978; Nelson 1981), the fountainhead of multiple modernities (Eisenstadt 2000), and the ideal or ideal-type to measure other civilizations, aspiring, deficient or both. Those with a more expansive optic (Braudel 1994; Cox 2000; Dallmayr 1996; O'Hagan 2002; Suzuki 2005) prove the exception: the hegemony of Western modernity is the hub in the analytical wheel. Dallmayr's magnanimous gesture to move beyond the West still takes the West as a point of reference. Eisenstadt's notion of 'multiple modernities' can escape neither the philosophical nor the sociological discourse of Western modernity. The paradigmatic centrality of Western civilization provides the master copy against which 'others' can be compared (Eisenstadt 2000), or 'alternative modernities' captured (Göle 2000). In the generous quest to go beyond the West, these accounts cannot proceed without acknowledging the original point of embarkation.

Voices from other geo-epistemological sites, on the other hand, either speak of a pre-modern 'Golden Age' to avoid the embarrassment of civilizational comparison or elect to acknowledge the tenor of the times, preferring a 'dialogue' to ensure ontological difference (Khatami 2000). Modernity rests on temporal and spatial distinctions (Fabian 1983), assigning the West a higher point on an ascending scale. To rethink civilizational discourse, therefore, requires strategies not only to de-essentialize but also dislodge the hegemony of modern forms of historicism. The latter resuscitate orientalism in two principal ways: privileging 'presentism' and promoting 'scientific-rational knowledge' (Nandy 1995). Presentism rests on the assumption of denying multiple histories within the past, some apparent, others concealed; some expressed, others repressed. Instead, it takes a singular known present, often produced by positivist methodology, as the known destination of the past. Historicism discards the past as a pre-modern, traditional vestige in the name of progress. As a *particular* form of knowledge, historicism also silences alternative expressions of knowing: myth, folklore and storytelling. Failure to meet the scientific criteria of verifiability disqualifies knowledge claims. Civilizational hierarchies rest on these twin operations of historicism, 'the cardinal principle of the mental culture of modernity' (Al-Azmeh 2001: 78).

Untying the non-West from the historicist imaginary allows recognition of multiple cultural instantiations – diverse expressions in time and space – without embracing the story of Western triumph or miracle. In this context, the idea of 'provincializing modernity' (or 'Europe' for Chakrabarty 2000) assigns modernity's career the status of a 'particularity' not the universal norm. This strategy offers the possibility to recover lost cognitive worlds either repressed in/with modernity (Nandy 1995; Inayatullah and Blaney 2004). On the other hand, the act of decoupling of modernity from the master narrative of Westernization, recognizing modernity's underside dampens the force of Eurocentrism.

Postorientalist critique largely avoids the reflexive turn within orientalism, misguided by the success of its 'seditious' (Prakash 1995) powers. Said's recognition of orientalism as an integral part of *modern* political-intellectual sensibility has not been fully appreciated: 'Orientalism is not a mere political subject matter of field that is reflected passively by culture, scholarship, or institutions; nor is it a large and "Western" imperial plot to hold down the "Oriental" world' (Said 1978: 12). Alternatively, Young's analysis of the critical reconsideration of colonial modernity as project and practice has contemporary relevance for extant mainstream civilizational analysis. An awareness of the mutual constitution of colonialism and orientalism organizes a different cognitive field to recognize similar projects in our own times, those that implicate hegemony with a refurbished civilizer/barbarian distinction (Al-Azmeh 2001). Colonial modernity, on this view, is not merely the domination of the non-West by the West, not simply 'a particular military and economic strategy of Western capitalist societies, but also as itself constituting and generated by a specific historical discourse of knowledge articulated with the operation of political power: colonization in short, involved epistemic as well as physical violence' (Young 2001: 383). Despite allusions to a power/knowledge nexus, postorientalist critiques downplay the effects of new power constellations.

The circulation of a mostly negative picture of Islam and Muslims is not divorced from the project of hegemonic consolidation. A purely functionalist account that sees the 'uses' of Islam to fulfil certain political needs is an insufficient guide to appreciate the demonization of Muslims and their faith. Western material and symbolic power *produces* a particular variant of the Islamic civilization. In turn, representations of the Islamic civilization contribute to producing Western power, giving coherence to the idea of Western civilizational identity and mobilizing the global symbolic economy to attain that end. This process has attained a familiar tonality in the current global climate of ontological insecurity. Less recognizable in received accounts, however, is the possibility of a *generalized* crisis of modernity and the difficulty of realizing the teleological promise of the Enlightenment without erasing difference through assimilation or cultural genocide. The safer and familiar terrain of civilizational apartheid appears as a firmer foundation to produce ontological security. Paradoxically, the enactment of the scopic regime of radical alterity only brings dread, anticipation and anxiety. Islam's presence *within* the West further complicates its location in this symbolic universe, an ontological nightmare for the liberal project of multicultural assimilation. Western society must now choose between relaxing pre-requisites of social and cultural inclusion and blatant prescriptions for instituting graded citizenship, surveillance and exclusion.

There are several facets to this process. In the global cultural economy, Muslims are represented; they cannot represent themselves (Marx, in Said 1978). The capacity to represent Islam globally is unevenly distributed. Hegemonic representations that enter the symbolic economy embrace an essentialized occidentalism as the mirror image of orientalism. Second, orientalist essentialism draws an unbridgeable wedge between the West and Muslims. This helps sanction strategies of containment, management and pre-emption. Demonization legitimates the uses of force. This is not a new story. Its repeats endlessly, stressing the stubbornness of cultural and religious cartographies. Recall Conrad's poignant statement:

> The conquest of the earth, which mostly means the taking it away from those who have a different complexion or slightly flatter noses than ourselves, is not a pretty thing when you look into it too much. What redeems it is the idea only. An idea at the back of it; not a sentimental pretense but an idea; an unselfish belief in the idea – something you can set up, and bow down before, and offer a sacrifice to …
>
> *(Cited in Said 1993: vii)*

Ultimately, as Said reminds us, power delimits the cognitive field; it also buttresses the divide between self and other. Appeals to unassimilable difference solidify civilizational boundaries (Neumann 1999). The current global climate is unimaginable without the continued deployment of notions of Islamic alterity both within and without the West's cultural containers. Alternatives to civilizational essentialism, hence, require negotiations with the question of boundaries, how they are set and maintained. They also necessitate an awareness of fractures *within* civilizational complexes that remain persistent irritants to notions of uniformity (see Introduction). Boundaries, however, are not static, but products of cultural practice and political struggle. The recognition of fractures within civilizational complexes helps challenge totalizing constructions of otherness. This observation is incontrovertible. The principal hurdle facing extant non-essentialist approaches to civilizational analysis, however, is the impossible task of mediating between notions of porous and core identities. On the one hand, repudiation of the civilizational identity may advance claims of theoretical anarchism or extreme relativism. On the obverse side, the assumption of civilizational rigidity reinforces standard orientalist tropes. Alternatives to these accounts are *relational* modes of civilizational thinking.

Relational modes presuppose neither relativism nor essentialism but processual vectors of civilizations – civilizations as products of interaction and cultural practice, but with operational codes that sustain continuity over time. Before attending to the relational framework, the next section probes the durable legacy of orientalism and the challenge of postorientalist thinking.

The scopic regimes of orientalism

The orientalist project has rested on familiar overlapping, if contradictory scopic regimes, giving durability to its structures. A brief accounting of these regimes would include *essentialism, stasis, othering, self-enclosure* and *historicism. Essentialism* relies on civilizational/cultural reductionism, locating otherness to a recognizable, monadic, self-subsistent essence. Anouar Abdel-Malek provides an incisive statement on essentialism:

> According to the traditional orientalists, an essence should exist – sometimes even clearly described in metaphysical terms – which constitutes the inalienable and common basis of all beings considered; this essence is both 'historical', since it goes back to the dawn of history, and fundamentally a-historical, since it transfixed the being, 'the object' of study, within its inalienable and non-evolutive specificity … Thus one ends with a typology – based on a real specificity, but detached from history, and consequently, conceived as being intangible, essential – which makes of the studied 'object' another being with regard to whom the studying subject is transcendent; we will have a homo Sinicus, a homo Arabicus (and why not a homo Aegyticus, etc.), a homo Africanus, the man – the 'normal man', it is understood – being the European man of the historical period, that is, since Greek antiquity.
>
> *(Abdel-Malek 1963: 107–108)*

Similarly, Al-Azmeh's critique of Gellner's essentialism also applies to other scholarly works that depict Islamic societies as unchanging, monadic wholes. Gellner's (1981) 'pendulum swing' theory of Islam, Al-Azmeh notes,

> postulates two forms of religiosity, the enthusiastic-rural and the puritanical-urban, in a primordial conflict and cyclical alternance which fundamentally constitutes Muslim history – so fundamentally, indeed, that the present condition of the Muslims can be conceived in no other terms, and which can have no outcome other than the triumph of urban Puritanism. Correlative with this religious characterization of a history, reduced to religious culture, is the proposition that no modernism for Muslims is inconceivable in terms other than those of the Muslim puritanical doctrine and its correlates.
>
> *(Al-Azmeh 2003: 43)*

Against the burden of essentialism, particular modes of consciousness or stable cultural patterns explain behavioural variations between discrete human communities or individuals, often on an ascending scale of progress (or a descending ladder of barbarism). Essentialism 'normally stresses the (over)-simplifying aspect of the cognitive process of constructing a Self-Other polarity … the role played by an "essence" is that of delimiting the field and the scope of the domestication of the Other' (Salvatore 1996: 459). Commonplace essentialist tropes include the traditional–modern divide, the separation between a private sphere of religiosity and a public sphere of the secular in the West, and an absence of separation of the two spheres in the ICZs, the pervasive colonization by religion of the social and lifeworlds of Muslims and the implausibility of social practice autonomous from faith. Al-Azmeh calls it the 'over-[I]slamization of Muslims, their endowment with a superhuman capacity for perpetual piety, the reduction of their history and their present life to a play and recovery of religious motifs, and hence a denial of their actual history' (Al-Azmeh 2003: 44).

To these elements can be added notions of cultural deficiency, want and emotive excess in coming to terms with the rationalizing processes of modernity. According to Pipes, for example:

> Future relations of Muslims and Westerners depend less on crude numbers or place of residence, and much more on beliefs, skills, and institutions. The critical question is *whether Muslims will modernize or not.* And the answer lies not in the Qur'an or in the Islamic religion, but in the attitudes and actions of nearly a billion individuals.
>
> *(Pipes 1990: 7, emphasis added)*

In the current global environment, the figure of Islamic terrorism dominates the cultural field. As Pipes puts it, 'Muslim countries host the most terrorists and the fewest democracies in the world' (Pipes 1990: 3). This sentiment is now widely shared, not merely within the community of Western organic intellectuals supplying counsel and prescription to the Prince, but broadly within Western civil societies, especially those that host immigrants from the ICZs including those who were born in the West. The equation of terrorism with the Muslim faith is a naturalized essentialist trope.

Essentialism is inconceivable without a notion of *stasis*, the attribution of fixity to otherness. Stasis links culture to nature; culture is reduced to its originary, changeless state – primordial, patterned, thick. Stasis denies both the idea of society and the idea of history; society collapses into nature. Social phenomena appear as the recurrence of nature phenomena, perhaps, with even greater rigidity and predictability. Once the inner principle of a culture or religion is grasped, the mind of a people captured within bounded spaces, time can be evacuated. The new and the old become indistinguishable like ghosts inhabiting cultural zones of innateness. Law-like regularity appearing in nature can also be found in cultural and religious communities, outside history, time or civilization. Lewis's essentialization of Islam as an unchanging faith pervades his mighty career as one of the authoritative representatives of orientalism. A key component of the misrecognition of Islam not as a faith, but as a total way of life. Hence, Islamic politics lacks the autonomy found in the West:

> Islamic law knows no corporate legal persons; Islamic history shows no councils or communes, no synods or parliaments, nor any other kind of elective or representative assembly ... the political experience of the Middle East [which Lewis often takes as the equivalent of the Islamic world] under the caliphs and sultans was one of almost unrelieved autocracy, in which obedience to the sovereign was a religious as well as a political obligation, and disobedience a sin as well as a crime.
>
> *(Lewis 1964: 64)*

Temporality dissolves into circularity. A classic example can be found in Pope Benedict XVI's (2006) remarks on the inextricable association between violence and faith as a durable feature of Islam, offering a striking example of essentialism's immunization against modernity or globalizing currents, economic integration, cultural flows or scientific exchange. Islam's past, present and future are simply identical. As Huntington stresses, '[c]ultures can change, and the nature of their impact on politics and economics can vary from one period to another. Yet the major differences in political and economic development among civilizations are clearly rooted in their different cultures' (Huntington 1996: 29).

The third scopic regime of orientalism is *othering*. Exoticism and demonization are two principal forms of othering (Žižek 1994). On this view, the strange and inscrutable world of the other can invite either wonder and awe, or merely repellent reaction – as the embodiment of heresy or totalizing sin. King's reading of orientalist constructions of Hinduism is relevant to the ICZs:

> Today, there are perhaps two powerful images in contemporary Western characterizations of Eastern religiosity. One is the continually enduring notion of the 'mystical East' – a powerful image precisely because of some of it represents what is most disturbing and outdated about Eastern culture, whilst for others it represents the magic, the mystery and the sense of the spiritual which they perceive to be lacking in modern Western culture ... The second image of Eastern religion – one indeed that is increasingly coming to the fore in Western circles, is that of the 'militant fanatic'.
>
> *(King 1999: 147)*

In the first instance, potential for parity remains, though rarely realized: otherness can apparently enclose mysterious wellsprings of wisdom; refined modalities of harnessing cognitive, spiritual or sexual energies; and pathways to escape materialism, pathologies of scientific reason, or psychic distress. Encounters with otherness can reveal limits of selfhood and its social constitution, or simply offer momentary reprieve from cultural boredom. The hyperexoticized world of *Arabian Nights*, a depoliticized and decontextualized Sufism (Islamic mysticism), Islamic art or the harem provide familiar tropes. On the other side, otherness affirms civilizational hierarchies. Daniel Pipes captures the ahistorical historicity of Islamic interaction with Christianity:

> The fear of Islam has some basis in reality. From the Battle of Ajnadayn in 634 until the Suez crisis of 1956, military hostility has *always* been the crux of the Christian-Muslim relationship. Muslims served as the enemy par excellence from the *Chanson de Roland* to the Rolando trilogy, from *El Cid* to *Don Quixote*. In real life, Arabs or Turks represent the national villains throughout southern Europe. Europeans repeatedly won their statehood by expelling Muslim overlords, from the Spanish *Reconquista* beginning in the early eleventh century to the Albanian war of independence ending in 1912.
>
> *(Pipes 1990: 3, emphasis added)*

At one extreme, otherness secures ontological certainty, confirming Western moral and material advance. However, otherness also produces deep anxieties about civilizational insecurity in the face of an irrational, fatalistic or fanatical adversary unimpressed by the modern apparatus of power, thought or conduct. Oriana Fallaci, the prominent Italian journalist and public intellectual, offers a compelling example of civilizational insecurity produced by othering Islam.

The fourth scopic regime of orientalism lies in the idea of *Self-enclosure*, which suggests the absence of significant contact between civilizations with the possibility of mutuality, learning, mimicry or synthesis. On this view, cultural difference acquires permanence within bounded universes imperious to the outside. Either connectedness between cultures is absent or it rarely produces change. A major implication of the notion of self-enclosure is naturalization of the other – other cultures not recognized as historical entities, but timeless entities. Once the endogeneity of the other is established, external contact can appear as progressive, civilizing and enlightening. However, the idea of self-enclosure can also generate the fiction that no amount of contact with the outside world can induce modernization and progress. Otherness is perpetually trapped in its own miserable state.

If the notion of stasis accords stability to the other, paradoxically though, orientalism acquires its élan only in/through *historicism*, the central plank of modern sensibility of space-time. Two aspects are crucial here: the shift in the idea of time from its divine realm to an objective, secular process involving earthly salvation *in* civilization; and the rise of the West within this imaginary (McNeill 1963). Historicism rationalizes Western hegemony by introducing the idea of *deficiency* as its master signifier for the non-West (Orient). Oriental deficiency appears as the constant feature in Western stories of progress, of modernization and development (Black 1966), of democracy and civil society (Diamond and Plattner 2001), or of quasi-states (Jackson 1990) or failed states (Fukuyama 2004). In the ICZs, as Al-Azmeh (1993: 168) puts it, Islam appears as 'a deficient order of things, and an order of deficient things'. A major proponent of Muslim cultural deficiency is Bernard Lewis (2002).

Civilization – as process – then becomes the supplanting of deficiency. To be 'civilized' is to escape, to overcome a lack – of reason, rationality, wealth or freedom. With the idea of deficiency, orientalism provides international relations the quality of recurrence. Hegemony, on this view, is a project of establishing leadership in the name of civilizing mission to release the non-Western sphere of the globe from its cultural deficiencies. The paradox lies, of course, in the realization that this is ultimately an impossible undertaking. Given the teleological underpinnings of historicism, recognizing no final endpoint (except in narratives of cultural hubris and triumphalism), the (deficient) other is locked in perpetuity into a circular web without an outlet. Conversely, the endpoint is merely a 'moment' reworked by/in time.

Agonism and postorientalism

Reflected in post-colonial theory (for distinctions among the various shades of this theory, see Loomba 2005), postorientalist reconstructions of Islamic otherness have offered fruitful pathways for recognizing difference *within* difference, fluidity and connectedness. The orientalist assumption of homogeneity produced by scriptural unity and its uniform instantiation in the Islamic world has yielded to appreciation of heterodoxy, the imprint of place, and cultural heterogeneity. In turn, the timeless universe of tradition in orientalist mythology engulfing Muslim mind and practice has opened up. Recognition of internal differentiation, contingency and the importance of locality have dissolved assumed unities. Against orientalist representations of the inseparability of religion and politics in Islam, postorientalism helps recognize separate and differentiated social spheres, relocating religion to local context and contingency. Orientalism conflates doctrine, belief and ritual. Postorientalism recognizes discriminations. In the Islamic instance, postorientalist reinterpretation helps distinguish between a contextualized and decontextualized Islam, an Islam of particularity and content versus an idealized, timeless and spatially homeless faith. As Asad suggests, conditions of the social world shape the experience of the spiritual world: 'There cannot be a universal definition of religion, not only because its constituent elements and relations are historically specific, but because that definition is itself the historical product of discursive processes' (Asad 1993: 29).

Postorientalism furnishes thinking spaces to capture the global experience of Islam. It deciphers how local Islam is interwoven into wider processes, and cautions against the tendency to subsume the local into the global. Furthermore, it resists privileging 'transnational Islam' above local processes of the social reproduction of Muslim identities. In turn, an appreciation of movement, malleability and transformation demystifies the notion of stasis. Orientalism eternalizes historical Islam. The orientalist trope 'fits with a widespread myth-making in Europe and America that operates in unintended collusion with fundamentalist Muslims' own different, but compatible, myths about themselves' (Fischer 2002: 65). Postorientalism frees Islam from timeless fetters. Building on Ibn Khaldun's insight that societies are human, not natural, entities with intersubjectivities and life-worlds (Ibn Khaldun

1950: 99; and Chapter 10), postorientalist (re)interpretation removes the orientalist guise of stagnant civilizational waters (Lewis 2002).

Recognition of change and changeability, however, without deconstructing the cultural logic of Western historicism only offers a halfway house. In refurbished orientalist narration (dubbed as neo-orientalism), represented by Daniel Pipes (2002) or Martin Kramer (1980), the Muslim pathway remains off course, devoid of the right ingredients for internalized transformation; modernity appearing as shallow externality. Unwittingly, the absence of internal elements for transformation echo themes in the philosophy of history, notably drawn in Hegelian accounts. Hegel's own interpretation of the Crusades offers an interesting benchmark. Spiritually deficient, crusaders can only fail to reach the Promised Land. The long passage that follows captures, albeit in a different context, the impossibility of development based entirely on an abstract principle:

> The great army of the Crusaders give us the best example of this. They march forth on a holy errand, but on their way they give free vent to all the passions, and in this the leaders show the example; the individuals allow themselves to fall into violence and heinous sin. Their march accomplished, though with an utter lack of judgment and forethought, and with the loss of thousands on the way, Jerusalem is reached: it is beautiful when Jerusalem comes in view to see them all doing penance in contrition of heart, falling on their faces and reverently adoring. But this is only a moment which follows upon months of frenzy, foolishness and grossness, which everyone displayed itself on the march. Animated by the loftiest bravery, they go on to storm and conquer the sacred citadel, and then they bathe themselves in blood, revel in endless cruelties, and rage with a brutal ferocity. From this they again pass on to contrition and penance; then they get up from their knees reconciled and sanctified, and once more they give themselves up to all the littleness of miserable passions, of selfishness and envy, of avarice and cupidity: their energies are directed to the satisfaction of their lusts, and they bring to naught the fair possession that their bravery had won. This comes to pass because the principle is only present in them in its implicitude as an abstract principle, and the actuality of man is not as yet spiritually formed and fashioned.
>
> *(Hegel 1995: 53)*

Eschewing the singular story of modernity, Eisenstadt offers an ecumenical narrative based on the idea of 'multiple modernities'. On the face of it, this idea repudiates the hubristic account of Western modernity. On closer inspection, however, the idea of 'multiple modernities' cannot escape the historicist burden, making the Western story the original masterpiece with 'other' civilizational complexes providing rough translations. The generic elements of modernity not only approximate Western experience but also take those elements as norm.

On the positive ledger, postorientalist interventions unveil exoticism in orientalist frames, but also undo the spell of demonization. Interrogating the mundane aspects of the ICZs, not merely the exoticized world of difference, provisions the possibility to move beyond culturalist accounts. Furthermore, postorientalist recognition of contingency and complexity in Islamic otherness functions as a form of exorcism. On this move, evil does not reside elsewhere, but is transported from a domestic source. Finally, the postorientalist emphasis on translocal connectivities disrupts orientalist fictions of self-enclosure and hermetically sealed borders. The ICZs no longer remain the home of incommensurable difference.

A major effect of postorientalist thinking on apprehending the ICZs is the intuition that *identities are relational*, a product of cross-contamination, mutual borrowing, mimicry and fusion. This intuition is nicely captured by Ismail:

> the identity constructed is relational: it shapes and is shaped by other social dimensions such as gender, class and lifestyles. Muslims, as actors, occupy different positions in their social settings and in relation to the processes of globalization. They do not engage, in a uniform manner, in the construction of Muslim selves. Nor do they reproduce a monolithic Muslim identity. Rather, their engagement in identity construction informs us of the power struggles that are embedded in material local conditions and global processes, and that make use of a multiplicity of registers and frames of reference.
>
> *(Ismail 2004: 630–631)*

The promise of postorientalism, however, has been largely ephemeral. In the face of dramatic events and a polarizing climate globally, there has been a consolidation of the natural attitude towards Islam. Hegemonic epistemic communities, despite dissent from many informed quarters, have elected to reproduce orientalist tropes about a presumably unified transnational Islam. This only goes to show the recursive character of knowledge production. Provoked by power, binaries can return. Strategies to domesticate otherness, once repudiated in postorientalist accounts, tend to rely on established classifications. No longer imbued with fluidity and flux, the ICZs re-emerge as islands of rigidity, closure and violence. On an alternative reading, however, orientalism never completely left the stage, nor did its hegemonic presence in the corridors of power come under any serious threat. Hence, a refurbished orientalism takes Islamic exceptionalism (see Chapter 1) as a natural state. The 'new-barbarian' variant (Al-Azmeh 2001) in which violence is the durable feature of Muslim society (Pope Benedict XVI 2006) circulated as common sense. If Western exceptionalism gave occidentalism its permanency, Islamic exceptionalism returns as the *raison d'être* of orientalism. Despite the push of globalizing modernity, the pull of religion keeps the ICZs trapped in inertia, irrationality and ignorance. As both religion and culture, Islam resists change. This metanarrative stresses the grip of oriental despotism (Lewis 2002). The ICZs have not only bypassed reformation but also have regressed. Once the envy of Europe, the ICZs have succumbed to cultural lethargy drawn from their faith. Bernard Lewis offers an unapologetic reworking of the orientalist theme of laggardness:

If the people of the Middle East continue on their present path, the suicide bombers may become a metaphor for the whole region, and there will be no escape from a downward spiral of hate and spite, rage and self-pity, poverty and oppression, culminating sooner or later in yet another alien domination; perhaps from a new Europe reverting to old ways, perhaps from a resurgent Russia, perhaps from some new, expanding superpower in the East. If they can abandon grievance and victimhood, settle their differences, and join their talents, energies, and resources in a common creative endeavor, then they can once again make the Middle East, in modern times as it was in antiquity and in the Middle Ages, a major center of civilization. For the time being, the choice is their own.

(Lewis 2002: 159)

Lewis does not sufficiently locate the sources of Islamic civilizational decline in the collapse of the medieval superstructure of learning. Nor do he and his scholarly fellow travellers address the displacement of knowledge in favour of the rise of shallower modes of thought drawn from superficial readings of Western modernity. Above all, Lewis and others of his scholarly bent fail to recognize the reasons for the 'shallow' responses under conditions not of Islam's own choosing. Neither colonialism nor imperialism enters the analysis. Hence, the 'what went wrong' (Lewis 2002) thesis elects to silence any appreciation of unequal power relations under colonial dispensation or the subalternity of the ICZs in relation to hegemony. Instead, orientalism offers the explanatory solution. As Al-Azmeh (2001: 89) states, '[w]e have seen that the primitive, the outsider, the laggard and a host of other antitheses of failures of civilization are bound together, as a generic group of cultural categories, with similar conditions of emergence in the civilized imaginary'.

Orientalism collapses heterogeneous spatial and cognitive worlds of the Islamic civilization. Selective examples of 'inertia' serve the entire topographical field, reinforcing the idea of Islamic mono-culturalism. Hence, a timeless essence of Islam, unshaken by history or politics, gives (neo-)orientalist accounts licence to speak of a singular zone of otherness. Once constructed, this zone follows a predicable logic. The failure to temporalize the Islamic civilization or to recognize agonistic tendencies within its diverse and changing worlds is unsurprising. Orientalism supplies the enabling and consolidated frame in the service of power. The process of conjoining orientalist knowledge structures with structures of institutional and political power seems effortless.

The failure of postorientalism, especially in its post-colonial iterations, is also linked to the former's latent commitment to a lure of authenticity drawn from celebratory accounts of indigeneity or nativism (Boehmer 1998). Seeking an empathetic engagement with otherness, this lure acquires the character of anti-essentialist essentialism. Some of the 'unspoken conventions and givens of post-colonialism', for instance, rest on 'the binaries that subsist beneath the challenge to Western dominance' (Boehmer 1998: 20). Despite its commitment to hetero-geneity, postorientalist interventions have been unable to avoid the use of binaries (self/other, metropolis/colony, West/non-West, centre/periphery) in their attempts to overcome essentialism. The fractured worlds of Islam, hence, have been defined principally by religion. The impulse of cultural empathy within postorientalism has largely taken the ICZs as 'distant cultures, exploited but with rich intact heritages waiting to be recovered' (Spivak 1988: 211–212).

Finally, postorientalist reinterpretations of ICZs also suffer from the tendency of an authentic/inauthentic dualism. This dualism is based on the assumption that an 'authentic' Islam can be recovered once liberated from Western modernity. Modernist Islamic hermeneutics in the fields of Quranic studies falls into this category. Attempts to 'reconcile' faith and modernity (Rahman 1982), or Islamic feminism (Afsaruddin 1999) seeking to recover gender-neutral readings of the word or tradition, for example, are premised on the idea of authenticity. Change, crosscontamination and transformation pose unorthodox challenges to Islamic social and life-worlds. The lure of authenticity may offer solace in the cultural economy of identity politics. However, it is an unreliable guide to shape the political terrain marked by subalternity.

Against critiques of orientalism and the constrictions of postorientalism, a more compelling avenue to de-essentialize the Islamic civilization is to recognize agonistic currents (Ben Jelloun 2002) within its heterodox real, imaginary and symbolic worlds. For instance, a deconstructive treatment of the Islamic civilization can afford sensitivity to differentiations and distinctions of locale, class, gender and ethnicity. Al-Azmeh suggests this pathway:

> the first step to be taken is critically to decompose the notion of Islam, and to look instead at the conditions of its recent emergence: social forces, historical mutations and developments, political conflicts, intellectual and ideological realities, devotional and theological styles, in addition to local ethnographic detail – it being clearly understood that ethnographic detail is to be regarded for what it is, and not simply as an instance or merely a concrete figure of a pervasive Islamism of life. Without this decomposition, the totalizing category of Islam will continue performing its phantasmatic role of calling things into being simply by naming them.
>
> *(Al-Azmeh 2003: 27)*

Al-Azmeh's counsel resonates with the preceding discussion, stressing the fractured character of Islam, which avoids the tradition–modernity split in ICZs. Religious attachment alone cannot serve as the cultural cipher of Muslim societies. Attachment takes on graded levels of intensity. The crucial point is to recognize the *political* context in which the image of a solidified Muslim identity materializes, in both self-representation of 'believers' (Euben 1999), but more significantly in relational processes involving Muslim selves and others. Self-representations do not spring from cultural essences, but emerge in/through political struggles over what it means to be a 'Muslim'. Often, the imposition of an image of a naturalized singular identity from the outside helps intensify religious commitment. The inside/outside nexus is central to the formation and consolidation of identities. Hence, the analysis returns to relational processes. Civilizational identities do not emerge in neutral spaces of culture, but within the conflictual terrain of politics.

On a related theme, intercivilizational encounters carry the twin possibility of simultaneously exposing the porous character of civilizations and solidifying identities. Attempting to overcome essentialism, hegemonic accounts of intercivilizational encounters (Huntington 1996) fail to resolve this basic paradox because they rest on essentialist understandings of civilizations. Alternatively, a recognition of *internal* political contestation within civilizations complicates 'encounters' and 'dialogues'. While the idiom and rules of contest are based on recognizable cultural codes, the assumption of agonistic politics challenges the fiction of harmony or coherence. This alternative reading obviates claims of civilizational essentialism. The impossibility of civilizational uniformity and the *political* nature of civilizational dynamics become intelligible on this view. Both Western and Islamic civilizations, hence, are products of international relations as much as international relations can ill afford civilizational encounters that merely serve as prehistory.

Conclusion

In globalizing times, fractures within the worlds of Islamic civilization have deepened and produced new forms of solidarities. The appearance of new ways of articulating religious identities (Gellner 1981; Robinson 2002), undermining established mores, confronts the usual orientalist narrative of cultural stagnation (Lewis 2002). However, the transformed representational field makes it painfully difficult to 'think past terror' (Buck-Morss 2003) with reference to Muslims or Islam. The naturalization of a consolidated image of Islam in the aftermath of recent dramatic global events, with strong historical antecedents (Daniel 1960), also abets in consolidating the West's own civilizational identity. Rather than going 'beyond orientalism' (Coronil 1996; Dallmayr 1996; Gran 1996), the 'new barbarians' frame (Tuastad 2003) better captures the West's ontological insecurity. Thinning cultural processes apparently yield to 'thicker' forms of identities. Yet, the identities and the processes that shape them remain in flux. Translocal relationality heightens tensions and agonistic pressures within assumed civilizational complexes. The constitutive politics of civilizational identity underscores the difficulty of securing borders, both real and imaginary. Neo-orientalist (re)inscription of 'Muslim rage' (Lewis 1990) as a singular marker of the Islamic civilization only regenerates potent malevolent effects globally. With wide institutional and representational support systems, the natural attitude toward 'repellent otherness' expressed in civilizational analysis (Huntington 1993, 1996; Lewis 1990, 2002) is not merely a minority view. Rather, it structures politics and policy.

On a different reading, the notion of contested civilizational identities, not a clash of essences, offers alternatives to self-serving claims of repellent otherness. The awkward language of the 'new crusades' or Just War (Elshtain 2003) captures the hegemonic stance towards the Islamic civilization. Authorization of established representations now provide self-reproducing rationales for an unending cycle of violence without spatial or temporal limits. The processes that mobilize symbolic resources to produce a uniform and repellent image of the Islamic civilization are largely of a *political* nature. The need to examine agonistic streams within the ICZs and to abandon the lure of Islamic civilizational authenticity are, therefore, not merely rhetorical exercises. Whilst the idea of 'multiple modernities' offers a corrective to modern historicist trajectories in which Western singularity reigns supreme, de-essentializing 'intercivilizational dialogue' offers more sturdy alternatives to place civilizational analysis on a more self-reflexive and critical footing.

Reflexive civilizational discourse unveils the epistemic blindness generated in hegemonic accounts – ideological interpretations that take culture as the defining feature of civilization. It challenges the notion that civilizations arise in the presumably neutral spaces of culture, *not* politics. A major implication here is the possibility of recognizing incommensurable cultural difference *itself* as a product of struggles to produce boundaries. Relational analysis allows an understanding of how distinctions between friend and enemy (Schmitt [1932] 1976) and strategies to produce hegemony as sources of civilizational difference work. Once politics contests the monadic nature of civilizations, the essentialist logic of civilizational analysis is also exposed.

In conclusion, the proposal for a 'dialogue among civilizations' also offers new pathways to move the analysis in non-hegemonic directions based on a repudiation of 'modular' notions of civilizations. These pathways are less opaque in Khatami's formulation:

> There are two ways to realize dialogue among civilizations. First, actual instances of the interaction and interpenetration of cultures and civilizations with each other, resulting from a variety of factors, present one mode in which this dialogue takes place. This mode of interaction is clearly involuntary and optional and occurs in an unpremeditated fashion, driven primarily by vagaries of social events, geographical situation and historical contingency. Second, alternatively, dialogue among civilizations would also mean a deliberate dialogue among representative members of various civilizations such as scholars, artists and philosophers from disparate civilizational domains. In the latter sense, dialogue entails a deliberate act based on premeditated indulgence and does not rise and fall at the mercy of historical and geographical contingency.
>
> *(Khatami 2000)*

Khatami's appeal to dialogue repudiates the political fiction of sealed borders, each (re)producing self-contained civilizational entities. Implicitly endorsing the notion of 'intertwined histories' (Said 1993), it offers an alternative to the hegemonic Western gaze. Rejecting the logic of a 'clash of civilizations', Khatami allows a pathway to overcome the West/Islam universe. However, the efficacy of his proposal cannot escape the brute force of politics, both within and without the ICZs.

10

IBN KHALDUN AND WORLD ORDER

> The world of the things that come into being as the result of action, materializes through thinking.
>
> *(Ibn Khaldun 1958, II: 413)*

The promise and challenge of globalization, with radical shifts in global economic activity, rearticulations in political space and the emergence of new forms of cultural identity, portend both opportunities and perils for international relations (IR) theory. Although existential dislocations may yield theoretical innovation, established patterns of thought – or what can be termed here the dominant orthodoxies of neo-realism and liberal institutionalism in IR theorizing – continue to discipline the imagination of those with power and privilege.

Against this dialectic of transformation in the world order and dominant thinking in IR lies the promise of an alternative approach. To realize this promise, it is important to identify fresh avenues for both innovation and emancipation. Appreciation of various civilizational complexes and their notions of world order in *their* present manifestation and reality is needed to fully understand and to reflect upon real historical change. Such complexes should be understood, not as entities outside the driving forces of historical transformation, or assigned the disparaging status of 'pre-history', but as a part of the movement of history. Also, to appreciate fully, for example, the complexities and contradictions of Islamic aspects of civilization may help free our imagination from the cultural fetters associated with prevailing orthodoxies. This would then enable us to move towards a universal conversation on international relations.

This chapter focuses on the writing and life of Ibn Khaldun as a modest step towards broadening IR to account more fully for those alternative conceptions that actually constitute the emerging world order. Ibn Khaldun's thought is apposite today inasmuch as it enables a reconstruction of our own intellectual and historical past. His philosophy of history, ideas on politics and society, and thoughts on culture and civilization provide signposts to understanding both the problems of constituting an alternative world order, and more specifically, the dilemmas of social transformation in the Islamic sphere of a globalizing world order.

Ibn Khaldun confronted a shifting ontological terrain similar to our own when his 14th-century world was being overturned. In our own times, a globalizing market-based order appears to unleash new forces with far-reaching implications for imagining and building collective or individual life (Gill 1995). The consolidation of 'new enclosures' also poses challenges that propel the need to engage other civilizational horizons. Resistance to such forces, as conceived by Ibn Khaldun, is recognizable less as an embodiment of tradition, irrationality or particularism, and more a rejection of the market's *social* form and the politics of exclusion. More generally, Ibn Khaldun's ideas reclaim the humanistic tradition in International Studies, a tradition salvaged from a Europeanized discourse of the Enlightenment. Ibn Khaldun thus reinforces non-positivist emphases on holistic thinking arising from an awareness of historical embeddedness.

History and the philosophy of history

Writing in a period that saw the basic structure of medieval Islamic civilization unravel, Ibn Khaldun experienced first-hand the shifting fortunes of Muslim political authority and material conditions. Yet, Ibn Khaldun's significance is not solely *as an Islamic thinker*, whose vision is bounded by the relativity of his circumstances, but a thinker *from* the Islamic world whose thought embodies the highest expression of human civilization.

Wali ad-Din 'Abd-ar-Rahman Ibn Khaldun was born in 1332 in Tunis, when North African civilization was in decline and the *reconquista* reduced Muslim Spain in size and influence. His eminent family background, combined with renown as a scholar-politician, gave Ibn Khaldun relative facility in negotiating power, wealth and status in various North African and Andalusian courts. However, realizing the futility of politics in effecting renewal, he sought – especially in his Universal History (*Kitab al-ibar*), and its Prolegomena (*The Muqaddima*) – an understanding of the meaning of history.

An astute observer of an age of Islamic-Arab decline, Ibn Khaldun is concerned with knowing the *actual conditions* in the life of a (political) community. Ibn Khaldun's reflections on world history emanate from the ontological spirit of his times. Yet, his general conception of social organization and development renders him a pioneer among the philosophers of history. Ibn Khaldun's 'science of culture' (*'ilm al-umran*) offers a synthesis of *falsafa* and the divine law as well as an attempt to provide general principles to understand particular circumstances, the actual unfolding of 'information about human social organisation' (Ibn Khaldun 1958: 71). Imbued in the Islamic philosophical tradition, Ibn Khaldun's primary object of study is to grasp the real meaning behind historical events.

By culture Ibn Khaldun meant the 'totality of conventionalized social habits, institutions, and arts' (Mahdi 1957: 289). The 'science of culture' included a study of all the religious and rational sciences, whose main object was to understand history. Ibn Khaldun was particularly interested in the effect of the environment on society and social organization and the relation between productive forces and social forms. Therefore, *'umran* covered a very wide range, from geography and demographics or the *oikoumene* (the populated world) to social relations. In this sense, *'umran* covered the totality of human phenomena. For analytical purposes, Ibn Khaldun distinguished between *'umran badawi* (primitive culture) and *'umran hadari* (civilization) (Mahdi 1957).

Ibn Khaldun is above all a theoretical synthesizer whose ideas violate established boundaries of modern social science. Practitioners in today's rival disciplines may claim Ibn Khaldun as one of their own – a sociologist, historian, philosopher, anthropologist or political theorist – but he escapes these disciplinary walls. His 'science of culture' deals with the totality of actual human existence. He is ultimately a theorist of *necessity*, where necessity is both a natural compulsion and natural condition. Ibn Khaldun paints a picture of a world with real constraints and possibilities, not a utopian or imaginary social order. An inner necessity, not tied to any idealized telos, pulls human society in specific directions.

Following the distinction in Islamic mysticism between things that are visible (exoteric) and those that are unseen (esoteric), Ibn Khaldun's reflections on history challenge knowledge claims that remain mired in recording appearances. Beneath external (*zahir*) events history, there is an internal (*batin*) logic. Multiplicity follows unity, an important Islamic belief (Leaman 1985). Whereas the method of collating historical information may take external data as a starting point in analysis (a favourite staple of contemporary positivist methodology), real knowledge flows from the rational structure that orders data. The *zahir* and *batin* aspects of history are intertwined: information yields the raw material to ascertain the causes; a knowledge of causes makes data intelligible. Philosophy and history, while based on different principles, are therefore unified in Ibn Khaldun's 'new science of culture'.

Combining philosophical concerns with theology, Islamic theorists had long recognized both divine revelation and natural reason as two modalities of knowledge. Contra dialectical theology in which tradition supersedes philosophy, Ibn Khaldun takes reason as the basis for approaching both theoretical and practical sciences. In his time, Islamic philosophy was preoccupied with the task of reconciling reason with religion. Prophecy and polity pulled the Muslim community in opposing directions. Identifying a rational element in both, Ibn Khaldun's work falls squarely within this Islamic philosophic tradition. Rejecting neo-Platonism, with its proclivity towards theoretical reasoning divorced from real history, Ibn Khaldun tackles real history, but he chooses 'not only to write history but also to write about history' (Mahdi 1957: 113). This section draws from several interpretations of Ibn Khaldun's thought, notably Mahdi (1957), Lacoste (1984) and Schmidt (1967).

For Ibn Khaldun, a universal pattern is discernible in social evolution. Acknowledging unity in human diversity, Ibn Khaldun sees history as a universal science which tries to grasp the essence of human organization. The 'science of culture' follows the logic of deductive reasoning to establish general principles before addressing specific instances, but experience also furnishes the basis for reworking categories. However, there is no definite telos or grand design in history leading up towards perfection. Ibn Khaldun also breaks with the annalistic method and would reject Vico's (1970) notion of a repetitive cycle of an ideal history to which human history must necessarily correspond. Essentially a theorist of transformation, Ibn Khaldun attempts to explain the cyclical pattern of history. Ultimately, the rise and fall of civilizations is not an iron law of history, but a principle that affirms the *changeability* of societal phenomena within a bounded structure. The necessary causes of change are distinguished from the contingent, the general from the particular. Only a longer view of historical evolution reveals a recognizable pattern. The seeds of development and destruction lie within the same social order.

By sensitizing readers to the susceptibility of *all* civilizations to enervation (attendant on the depletion of creative and consolidating capacities), Ibn Khaldun draws attention to an *historical* consciousness. To the extent that civilizations are historical (and thereby human) constructions, he offers none of the promise of transcendental orders.

Ibn Khaldun situates his science within Islamic metaphysics, which stresses the transitory character of human existence. Islamic cosmology places men and women in an intermediate position – God on one side, nature (and the animal world) on the other (Khalidi 1985). In developing this idea, Ibn Khaldun proposes a symbiotic relationship between the various parts of a human being (body and soul) and the elements of the universe, establishing an organic link between humans and the environment. Islamic epistemology, in Ibn Khaldun's terms (following Aristotle), distinguished the theoretical, practical and productive sciences, each with a distinct object. Ibn Khaldun accepts this distinction, but seeks to understand real history as an autonomous object of study. His break lies in treating history not as a chronicle of events, but as a science geared towards understanding the different forms of culture. Taking the distinction among the essential, the accidental and the implausible causes, Ibn Khaldun's project is to penetrate the inner workings of culture. Throughout, he underscores the need for *historical*, not formal understanding. Implicit here is a critique of pure exegetical reasoning that fails to address the real conditions of humanity, and of formal dialectics in favour of historical dialectics. In Ibn Khaldun, both genetic and analytical methods are blended. The former yields an understanding of culture through its various phases of development; the latter helps comprehend the particular aspects of culture.

Politics and society

Ibn Khaldun posits the rationality of historical processes. Extending Islamic metaphysics, he sees reason as the distinguishing mark of human beings. Human intentionality – the capacity for purposeful activity – lies at the root of any social order and its cultural manifestations. Intentionality covers human capacity to order acts in both social relations and in relations with nature. The basis of intentionality, however, is not self-interest and a prefabricated human nature, but action. Unlike social contractarians, Ibn Khaldun rejects the idea of a state of nature. Cooperation *in* society is the human condition. Material existence is the common problem facing different human collectivities. Anarchy may follow given competition and social strife, resulting in new forms of social control, but it is not (as in neo-realism) the defining metaphor of society. Indeed, Ibn Khaldun has a complex, multifaceted conception of human nature, which combines animal and human attributes. Proposing a hierarchy of desires, linked to human capacity, habit and learning, Ibn Khaldun sees perfectibility and its realization as intrinsic to the human condition.

A central concern for Ibn Khaldun is the tripartite relationship between the rise of civilization, economic prosperity and social disintegration. For him, human society is the collective product of three basic elements: reason, social reproduction *and* social cohesion. Both nature and nurture must coalesce to ensure the existence and development of society.

Anticipating Adam Smith, Ibn Khaldun links the division of labour to wealth creation: in the shape of a division of labour, human cooperation satisfies greater needs. What begins as an initial step towards survival advances social wealth. Cooperation and the need to keep society cohesive leads to the rise of the state. Hence, the state is the natural outcome of cooperation, not anarchy. Society must take a state form to subsist. Society and state are, therefore, natural, not in a primordial sense alone, but in a rational sense of having a primary cause. Wealth creation and cultural identity, in turn, interact at multiple levels.

The focal point of Ibn Khaldun's analysis is the state (*dawla*), which is quintessentially the form civilized culture must take. The rise and decline of states, his primary concern, is neither the consequence of great personages in history nor dependent upon individual human action. All states experience five phases in their evolutionary path: establishment, consolidation, prosperity, complacency and decline. A similar, though not the same, trajectory is followed by the city, economic life, and the relation between sedentary and primitive forms of culture.

Unlike his Greek predecessors, Ibn Khaldun does not seek an ideal state (*madina fadīla*), but an analysis of *historical* states distinguished by the ends regimes pursue. Broadly conceived, forms of governance are tied to the animating spirit of the regimes. Hence, regimes of law are characterized by an inner justification sanctioned by divine law. By contrast, rational regimes pursue either the public good or the good of the ruler. Actual states are gradations of different hues, combining elements from these modular forms. Hence, Ibn Khaldun's criterion for classifying states emanates from an internal principle, not imposed from an *a priori* typological scheme as in discourses on non-Western democracies.

Culture and civilization

In a hierarchically arranged order of principles, Ibn Khaldun places human beings in a twofold relation to nature and the spiritual world. Within this scheme, he sees culture as a product of human existence and endeavour; he seeks to lay out the foundations of the rise of primitive culture and its transition to civilized culture, the development of culture through different modalities (economic activity, for instance) and its formal aspect – the state. In turn, culture develops in distinct phases, each phase characterized by a distinct ethos. Culture is the outcome of material necessity, desire and reason. To the extent that culture embodies reason, it can be rationally apprehended. Whether in institutions or the arts, individual or collective habits, or economic life, culture is ultimately a reflection of the application of human capacity to think.

Ibn Khaldun repudiates the notion of culture as a primordial substance. Culture, for him, is never static. Distinctive in the manner in which he construes the evolution of culture in different historical contexts, Ibn Khaldun would not share the orientalist predilection to view culture in monadic terms. In terms of quality, quantity and space, mutation is the natural state of culture. Hence, the forms of *'asabiyya* (social solidarity that underpins each political order) change when religion reinforces mechanical solidarities, as does culture in primitive or civilized contexts, or the character of material production. The concept of *'asabiyya*, like most other concepts in Ibn Khaldun's philosophy of history, is a highly contested term. Two broad lines of interpretation are recognizable in the literature. In the first sense, *'asabiyya* refers to social solidarity of a group. Durkheim's concept of *mechanical solidarity* comes closest to this sense (Gellner 1981). Other scholars treat *'asabiyya* as a more flexible concept which refers to the animating spirit of any social or political order – for example, Machiavelli's notion of *virtù*. In this chapter, *'asabiyya* is understood as a dialectical term which develops in the logical sequence from generality to particularity. *Hence*, depending upon the specific context, *'asabiyya* evolves: different elements combine to constitute the spirit or solidarity that undergirds a community, state or civilization. Islamic intersubjectivity affords only one important synthesis of materialist and spiritual components of (human) social association. Demographic change, the rise and decline of urban culture, also heralds transformations. The rearticulation of territorial boundaries, in turn, alters the ethos of human society.

In this elaborate theoretical structure, *'asabiyya* and its formal organization in the state are the motor-force of historical change. As forms of social solidarity change, so does culture. Ibn Khaldun sees a dialectical link between *'asabiyya* and human capacity: without *'asabiyya*, the possibility for a culture to last for a very long time is negligible. All civilizations must experience growth, limits and decline; civilizations obey laws of change; so do elements that compose them. Yet, aware of their dynamic nature, Ibn Khaldun accords relative autonomy to these elements. In the concept of *'asabiyya* lies the potential for tracing the genealogy of civilizations but also (in a contemporary sense), the source of inner weakness in Muslim society as it negotiates a market-based order in the opening decades of the 21st century.

Ibn Khaldun and world order

What guidance can the ideas of a 14th-century thinker provide for rethinking an emerging world order in the 21st century? Ibn Khaldun is a bridge between the past and the present, but in more poignant terms, a link between a more inclusive historical consciousness and a hegemonic (and therefore, exclusivist) stance in Western IR.

To begin with, Ibn Khaldun represents an embedded consciousness of the Islamic world. Recognizing alternative intersubjectivities means to acknowledge the *internality* of social development in other contexts, processes integral to the realization of universal history. From this vantage point, Ibn Khaldun affords the opportunity to recover Islam's internal dialectic, both as it predates European hegemony and as it was radically reconstituted with the rise of the West. In examining the particularity of distinct civilizations within the common framework of universal history, Ibn Khaldun provides insight into the Islamic world, understood in the context of world history. In this sense, Ibn Khaldun allows an appreciation of the deeper reasons for the ferment in the Islamic cultural zones (ICZs). At the same time, Ibn Khaldun is a philosopher of world history, a universal thinker, one whose thought engages a much wider object: human society in the aggregate. He provides a *synthesis* of human civilization at a particular moment in time.

Next, Ibn Khaldun's 'pre-scientific' thought anticipates the post-positivist humanist current of historicism. Social orders are neither eternal nor natural, but historical. In Ibn Khaldun's worldview, material forces, states and civilizations are subject to dialectical change. Therefore, the present world order is ultimately a congealed form of social relations on a global scale, imbued with human inten-tionality. In comparison, positivism often creates the fiction of permanence or order. One implication of stasis – the world of neo-realists – pertains to under-standings of cultural encounters: a temporal separation is maintained between epochs organized under alternative civilizational principles. The past survives, but as under-theorized history, with neither movement nor consequence. Hence, Columbus's voyage, the rise of Western capitalism, or Westphalia become familiar signposts to modernity, lacking in conceptual underpinnings for what drives these momentous occurrences. Another implication is to mistake alternatives to an existing order as chaos or anarchy, or to fail to pose the possibilities for transformation.

Additionally, on Ibn Khaldun's reading, an acceptance of other civilizational principles, especially those that combine reason and faith, may temper economic development with spiritual concerns. Ibn Khaldun saw no contradiction between his 'science of culture' and the divine scheme. In the context of profound ecological challenges, largely the consequence of a basic disregard for nature in extant 'models' of development, a moderated notion of technological progress may be entirely legitimate.

Finally, from Ibn Khaldun's perspective, social solidarity or *'asabiyya* is not determined *a priori*, but is historically embedded. Ibn Khaldun's realism (not mainstream realism in Western IR) makes ethics contingent upon social forces and their resolution in particular forms of social and political community. Hence, he would dismiss claims on ethics in discussions of a global civil society, cosmopoli-tanism or global democracy as utopias, failing to recognize the importance of historical causes. For Ibn Khaldun, all *a priori* claims about idealized and preferred worlds disown the societal context of their inception. The basis of a universal civilization lies in *the world as it is*, but also a world that is made with human intentionality that congeals divine purpose. On Ibn Khaldun's reading, an understanding of history is a basic precondition for speculation about better worlds, and on that basis, one may add, an awareness of the consciousness that undergirds social orders.

The Islamic world

The significance of Ibn Khaldun's thoughts on universal history becomes pronounced against the background of rethinking the relation of the Islamic world to the emerging world order. Following Ibn Khaldun, the reassertion of Islamic consciousness is placed within a framework that avoids either essentialism or relativism, the former treating Islam in fixed, unchanging terms, and the latter viewing Islam as particularistic and standing outside universal history. Ibn Khaldun would recognize that the Islamic world in the opening decades of the 21st century, as in his times, is enmeshed in a crisis. A source of the crisis in the 19th and 20th centuries was the assault of the West on Islamic society, producing new tensions and conflicts. However, Ibn Khaldun would also acknowledge that the roots of this crisis are primarily *internal* to Islamic civilization, only reinforced by outside forces. Western impact on Muslim society appears in the form of economic subordination, but significantly, it is provoking a shift in the terms of political and social discourse. Externally driven norms of conduct have captured the imagination of Muslim dominant classes, while the vast majority seek meaning and succour in uncolonized sensibilities. Replacing an internal dialectic with a potential for resolution, rival notions of politics, ethics or civility abound. In their encounter with the West, Muslims began to see themselves not in their own civilizational terms, with an appreciation of *their own history*, but as a subordinate, subaltern community of believers. Even the forms of Islamic reform and renewal became mere reactions to the West, not responses to internally driven historical forces.

The crisis of Muslim society encompasses a number of factors, including the loss of *'asabiyya*; economic degeneration; political corruptions, schisms and state decline; and the enervation of a culture that is unable to renew itself. There are no guarantees that the impetus of change would correspond to piety, but to a combination of *'asabiyya* and divine law. However, on Ibn Khaldun's reading, there are no remedies; history can only be understood, not escaped. Ibn Khaldun's Islamic civilization in the Maghreb could not transcend its historical constraints. The last great Almohad Empire in the Maghreb had ceased to exist even before Ibn Khaldun's birth in 1332. Until his death in 1406, he personally observed the passing of an era in which he had played an important role as a prime minister, adviser, and political counsel to several monarchs. His deep historical consciousness led him to see political reform in the Islamic community constrained by the materiality of the times. Ibn Khaldun writes in *The Muqaddima:* 'When there is a general change in conditions, it is as though the whole world has been altered ... Therefore there is need at this time that someone should systematically set down the situation of the world among all regions and races' (Ibn Khaldun 1958: I:65). Neither good intentions nor shifting political fortunes could surmount these conditions.

In the time separating Ibn Khaldun's world from our own, the Muslims have not only lost their former glory, but the crisis that once inflicted the Arab-Islamic Maghreb is now *globalized* to affect the Islamic civilization as a whole. Once a thriving culture and trading civilization straddling three continents, Islam had lost its momentum due to internal fragmentation. Similarly, despite individual achievements, the Islamic civilization today also seems unable to establish a material basis for realizing an alternative vision. The quest for a perfect Islamic state appears remote.

Following Ibn Khaldun into the present implies a repudiation of an *external* reading of Islamic history in favour of an investigation of the *internal* debate and conjuncture within Islam: between various strands of philosophy and revealed law; between Islamic *shari'ah* and *kanun*; between faith and reason (Fakhry 1970; Corbin 1993). International relations sustains or diminishes the *internally* structured dialectic. Though a commitment to Islam appears non-negotiable, the quotidian practices of Muslim society reveal heterogeneous expression. In this internal debate, reform is neither new to Islam nor singularly propelled by external determinants, notably Westernization. Efforts to reconcile a living faith with the imperatives of reason or philosophy are intrinsic to Islamic history, an essential backdrop to Ibn Khaldun's 'new science of culture'. Closure in the debate within the Islamic community, on the other hand, reflects the perceived threat by some Muslims of an imminent harm to the *Ummah*, to the vital sources of Islamic belief and practice. Reform treats Islam as a dynamic faith, whose true realization is historical, underlining the unfinished nature of history; closure freezes the dialectic. In the name of recapturing the 'golden past', it privileges an uncompromising faith in the texts and implementation of the *shari'ah* in virtually all walks of Muslim social life (Pasha and Samatar 1996).

Beyond Islamic reform or closure, Muslim anxieties are real: how to reverse an historical tide that has pitted Western modernity against their civilization. Generally, in times of acute crisis, Muslims have been willing to trade in their local traditions in favour of more abstract and universal interpretations of the *Qur'an*, *Sunnah* and *Hadith* (Gellner 1981). The presumption that local traditions are usually the product of a compromise in the original teachings of the faith, could only yield closure in debate, but provide a simpler explanation of societal ills. Appreciating the character of heated debates over different modalities of reason and faith *within* the totality of Muslim sensibilities averts external interpretations of Muslim society. This also prevents orientalist constructions of Islamic politics and its apparently unrecognizable patterns.

How can Muslims constitute *'asabiyya* so that it recognizes the challenges and constraints of globalization or the compulsions of international relations? This may be the central question facing the Islamic world in our times. As Ibn Khaldun recognized, religion does not exhaust the compass of social cohesion. In the context of a global order, Muslims cannot expect the *Shari'ah* alone to help over-come centuries of subordination, misrule, neglect and economic marginalization. To realize the law would depend upon rational principles of administering both economy and state. Islamic culture, like any sedentary culture, for Ibn Khaldun, was a complex structure of its productive capacity and urban institutions; forms of state that had arisen throughout Islamic history; *'asabiyya*, which made it possible to coalesce; and the notion of the common good.

Yet, in times of crisis, those who are at the margins of world order may be better situated to propose alternatives. Removed from a closer ideological commitment to that order's survival, their intersubjectivity may capture opposing elements. In addition, as in Ibn Khaldun's times, when 'the material foundations of Islamic hegemony were much weakened', while its 'cultural pre-eminence' remained (Cox 1992: 147), Islamic resurgence today appears more conspicuous in the cul-tural arena than in the materiality of its political economy. This unequal dialectic between accumulation and Islamic culture unveils *new* global dynamics, mis-conceived either as a 'clash of civilizations' (Huntington 1993) or a 'return of Islam' (Lewis 1976).

In the context of global political economy, the Islamic civilization must redis-cover the sources of vitality, not only in faith, but also in new constellations of politics that afford the rise of a new *'asabiyya*. Extrapolating from Ibn Khaldun's basic distinction between nomadic and sedentary groups, with *'asabiyya* being stronger in the former but corrupted by the development of civilization and luxury, a key feature of Islamic societies in our own times appears to be the per-verse relation between wealth and culture. The sources of renewal tend to coalesce around sectors of the population who find themselves marginalized; the affluent seem removed from the wellsprings of Islamic culture, preferring the materialist and often shallow accoutrements of West-centred modernity.

Ibn Khaldun's distinction between theoretical and lived Islam also finds a parallel in extant Islamic states, those with a token commitment to Islam and the larger Muslim society that takes Islam's ethos as its motor. The rupture between those who seek comfort and those with the capacity to establish *'asabiyya* may have grown with the advent of market civilization. The compression of space and time, a crucial element of globalization (Mittelman 1996), adds yet another dimension to the dialectic between the need to preserve and renew the faith and establish a self-sustaining material civilization. In several ICZs, there is lively conversation and contestation on these issues without a definite resolution.

A new synthesis of faith and *'asabiyya* alone, recognizing material constraints and the resources of culture, can yield pathways towards a reconstitution of an unequal world order. Yet, the primary impetus for innovation and transformation must arise from *within* the ICZs with a rethinking of the state, patterns of justice, economic organization and cultural development. However, the burdens placed on those who are least prepared to withstand them, an integral feature of a market order, must be redistributed in the reverse direction. Injustice and decline of a civilization are inextricably related, in that the former creates the conditions of division and dissension, undermining *'asabiyya*. Without addressing the issue of justice within the *Ummah*, calls for redressing history may be irrelevant.

Conclusion

In the face of capitalism's homogenizing, if socially disintegrative, force, the task of harmonizing the demands of accumulation with the yearning for cultural autonomy appears more tenuous. Although riddled with irreconcilable contradictions, often concealed in proclamations of the 'end of history' (Fukuyama 1992) or calls for a new world order, global neoliberalism presents itself as the new heavy artillery in our own era to batter down all cultural walls. Offering little solace to those who resist its path, the thrust towards homogenization leaves room for a shallow vision for mutual cultural recognition. Without a durable social base, the global reach of market civilization is unable to realize its imaginary future, giving the struggles for cultural heterogeneity and autonomy both purpose and salience. On this reading, political assertiveness in the ICZs becomes recognizable as an aspect of globalization itself, rather than simply a reaction to globalization.

Ibn Khaldun's analysis of a declining Islamic civilization yields a closer scrutiny of the historical context and logic of Muslim sensibilities. It also gives the quest for a supra-intersubjectivity a rational and real foundation. By appreciating the internal dialectic of other civilizations, the nominalism of recognizing difference can give way to a genuine acknowledgement of their agency and development. Islam's historical structures have rarely entered the study of world politics, emptied out in the problematic of anarchy that homogenizes space and time, or appended to West-centred global capitalism, *merely* following its drumbeat. Instead, denying the received temporal sequence of history is to recognize its partiality, not particularity.

Many extant readings of Islam often fail to recognize the integrity of Muslim civilization. Ibn Khaldun allows us to understand the wholeness of Islam's internal dialectic, an alternative to partial readings that arbitrarily connect different aspects of phenomena without capturing their embeddedness. The real causes of the Muslim predicament may not be so readily apparent; they require careful theoretical scrutiny, as in Ibn Khaldun's 'science of culture', not solely for immediate practical purposes. The *longue durée* of Islamic history furnishes an understanding of the mutual interaction and development of different, but interconnected, elements.

Recently, culture has appeared as an alternative to *both* 'anarchy' and 'political economy' as the grand metaphor for explaining a post-Cold War world order. In place of an appreciation of intercivilizational dialogue, established on an acknowledgement of the diversity of *internal* principles embodied in *particular* historical-structural contexts, liberal triumphalism (Fukuyama 1992), or an imminent 'clash of civilizations' (Huntington 1993) emerge as successors to the received paradigms – the new organizing principles. In these constructions, however, the stasis of Western hegemony has been recycled. Alternatively, recognition of 'difference' has assumed a ceremonial status in numerous poststructuralist and post-colonial writings – the recognition of particularism as the defining motif of conceptualization. In these formulations, contra Ibn Khaldun, the universal character of human civilizations is overlooked.

Avoiding particularism, critical forms of theoretical innovation are embedded in a recognition of the universal nature of human association *and* its spatio-temporal realization. On Ibn Khaldun's historicist terms, this would involve a repudiation of mere exegetical reasoning and an appreciation of actual historical conditions as a starting point for conceptualization. The main purpose of Ibn Khaldun's 'science of culture' is to furnish an awareness of the real reasons behind events history. However, this seemingly elementary task can also become the source of critical reflection. Every epoch is imbued with a distinctive logic, yet the common problem of human association gives history a universal configuration. Assuming the rationality of historical phenomena, an understanding of the spirit of the times provides the basis for transcending the immediate world of sensory data. Historical consciousness affords reflexivity. Taking this initial premise, Ibn Khaldun's historicist thinking laid the path for subsequent theoretical innovations prominent in Vico, Machiavelli and Gramsci.

Following Aristotle and anticipating future generations of philosopher-historians, Ibn Khaldun locates the meaning of any epoch only in the completion of its historical cycle. Once an historical process has exhausted its possibilities, understandings of its latent structure become plausible. Ordinarily, with 'a general change of conditions', as Ibn Khaldun notes, a world may be 'brought into existence anew'. Reflexivity is often the main harvest of structural transformations.

Ibn Khaldun's 'science of culture' appears to originate necessarily with the decline of Islamic civilization in North Africa. Yet, on a careful reading of Ibn Khaldun, theoretical innovations are not linked to crises in a linear relationship. Indeed, as any mindful study of civilizations would show, social dislocations have even suppressed reflexivity or dislocated embryonic transformation. Great transformations in social and political association or imagination rarely follow the same trajectory. Innovation does not hinge only upon an awareness of the actual conditions of our own world, but is contingent on propitious social forces. The meaning of history lies precisely in rejecting the notion that there are direct pathways from here to there. Thus, Ibn Khaldun's 'science of culture' is not only a product of a crisis of North Africa, but it draws heavily from heterodox intellectual achievements of Islamic civilization *in its totality*. Perhaps the brilliance of Ibn Khaldun lies in his ability to respond simultaneously to a crisis of a specific historical epoch, *and* to synthesize Muslim thought in its advanced permutations.

In our times, a globalizing economy appears to produce a unified material world. An awareness of its basic contradictory impulses offers an *initial* step towards innovation. A recognition of different intersubjectivities and *their* constitutive principles, distributed across space and time, may create the intellectual spaces to identify the diverse cultural expressions of globalization. Paradoxically, globalization also occasions a recognition of the particularistic nature of extant IR theory. In this context, theoretical innovation may require a synthesis of different civilizational perspectives. Specific investigations of multiple modes of thought from a variety of perspectives may help overcome the constrictions of the basic categories of (Western) social thought, reveal the cultural foundations of both 'normative' and 'positive' social science, and challenge the hegemony of normalized epistemologies. Nevertheless, the process of theoretical innovation must be discerned as open-ended: as an integral aspect of the social process itself.

With a dislocation in the nature of the world comes the hope of new imaginings. However, the new need not originate with the present. A rediscovery of the past and the recognition of its repressed consciousness may yield openings to rethink how we envision and remake our world. With such a rediscovery, epochs, artificially sealed off from one another, may be reconnected, and the possibility of transcending the constrictions of the present may arise.

BIBLIOGRAPHY

Abaza, Mona and Georg Stauth (1990) Occidental Reason, Orientalism, Islamic Fundamentalism: A Critique, in *Globalization, Knowledge and Society*, ed. Martin Albrow and Elizabeth King. London: Sage.

Abdel-Malek, Anouar (1963) Orientalism in Crisis. *Diogenes* 11(44): 103–140.

Abootalebi, Ali R. (1995) Democratization in Developing Countries: 1980–1989. *Journal of Developing Areas* 29(4): 507–530.

Abrahamian, Ervand (2003) The US Media, Huntington and September 11. *Third World Quarterly* 24(3): 529–544.

Abu-Lughod, Lila (2002) Do Muslim Women Need Saving? Reflections on Cultural Relativism and its Others. *American Anthropologist* 104(3): 783–790.

Adamson, Walter L. (1980) *Hegemony and Revolution: A Study of Antonio Gramsci's Political and Cultural Theory*. Berkeley, CA: California University Press.

Addi, Lahouari (1992) Islamicist Utopia and Democracy. *Annals of the American Academy of Political and Social Science* 524: 120–130.

Advisory Group on Public Diplomacy for the Arab and Muslim World (2003) *Changing Minds, Winning Peace: A New Strategic Direction for U.S. Public Diplomacy in the Arab & Muslim World*. Submitted to the Committee on Appropriations, US House of Representatives, 1 October. Washington, DC: The Advisory Group on Public Diplomacy.

Afsaruddin, Asma (1999) *Hermeneutics and Honor: Negotiation of Female 'Public Space' in Islamic/ate Societies*. Cambridge, MA: Harvard University Press.

Agamben, Giorgio (1998) *Homo Sacer: Sovereign Power and Bare Life*. Stanford, CA: Stanford University Press.

Agamben, Giorgio (2001) On Security and Terror. *Frankfurter Allgemeine Zeitung*, trans. Soenke Zehle, 20 September.

Agamben, Giorgio (2005) *State of Exception*. Chicago, IL: University of Chicago Press.

Akhavi, Shahrough (2003) Islam and the West in World History. *Third World Quarterly* 24: 545–562.

Al-Azmeh, Aziz (1993) *Islams and Modernities*. London: Verso.

Al-Azmeh, Aziz (1996 [1993]) *Islams and Modernities*. London: Verso.

Al-Azmeh, Aziz (2001) Civilization, Culture and the New Barbarians. *International Sociology* 16(1): 75–93.

Al-Azmeh, Aziz (2003) Postmodern Obscurantism and 'The Muslim Question'. *Journal for the Study of Religions and Ideologies* 5: 21–46.

Alinejad, Mahmoud (2002) Coming to Terms with Modernity: Iranian Intellectuals and the Emerging Public Sphere. *Islam and Christian-Muslim Relations* 13(1): 25–47.

Anderson, Perry (1974a) *Passages from Antiquity to Feudalism.* London: New Left Books.

Anderson, Perry (1974b) *Lineages of the Absolutist State.* London: New Left Books.

Ansari, Humayun (2002) *Muslims in Britain.* London: Minority Rights Group International.

Appadurai, Arjun (1996) *Modernity at Large: Cultural Dimensions of Globalization.* Minneapolis: University of Minneapolis.

Appleby, Scott (2000) *The Ambivalence of the Sacred: Religion, Violence, and Reconciliation.* MD: Rowman and Littlefield.

Arjomand, Said A. (2004) Islam, Political Change and Globalisation. *Thesis Eleven* 76 (February): 9–28.

Arnason, J.P. (2001) Civilizational Patterns and Civilizing Processes. *International Sociology* 16(3): 387–405.

Arrighi, Giovanni (1993) The Three Histories of Historical Materialism, in *Gramsci, Historical Materialism and International Relations*, ed. Stephen Gill. Cambridge: Cambridge University Press, pp. 148–185.

Asad, Talal, ed. (1973) *Anthropology and the Colonial Encounter.* London: Ithaca Press.

Asad, Talal (1993) *Genealogies of Religion: Discipline and Reasons of Power in Christianity and Islam.* Baltimore, MD: Johns Hopkins University Press.

Asad, Talal (2003) *Formations of the Secular: Christianity, Islam, Modernity.* Stanford, CA: Stanford University Press.

Augelli, Enrico and Craig N. Murphy (1988) *America's Quest for Supremacy and the Third World: A Gramscian Analysis.* London: Pinter.

Augelli, Enrico and Craig N. Murphy (1993) Gramsci and International Relations: A General Perspective with Examples from Recent US Policy toward the Third World, in *Gramsci, Historical Materialism and International Relations*, ed. Stephen Gill. Cambridge: Cambridge University Press, pp. 127–147.

Ayoob, Mohammed (2008) *The Many Faces of Political Islam: Religion and Politics in the Muslim World.* Ann Arbor: University of Michigan Press.

Ayubi, Nazih (1991) *Political Islam: Religion and Politics in the Arab World.* London and New York: Routledge.

Badiou, Alain (2003) *St. Paul: The Foundations of Universalism*, trans. Ray Brassier. Stanford, CA: Stanford University Press.

Balibar, Etienne (2002) *Politics and the Other Scene.* London: Verso.

Ball, Karyn (2005) Paranoia in the Age of the World Picture: The Global 'Limits of Enlightenment'. *Cultural Critique* 61 (Fall): 115–147.

Barazangi, Nimat Hafez, M. Raquibuz Zaman and Omar Afzal, eds (1996) *Islamic Identity and the Struggle for Justice.* Gainesville, FL: University of Florida Press.

Barber, Benjamin (1996) *Jihad versus McWorld.* New York: Ballantine Books.

Bassiouni, M. Cherif (2007) Evolving Approaches to Jihad: From Self-defense to Revolutionary and Regime Change Political Violence. *Chicago Journal of International Law* 8: 119–146.

Beck, Ulrich (2000) *What is Globalisation?*, trans. Patrick Camiller. Cambridge: Polity Press.

Beck, Ulrich (2006) *The Cosmopolitan Vision.* Cambridge: Polity.

Bellamy, Richard (1990) Gramsci, Croce and the Italian Tradition. *History of Political Thought* 11(2): 313–337.

Bellamy, Richard and Darrow Schecter (1993) *Gramsci and the Italian State*. Manchester: Manchester University Press.

Benedict XVI, His Holiness the Pope (2006) *Faith, Reason and the University: Memories Reflections. Lecture by Pope Benedict XVI at the University of Regensburg in Germany on 12 September*. www.guardian.co.uk/pope/story/0,,1873277,00.html

Benhabib, Seyla (2002) Unholy Wars. *Constellations: An International Journal of Critical and Democratic Theory* 9: 34–45.

Ben Jelloun, Mohammed (2002) Agonistic Islam. *Jouvert* 6(3): 1–10. https://english.chass.ncsu.edu/jouvert/v613/agon.htm (accessed 21 December 2016).

Berger, Peter L., ed. (1999) *The Desecularization of the World: Resurgent Religion and World Politics*. Washington, DC: Ethics and Public Policy Center.

Beyer, Peter (1992) The Global Environment as a Religious Issue: A Sociological Analysis. *Religion* 2(1): 1–19.

Beyer, Peter (1994) *Religion and Globalization*. London: Sage.

Bhabha, Homi K. (1994) *The Location of Culture*. London and New York: Routledge.

Bhagwati, Jagdish N. (2004) *In Defense of Globalization*. New York: Oxford University Press.

Bhargava, Rajeev, ed. (1998) *Secularism and its Critics*. Oxford: Oxford University Press.

Bhuta, Nehal (2003) A Global State of Exception? The United States and World Order. *Constellations* 10(3): 371–391.

Bieler, Andreas and Adam D. Morton, eds (2001a) *Social Forces in the Making of the New Europe: The Restructuring of European Social Relations in the Global Political Economy*. London: Palgrave.

Bieler, Andreas and Adam D. Morton (2001b) The Gordian Knot of Agency-Structure in International Relations: A Neo-Gramscian Perspective. *European Journal of International Relations* 7(1): 5–35.

Bieler, Andreas and Adam D. Morton (2003) Globalisation, the State and Class Struggle: A 'Critical Economy' Engagement with Open Marxism. *British Journal of Politics and International Relations* 5(4): 467–499.

Bigo, Didier (2002) Security and Immigration: Toward a Critique of the Governmentality of Unease. *Alternatives* 27: 63–92.

Bigo, Didier (2006) Globalized (In)Security: The Field and the Ban-opticon. In *Illiberal Practices of Liberal Regimes: The (In)Security Games*, eds Didier Bigo and Anastassia Tsoukala. Paris: L'Harmattan.

Bilgin, Pinar and Adam David Morton (2004) From 'Rogue' to 'Failed' States? The Fallacy of Short-Termism. *Politics* 24(3): 169–180.

Binder, Leonard (1988) *Islamic Liberalism: A Critique of Development Ideologies*. University of Chicago Press.

Black, Cyril E. (1966) *The Dynamics of Modernization: A Study in Comparative History*. New York: Harper & Row.

Blair, Tony (2005) Speech on the London Bombings Delivered at the Labour Party National Conference. BBC, 9 July. http://news.bbc.co.uk/l/hi/uk/4689363.stm

Blair, Tony (2006) Speech to the World Affairs Council in Los Angeles, 2 August. http://news.bbc.co.uk/1/hi/uk/5236896.stm (accessed 21 December 2016).

Blaney, David L. and Mustapha Kamal Pasha (1993) Civil Society and Democracy in the Third World: Ambiguities and Historical Possibilities. *Studies in Comparative International Development* 18(1): 3–24.

Blaut, J.M. (1993) *The Colonizer's Model of the World: Geographical Diffusionism and Eurocentric History*. New York and London: Guilford Press.

Bleiker, Roland (2001) The Aesthetic Turn in International Political Theory. *Millennium: Journal of International Studies* 30(3): 509–538.

Blond, Philip, ed. (1998) *Post-Secular Philosophy: Between Philosophy and Theology*. London: Routledge.

Boehmer, Elleke (1998) Questions of Neo-orientalism. *Interventions: International Journal of Postcolonial Studies* 1(1): 18–21.

Bonnell, Victoria E. and Lynn Hunt, eds. (1999) *Beyond the Cultural Turn: New Directions in the Study of Society and Culture*. Berkeley: University of California Press.

Bourricaud, François (1985) Modernity, 'Universal Reference' and the Process of Modernization, in *Patterns of Modernity: Volume I: The West*, ed. S.N. Eisenstadt. London: Frances Pinter.

Braudel, Fernand (1994) *A History of Civilizations*. Penguin Press.

Brennan, Timothy (1988–89) Literary Criticism and the Southern Question. *Cultural Critique* 11: 87–114.

Buci-Glucksmann, C. (1980) *Gramsci and the State*, trans. David Fernbach. London: Lawrence & Wishart.

Buck-Morss, Susan (2003) *Thinking Past Terror: Islamism and Critical Theory on the Left*. London: Verso.

Bull, Hedley (1977) *The Anarchical Society: A Study of Order in International Politics*. London: Macmillan.

Burckhardt, Jacob (1955 [1889]) Letter to Friedrich von Preen, in *The Letters of Jacob Burckhardt*, ed. A. Dru. London: Routledge and Kegan Paul.

Buruma, Ian and Avishai Margalit (2004) *Occidentalism: The West in the Eyes of its Enemies*. New York: Penguin Press.

Butko, Thomas J. (2004) Revelation or Revolution: A Gramscian Approach to the Rise of Political Islam. *British Journal of Middle Eastern Studies* 31(1): 41–62.

Butler, Judith (2008) Sexual Politics, Torture, and Secular Time. *The British Journal of Sociology* 59: 1–23.

Butterworth, Charles E. (1992) Political Islam: The Origins. *Annals of the American Academy of Political and Social Science* 524: 26–37.

Buttigieg, Joseph A. (1986a) The Legacy of Antonio Gramsci. *Boundary 2* 14(3): 1–17.

Buttigieg, Joseph A. (1986b) Gramsci's Method. *Boundary 2* 17(2): 60–81.

Buzan, Barry and Richard Little (2001) Why International Relations has Failed as an Intellectual Project and What to do About it. *Millennium: Journal of International Studies* 30(1): 19–39.

Buzan, Barry and Ole Wæver (2005) *Liberalism and Security: The Contradictions of the Liberal Leviathan*. Copenhagen: Copenhagen Peace Research Institute, Working Paper, April 1998. www.cianet.org/wps/bub02

Buzan, Barry, Ole Waever and Jaap de Wilde (1998) *Security: A New Framework*. Lynne Rienner Publishers.

Calhoun, Craig (2010) Rethinking Secularism. *The Hedgehog Review* (Fall).

Calhoun, Craig, Paul Price and Ashley Timmer, eds (2002) *Understanding September 11*, Project coordinated by the Social Science Research Council. New York: New Press.

Camilleri, Joseph (2012) Postsecularist Discourse in an 'Age of Transition'. *Review of International Studies* 38(4): 1019–1039.

Campbell, David (1998) *Writing Security: United States Foreign Policy and the Politics of Identity*. Minneapolis: University of Minnesota Press.

Caputo, John (2001) *On Religion*. London and New York: Routledge.

Caputo, John D. and Gianni Vattimo (2007) *After the Death of God*, ed. Jeffrey W. Robbins, Afterword Gabriel Vahanian. New York: Columbia University Press.

Casanova, José (1994) *Public Religions in the Modern World*. Chicago: University of Chicago Press.

Casanova, José (2001) Civil Society and Religion: Retrospective Reflections on Catholicism and Prospective Reflections on Islam. *Social Research* 68: 1041–1080.

Casanova, José (2006) Secularization Revisited: A Reply to Talal Asad, in *Powers of the Secular Modern: Talal Asad and his Interlocutors*, ed. Charles Hirschkind and David Scott. Palo Alto, CA: Stanford University Press.

Castells, Manuel (1996) *The Rise of the Network Society*. Oxford and Malden, MA: Blackwell.

CBC News (2005) Hate Crimes against U.K. Muslims Soar. CBC News, 3 August. www.cbc.ca/story/world/national/2005/08/03racism050803.html

Chakrabarty, Dipesh (2000) *Provincializing Europe: Postcolonial Thought and Historical Difference*. Princeton, NJ: Princeton University Press.

Chatterjee, Partha (1986) *Nationalist Thought and the Colonial World: A Derivative Discourse*. Tokyo: United Nations University, Zed Press.

Chatterjee, Partha (1988) On Gramsci's 'Fundamental Mistake'. *Economic and Political Weekly* 23(5): PE, 24–26.

Chatterjee, Partha (1998) Beyond the Nation? Or Within? *Social Text* 56: 57–69.

Checkel, Jeffrey (1998) The Constructivist Turn in International Relations Theory. *World Politics* 50(1) (January): 324–348.

Chen, Xiaomei (1992) Occidentalism as Counterdiscourse: 'He Shang' in Post-Mao China. *Critical Inquiry* 18(4): 686–712.

Clague, Christopher, Suzanne Gleason and Stephen Knack (2001) Determinants of Lasting Democracy in Poor Countries: Culture, Development and Institutions. *Annals of the American Academy of Political and Social Science* 573: 16–41.

Clifford, James (1988) *The Predicament of Culture: Twentieth-Century Ethnography, Literature, and Art*. Cambridge, MA: Harvard University Press.

Coker, Christopher (1998) *Twilight of the West*. Boulder, CO: Westview.

Colas, Dominique (1997) *Civil Society and Fanaticism: Conjoined Histories*, trans. Amy Jacobs. Stanford, CA: Stanford University Press.

Commission on Human Security (CHS) (2003) *Human Security Now*. New York: Oxford University Press.

Connerton, Paul, ed. (1976) *Critical Sociology*. Harmondsworth: Penguin.

Connolly, William E. (1995) *The Ethos of Pluralization*. Minneapolis: University of Minnesota Press.

Connolly, William E. (1997) *Why I am Not a Secularist*. Chicago: Chicago University Press.

Connolly, William E. (1998) The New Cult of Civilizational Superiority. *Theory and Event* 2(4): 1–7.

Cooper, R. (2003) *The Breaking of Nations: Order and Chaos in the Twenty-First Century*. New York: Atlantic Monthly Press.

Corbin, Henry (1993) *History of Islamic Philosophy*, trans. Laidain Sherrard. London: Kegan Paul. First edn in French, 1964.

Coronil, Fernando (1996) Beyond Occidentalism: Toward Nonimperial Geohistorical Categories. *Cultural Anthropology* 11: 51–87.

Coward, Martin (2005) The Globalisation of Enclosure: Interrogating the Geopolitics of Empire. *Third World Quarterly* 26(6): 855–871.

Cox, Michael (2004a) Empire by Denial. *Security Dialogue* 35(2): 228–236.

Cox, Robert W. (1981) Social Forces, States and World Orders: Beyond International Relations Theory. *Millennium: Journal of International Studies* 10(2): 126–155.

Cox, Robert W. (1983) Gramsci, Hegemony and International Relations: An Essay in Method. *Millennium: Journal of International Studies* 12(2): 162–175.

Cox, Robert W. (1987) *Production, Power and World Order: Social Forces in the Making of History*. New York: Columbia University Press.

Cox, Robert W. (1992) Towards a Post-Hegemonic Conceptualization of World Order: Reflections on the Relevancy of Ibn Khaldun, in *Governance without Government: Order and Change in World Politics*, ed. J.N. Rosenau and E.-O. Czempiel. Cambridge: Cambridge University Press.

Cox, Robert W. (2000) Thinking about Civilizations. *Review of International Studies* 26: 217–234.

Cox, Robert W. (2004b) Beyond Empire and Terror: Critical Reflections on the Political Economy of World Order. *New Political Economy* 9(3): 307–323.

Cox, Robert W. and Michael G. Schecter (2002) *The Political Economy of a Plural World: Critical Reflections on Power, Morals and Civilisation*. London: Routledge.

Crehan, Kate (2002) *Gramsci, Culture and Anthropology*. London: Pluto Press.

Crone, Patricia (1980) *Slaves on Horses: The Evolution of the Islamic Polity*. New York: Cambridge University Press.

Curtis, S. (1996) The Sovereignty of the Secular and the Power of Religion. *American Literary History* 8(2): 328–340.

Cutler, A. Claire, Virginia Haufler and Tony Porter, eds (1999) *Private Authority and International Affairs*. Albany: State University of New York Press.

Dalacoura, Katerina (2002) Violence, September 11 and the Interpretations of Islam. *International Relations* 16(2): 269–273.

Dallmayr, Fred R. (1996) *Beyond Orientalism: Essays on Cross-Cultural Encounter*. Binghamton, NY: SUNY Press.

Dallmayr, Fred R. (2002) Globalization and Inequality: A Plea for Global Justice. *International Studies Review* 4(2): 137–156.

Daniel, Norman (1960) *Islam and the West: The Making of an Image*. Edinburgh: The University Press.

Davies, Matt (1999) *International Political Economy and Mass Communication in Chile: National Intellectuals and Transnational Hegemony*. London: Macmillan.

Davis, Creston, John Milbank and Slavoj Žižek, eds (2005) *Theology and the Political: The New Debate*. Durham, NC and London: Duke University Press.

Davis, Nancy J. and Robert V. Robinson (2006) The Egalitarian Face of Islamic Orthodoxy: Support for Islamic Law and Economic Justice in Seven Muslim-Majority Nations. *American Sociological Review* 71 (April): 167–190.

Davutoglu, Ahmet (1994) *Alternative Paradigms: The Impact of Islamic and Western Weltanschauungs on Political Theory*. New York and London: University Press of America.

Dean, Mitchell (2006) A Political Mythology of World Order: Carl Schmitt's Nomos. *Theory, Culture & Society* 23(5): 1–22.

De Benoist, A. (2007) Global Terrorism and the State of Permanent Exception: The Significance of Carl Schmitt's Thought Today, in *The International Political Thought of Carl Schmitt: Terror, Liberal War and the Crisis of Global Order*, ed. L. Odysseos and F. Petito. New York and Abingdon, UK: Routledge.

De Carvalho, Benjamin, Halyard Leira and John B. Hobson (2011) The Big Bangs of IR: The Myths that Your Teachers Tell You about 1648 and 1919. *Millennium: Journal of International Studies* 39: 735–758.

Deeb, Mary-Jane (1992) Militant Islam and the Politics of Redemption. *Annals of the American Academy of Political and Social Science* 524: 52–65.

Derlugiuan, Georgi M. and Scott L. Greer, eds (2000) *Questioning Geopolitics: Political Projects in a Changing World-System*. Westport, CT: Praeger.

Derrida, Jacques (1976) *Of Grammatology*, trans. Gayatri Chakravorty Spivak. Baltimore, MD: The Johns Hopkins University Press.

Derrida, Jacques (2002) *Acts of Religion*, ed. and Introduction Gil Anidjar. New York and London: Routledge.

Devji, Faisal (2005) *Landscapes of the Jihad*. Ithaca, NY: Cornell University Press.

de Vries, Hent and Lawrence Sullivan, eds (2006) *Political Theologies in a Post-Secular World*. New York: Fordham University Press.

Diamond, Larry and Marc F. Plattner (2001) *The Global Divergence of Democracy*. Baltimore, MD: Johns Hopkins University Press.

Doyle, Michael (1983) Kant, Liberal Legacies, and Foreign Affairs. *Philosophy and Public Affairs* 12(2 and 3) (Summer and Fall and Fall): 205–235, 323–353.

Edkins, Jenny (2002) Forget Trauma: Responses to September 11. *International Relations* 16(2): 243–256.

Eickelman, Dale F. (2000) Islam and the Languages of Modernity. *Daedalus* 129(1): 119–133.

Eisenstadt, Shmuel N. (1966) *Modernization: Protest and Change*. Englewood Cliffs, NJ: Prentice-Hall.

Eisenstadt, Shmuel N. (1984) Heterodoxies and Dynamics of Civilizations. *Proceedings of the American Philosophical Society* 128(2): 104–113.

Eisenstadt, Shmuel N. (2000) Multiple Modernities. *Daedalus* 129: 1–29.

Eisenstadt, S.N. (2001) The Civilizational Dimension of Modernity: Modernity as a Distinct Civilization. *International Sociology* 16: 320–340.

Elias, Norbert (1978) *The Civilizing Process*, trans. Edmund Jephcott. Oxford: Basil Blackwell.

Elshtain, Judith Bethke (2003) *Just War Against Terror: The Burden of American Power in a Violent World*. New York: Basic Books.

Esposito, John L., ed. (1983) *Voices of Resurgent Islam*. New York: Oxford University Press.

Esposito, John L. (1998) *Islam: The Straight Path*, third edn. New York: Oxford University Press.

Esposito, John L. and John O. Voll (1996) *Islam and Democracy*. New York: Oxford University Press.

Esposito, John L. and Michael Watson, eds (2000) *Religion and the Global Order*. Cardiff: University of Wales Press.

Euben, Roxanne L. (1997) Comparative Political Theory: An Islamic Fundamentalist Critique of Rationalism. *Journal of Politics* 59(1): 28–55.

Euben, Roxanne L. (1999) *Enemy in the Mirror: Islamic Fundamentalism and the Limits of Modern Rationalism*. Princeton, NJ: Princeton University Press.

Euben, Roxanne L. (2002a) The New Manicheans. *Theory and Event* 5(4): 561–594.

Euben, Roxanne L. (2002b) Killing (for) Politics: Jihad, Martyrdom and Political Action. *Political Theory* 30(1): 4–35.

Fabian, Johannes (1983) *Time and the Other: How Anthropology Makes its Object*. New York: Columbia University Press.

Fabio, Petito and Pavlos Hatzopoulos, eds (2003) *Religion in International Relations: The Return from Exile*. New York: Palgrave.

Fakhry, Majid (1970) *A History of Islamic Philosophy*. New York: Columbia University Press.

Falk, Richard (1992/1993) The Making of Global Citizenship, in *Global Visions: Beyond the New World Order*, ed. Jeremy Brecher, John Brown Childs and Jill Cutler. Boston: South End Press.

Falk, Richard (1997) The Critical Realist Tradition and the Demystification of Interstate Power: E.H. Carr, Hedley Bull, and Robert Cox, in *Innovation and Transformation in International Studies*, S. Gill and J.H. Mittelman. Cambridge: Cambridge University Press, pp. 39–55.

Falk, Richard (1999) *Predatory Globalization: A Critique*. Oxford: Polity.

Falk, Richard et al., eds (2002) *Reframing the International: Law, Culture, Politics*. London: Routledge.

Fanon, Frantz (1963/1967) *The Wretched of the Earth*. New York: Grove Press.

Featherstone, Mike, Scott Lash and Roland Robertson, eds (1995) *Global Modernities*. London and Thousand Oaks, CA: Sage.

Femia, Joseph V. (1981) *Gramsci's Political Thought: Hegemony, Consciousness and the Revolutionary Process*. Oxford: Clarendon Press.

Ferguson, Niall (2003) *Empire: How Britain Made the Modern World*. London: Allen Lane.

Ferguson, Niall (2011) *Civilization: The West and the Rest*. London: Allen Lane.

Finocchiaro, Maurice A. (1988) *Gramsci and the History of Dialectical Thought*. Cambridge: Cambridge University Press.

Fischer, Michael M.J. (2002) Islam: The Odd Civilization Out? *New Perspectives Quarterly* (Winter): 62–71.

Fontana, Benedetto (1993) *Hegemony and Power: On the Relation between Gramsci and Machiavelli*. Minneapolis, MN: University of Minnesota Press.

Fox, Jonathan and Shmuel Sandler (2004) *Bringing Religion into International Relations*. New York: Palgrave Macmillan.

Freitag, Sandria B. (1996) Contesting in Public: Colonial Legacies and Contemporary Communalism, in *Making India Hindu: Religion, Community, and the Politics of Democracy in India*, ed. David Ludden. New Delhi: Oxford University Press, pp. 211–234.

Friedman, Thomas L. (1999) *The Lexus and the Olive Tree*. London: HarperCollins.

Friedman, Thomas L. (2002) Moderate Muslim Voices Must be Heard. *The New York Times*, 4 June.

Friedman, Thomas L. (2005) *The World is Flat: A Brief History of the Globalized World in the Twenty-First Century*. London: Allen Lane.

Fukuyama, Francis (1989) The End of History? *The National Interest* 16: 3–18.

Fukuyama, Francis (1992) *The End of History and the Last Man*. New York: Free Press.

Fukuyama, Francis (2001) The West Has Won. *The Guardian*, 11 October, electronic version.

Fukuyama, Francis (2004) *State-Building: Governance and World in the 21st Century*. New York: Cornell University Press.

Gellner, Ernest (1981) *Muslim Society*. Cambridge: Cambridge University Press.

Gellner, Ernest (1990) *The Civil and the Sacred*, The Tanner Lectures on Human Values, delivered at Harvard University (20 February–1 March 1990), p. 318. http://stevereads.com/papers to read/civil and the, sacred gellner.pdf

Gellner, Ernest (1992) *Postmodernism, Reason and Religion*. London and New York: Routledge.

Gellner, Ernest (1994) *Conditions of Liberty: Civil Society and its Rivals*. London: Hamish Hamilton.

Gellner, Ernest (2000) Religion and the Profane. *Eurozine* (28 August). www.eurozine.com/articles/2000-8-28-gellner-en.htmf

Germain, Randall D. and Michael Kenny (1998) Engaging Gramsci: International Relations and the New Gramscians. *Review of International Studies* 5(2): 252–283.

Ghalioun, Burhan (2004) The Persistence of Arab Authoritarianism. *Journal of Democracy* 15(4): 126–132.

Gill, Stephen (1990) *American Hegemony and the Trilateral Commission*. Cambridge: Cambridge University Press.

Gill, Stephen, ed. (1993) *Gramsci, Historical Materialism and International Relations*. Cambridge: Cambridge University Press.

Gill, Stephen (1995) Globalization, Market Civilization, and Disciplinary Neoliberalism. *Millennium* 23(3): 399–423.

Gill, Stephen (2000) Globalising Capital and Political Agency in the Twenty-first Century, in *Questioning Geopolitics: Political Projects in a Changing World-System*, ed. G. Derlugiuan and S.L. Greer. Westport, CT: Praeger, pp. 15–32.

Gill, Stephen (2002) Constitutionalizing Inequality and the Clash of Globalizations. *International Studies Review* 4(2): 47–65.

Gill, Stephen and David Law (1988) *The Global Political Economy: Perspectives, Problems and Policies*. Baltimore, MD: Johns Hopkins University Press.

Gill, Stephen and James H. Mittelman, eds (1997) *Innovation and Transformation in International Studies*. Cambridge: Cambridge University Press.

Gismondi, Mark David (2004) Civilisation as Paradigm: An Inquiry into the Hermeneutics of Conflict. *Geopolitics* 9: 402–425.

Göle, Nilüfer (2000) Snapshots of Islamic Modernities. *Daedalus* 129(1): 91–117.

Göle, Nilüfer (2002) Close Encounters: Islam, Modernity, and Violence, in *Understanding September 11*, ed. Craig Calhoun, Paul Price and Ashley Timmer. Project coordinated by the Social Science Research Council. New York: New Press.

Gong, Geritt W. (1984) *The Standard of 'Civilization' in International Society*. Oxford: Clarendon Press.

Gramsci, Antonio (1971) *Selections from the Prison Notebooks*, ed. and trans. Quintin Hoare and Geoffrey Nowell-Smith. London: Lawrence & Wishart.

Gramsci, Antonio (1992 [1891–1937]) *Prison Notebooks*, Vol. 1, ed. with Introduction by J.A. Buttigieg and A. Callari. New York: Columbia University Press.

Gramsci, Antonio (1994) *Pre-Prison Writings*, ed. R. Bellamy, trans. V. Cox. Cambridge: Cambridge University Press.

Gramsci, Antonio (1996) *Prison Notebooks*, Vol. 2, ed. and trans. J.A. Buttigieg. New York: Columbia University Press.

Gran, Peter (1996) *Beyond Eurocentrism: A New View Modern World History*. New York: Syracuse University Press.

Gray, John (2002) The Era of Globalisation is Over. *New Statesman and Society* (24 September): 25–27.

Gregory, Derek (2004) *The Colonial Present: Afghanistan, Palestine, Iraq*. Maldon and Oxford: Blackwell.

Grovogui, Siba N. (2002) Regimes of Sovereignty: International Morality and the African Condition. *European Journal of International Relations* 8(3): 315–338.

Guha, Ranajit (1997) *Dominance without Hegemony: History and Power in Colonial India*. Cambridge, MA: Harvard University Press.

Guilhot, Nicholas (2008) Postwar American Political Science and the Birth of IR Theory. *International Political Sociology* 2.

Guilhot, Nicholas (2010) American Katechon: When Political Theology Became International Theory. *Constellations* 17: 224–253.

Habermas, Jürgen (1987) *The Philosophical Discourse of Modernity*, trans. Frederick G. Lawrence. Cambridge: The MIT Press.

Habermas, Jürgen (2006) Religion in the Public Sphere. *European Journal of Philosophy* 14: 1–25.

Habermas, Jürgen (2008) *Between Naturalism and Religion: Philosophical Essays*, trans. Ciaran Cronin. Cambridge: Polity Press.

Hall, John A. (1985) *Powers and Liberties: The Causes and Consequences of the Rise of the West*. Oxford: Basil Blackwell.

Halliday, Fred (1993) 'Orientalism' and its Critics. *British Journal of Middle Eastern Studies* 20: 145–163.

Hampson, Fen Osler, Jean Daudelin, John Hay, Holly Reid and Todd Martin (2002) *Madness in the Multitude: Human Security and World Disorder*. New York: Oxford University Press.

Hardt, Michael and Antonio Negri (2000) *Empire*. Cambridge, MA: Harvard University Press.

Hashmi, Sohail H., ed. (2002) *Islamic Political Ethics: Civil Society, Pluralism, and Conflict*. Princeton, NJ: Princeton University Press.

Hatzopoulos, Pavlos, ed. (2003) *Religion in International Relations: The Return from Exile*. New York: Palgrave Macmillan.

Haynes, Jeffrey, eds (2009) *Religion and Politics: Critical Concepts*, 4 vols. London and New York: Routledge.

Hegel, Georg Wilhelm Friedrich (1995 [1892–96]) *Lectures on the Philosophy of History: Vol. 3: Modern and Medieval Philosophy*, trans. E.S. Haldane and Frances H. Simson. Lincoln and London: University of Nebraska Press.

Held, David et al. (1999) *Global Transformations: Politics, Economics and Culture*. Cambridge: Polity Press.

Hodgson, Marshall G.S. (1974) *The Venture of Islam: Conscience and History in a World Civilization*, 3 vols. Chicago and London: University of Chicago Press.

Holton, Robert (2000) Globalization's Cultural Consequences. *Annals of the American Academy of Political and Social Science* 570: 140–152.

Homeland Security (2006) The Second Annual European Homeland Defence Conference. www.wbresearch.com/homelandsecurityeurope/index.html

Hoodbhoy, Pervez (1991) *Islam and Science: Religious Orthodoxy and the Battle for Rationality*. London-Atlantic Highlands: Zed Books.

Howell, Sally and Andrew Shryock (2003) Cracking Down on Diaspora: Arab Detroit and America's 'War on Terror'. *Anthropological Quarterly* 76(3): 443–462.

Huntington, Samuel P. (1993) The Clash of Civilizations. *Foreign Affairs* 72(3) (Summer): 22–49.

Huntington, Samuel P. (1996) *The Clash of Civilizations and the Remaking of World Order*. New York: Simon and Schuster.

Hurd, Elizabeth Shakman (2003) Appropriating Islam: The Islamic Other in the Consolidation of Western Modernity. *Critique: Critical Middle Eastern Studies* 12(1): 25–41.

Hurd, Elizabeth Shakman (2004) The Political Authority of Secularism in International Relations. *European Journal of International Relations* 10(2): 235–262.

Hurd, Elizabeth Shakman (2007) *The Politics of Secularism in International Relations*. Princeton, NJ: Princeton University Press.

Huysmans, Jef (2004) Minding Expectations: The Politics of Insecurity and Liberal Democracy. *Contemporary Political Theory* 3(3): 321–341.

Huysmans, Jef (2008) The Jargon of Exception – On Schmitt, Agamben and the Absence of Political Society. *International Political Sociology* 2(2): 165–183.

Huysmans, Jef and Alessandra Buonfino (2008) Politics of Exception and Unease: Immigration, Asylum and Terrorism in Parliamentary Debates in the UK. *Political Studies* 56(4): 766–788.

Ibn Khaldun (1950) *An Arab Philosophy of History. Selections from the Prolegomena of Ibn Khaldun of Tunis (1332–1406)*, trans. and arranged by Charles Issawi. Princeton: The Darwin Press.

Ibn Khaldun (1958) *The Muqaddimah: An Introduction to History*, trans. Franz Rosenthal, abridged and ed. J. Dawood. Princeton, NJ: Princeton University Press.

Ibn Khaldun (1967 [1332–1406]) *The Muqaddimah: An Introduction to History*, trans. Franz Rosenthal, second edn. London: Routledge and Kegan Paul.

Ignatieff, Michael (2005) *The Lesser Evil: Political Ethics in an Age of Terror*. Edinburgh: Edinburgh University Press.

Inayatullah, Naeem and David L. Blaney (2004) *International Relations and the Problem of Difference*. New York: Routledge.

Irigaray, Luce (1993) *Sexes and Genealogies*, trans. G.C. Gill. New York: Columbia University Press.

Ismail, Salwa (2004) Being Muslim: Islam, Islamism and Identity Politics. *Government and Opposition* 39(4): 614–631.

Jackson, Robert H. (1990) *Quasi-States: Sovereignty, International Relations and the Third World*. Cambridge: Cambridge University Press.

Jahn, Beate (2000) *The Cultural Construction of International Relations: The Invention of the State of Nature*. New York: Palgrave Macmillan.

Jakobsen, Janet R. and Ann Pellegrini, eds (2008) *Secularisms*. Durham, NC and London: Duke University Press.

Jay, Martin (1988) Scopic Regimes of Modernity, in *Vision and Visuality*, ed. H. Foster. Seattle, WA: Dia Art Foundation.

Joas, Hans (2008) *Do We Need Religion? On the Experience of Self-Transcendence*, trans. Alex Skinner. Boulder, CO and London: Paradigm Publishers.

Johns, Fleur (2005) Guantanamo Bay and the Annihilation of the Exception. *The European Journal of International Law* 16(4): 613–635.

Juergensmeyer, Mark (2003) *Terror in the Mind of God: The Global Rise of Religious Violence*, third edn, revised and updated. Berkeley and London: University of California Press.

Kagay, Donald J. (1999) The Essential Enemy: The Image of the Muslim as Adversary and Vassal in the Law and Literature of the Medieval Crown of Aragon, in *Western Views of Islam in Medieval and Early Modern Europe: Perception of the Other*, ed. David R. Blanks and Michael Frassetto. Houndmills, Basingstoke and London: Palgrave Macmillan.

Kalyvas, Andreas (1998) Hegemonic Sovereignty: Carl Schmitt, Antonio Gramsci and the Constituent Prince. *Journal of Political Ideologies* 5(3): 343–376.

Kant, Immanuel (1983) Perpetual Peace, in *Immanuel Kant, Perpetual Peace and Other Essays*, trans. Ted Humphrey. Cambridge: Hackett Publishing Company, pp. 107–143.

Katzenstein, Peter J. (2006) Multiple Modernities as Limits to Secular Europeanization, in *Religion in an Expanding Europe*, ed. Timothy A. Byrnes and Peter J. Katzenstein. Cambridge: Cambridge University Press, pp. 1–33.

Keane, John (2003) *Global Civil Society?* Cambridge: Cambridge University Press.

Keddie, Nikki R. (1994) The Revolt of Islam, 1700 to 1993: Comparative Considerations and Relations to Imperialism. *Comparative Studies in Society and History* 36(3) (July): 463–487.

Keddie, Nikki R. (1998) The New Religious Politics: Where, When, and Why Do 'Fundamentalisms' Appear? *Comparative Studies in Society and History* 40(4): 696–723.

Kedourie, Elie (1992) *Politics in the Middle East*. Oxford: Oxford University Press.

Keebel, Edna (2005) Immigration, Civil Liberties and National/Homeland Security. *International Journal* 60(2): 359–372.

Kepel, Gilles (2003) *Jihad: The Trail of Political Islam*, trans. Anthony F. Roberts. London: I.B. Tauris.

Khalidi, Tarif (1985) *Classical Arab Islam: The Culture and Heritage of the Golden Age*. Princeton, NJ: The Darwin Press.

Khatami, Mohammad (2000) *Dialogue Among Civilizations* [provisional verbatim transcription]. Round table, New York, 5 September. unesco.org/dialogue/en/khatami.htm

King, Richard (1999) Orientalism and the Modern Myth of 'Hinduism'. *Numen* 46: 146–185.

Kramer, Martin S. (1980) *Political Islam*. Beverly Hills, CA: Sage Publications.

Kramer, Martin (1993) Where Islam and Democracy Part Ways, in *Democracy in the Middle East: Defining the Challenge*, ed. Yehuda Mirsky and Matt Ahrens. Washington, DC: Washington Institute for Near East Policy.

Kramer, Martin, ed. (1997) *The Islamism Debate*. Tel Aviv: Moshe Dayan Center for Middle Eastern and African Studies.

Kratochwil, Friedrich (2005) Religion and (Inter-)National Politics: On the Heuristics of Identities, Structures, and Agents. *Alternatives* 30: 113–140.

Kuhn, Thomas S. (1970) *The Structure of Scientific Revolutions*, second edn. Chicago: University of Chicago Press.

Laclau, Ernest and Chantal Mouffe (1985) *Hegemony and Socialist Strategy: Towards a Radical Democratic Politics*, trans. W. Moore and Paul Cammack. London: Verso.

Lacoste, Yves (1984) *Ibn Khaldun: The Birth of History and the Past of the Third World*. London: Verso.

Lakoff, Sanford A. (2004) The Reality of Muslim Exceptionalism. *Journal of Democracy* 15(4): 133–139.

Lal, Deepak (2004) *In Praise of Empires: Globalization and Order*. New York: Palgrave Macmillan.

Lapid, Yosef and Friedrich Kratochwil, eds (1996) *The Return of Culture and Identity in IR Theory*. Boulder, CO and London: Lynne Rienner.

Lapidus, Ira M. (1975) The Separation of State and Religion in the Development of Early Islamic Society. *International Journal of Middle East Studies* 6(4): 363–385.

Lapidus, Ira M. (1992) The Golden Age: The Political Concepts of Islam. *The Annals of the American Academy of Political and Social Science* 524: 13–25.

Lapidus, Ira M. (2002) *A History of Islamic Societies*, second edn. Cambridge: Cambridge University Press, especially chapters 5–7, pp. 67–102.

Lawrence, Bruce B., ed. (1984) *Ibn Khaldun and Islamic Ideology*. Leiden: E.J. Brill.

Leaman, Oliver (1985) *An Introduction to Medieval Islamic Philosophy*. Cambridge: Cambridge University Press.

Levy, Carl (2005) The European Union after 9/11: The Demise of a Liberal Democratic Asylum Regime. *Government and Opposition* 40(1): 26–59.

Lewis, Bernard (1964) *The Middle East and the West*. New York: Harper Torchbooks.

Lewis, Bernard (1976) The Return of Islam. *Commentary* 61: 39–49.

Lewis, Bernard (1988/1991) *The Political Language of Islam*. Chicago, IL: University of Chicago Press.

Lewis, Bernard (1990) The Roots of Muslim Rage. *Atlantic Monthly* 266(3): 47–60.

Lewis, Bernard (1993) Islam and Liberal Democracy. *Atlantic Monthly* (February): 89–98.

Lewis, Bernard (2001) The Revolt of Islam. *The New Yorker* (19 November): 50–63.

Lewis, Bernard (2002) *What Went Wrong? The Clash Between Islam and Modernity in the Middle East*. London: Weidenfeld & Nicholson.

Lewis, Bernard (2003) *The Crisis of Islam: Holy War and Unholy Terror*. London: Weidenfeld & Nicolson.

Loomba, Ania (2005) *Colonialism/Postcolonialism*. London: Routledge.

Lubeck, Paul M. (2000) The Islamic Revival: Antinomies of Islamic Movements Under Globalization, in *Global Social Movements*, ed. Robin Cohen and Shirin M. Rai. London and New Brunswick, NJ: Athlone Press.

Luomaaho, Mika (2009) Political Theology, Anthropomorphism, and Person-hood of the State: The Religion of IR. *International Political Sociology* 3: 293–309.

Mahdi, Mohsin (1957) *Ibn Khaldun's Philosophy of History: A Study in Philosophical Foundations of the Science of Culture*. London and Chicago: Phoenix Books, University of Chicago Press.

Mamdani, Mahmood (2004) *Good Muslim, Bad Muslim: America, the Cold War, and the Roots of Terror*. New York: Pantheon Books.

Mandaville, Peter (1999) Territory and Translocality: Discrepant Idioms of Political Identity. *Millennium: Journal of International Studies* 28(3): 653–673.

Mandaville, Peter (2007) *Global Political Islam*. London: Routledge.

Mann, Michael (2001) Globalization and September 11. *New Left Review* 112 (November–December): 51–72.

Mardin, Şerif (1991) The Just and the Unjust. *Daedalus* 120: 113–129.

Marlow, Louise (1997) *Hierarchy and Egalitarianism in Islamic Thought*. Cambridge: Cambridge University Press.

Marr, Timothy (2006) *The Cultural Roots of American Islamicism*. Cambridge: Cambridge University Press.

Marty, Martin E. and R. Scott Appleby, eds (1991) *Fundamentalism Observed*. Chicago: University of Chicago Press.

Maruyama, Masao (1974 [1952]) *Studies in the Intellectual History of Togugawa Japan*, trans. Mikiso Hane. Tokyo: University of Tokyo Press.

Marx, Karl (2001 [1952]) *The Eighteenth Brumaire of Louis Bonaparte*. London: The Electric Book Company.

Mavelli, Luca (2012) *Europe's Encounter with Islam: The Secular and the Postsecular*. Abingdon, UK: Routledge.

Mavelli, Luca (2012) 'Postsecular Resistance, the Body and the 2011 Egyptian Revolution', *Review of International Studies* 38(5): 1057–1078.

Mazlish, Bruce (2004) *Civilization and its Contents*. Stanford: Stanford University Press.

Mazrui, Ali A. (1991) The Resurgence of Islam and the Decline of Communism. *Futures* 23(3) (April): 273.

McNeill, William H. (1963) *The Rise of the West: A History of the Human Community*. Chicago, IL: University of Chicago Press.

Mearsheimer, John J. (1990) Back to the Future: Instability in Europe after the Cold War. *International Security* 15(1): 5–56.

Mégret, Frédéric (2002) 'War'? Legal Semantics and the Move to Violence. *European Journal of International Law* 13(2): 361–399.

Milbank, John (1991) *Theology and Social Theory: Beyond Secular Reason*. Cambridge, MA: Blackwell.

Mitchell, Timothy (1988) *Colonising Egypt*. New York and Cambridge: Cambridge University Press.

Mittelman, James H., ed. (1996) *Globalization: Critical Reflections*. Boulder, CO and London: Lynne Rienner.

Mittelman, James (2000) *The Globalization Syndrome: Transformation and Resistance*. Princeton, NJ: Princeton University Press.

Mittelman, James H. (2010) *Hyperconflict: Globalization and Insecurity*. Stanford, CA: Stanford University Press.

Moaddel, Mansoor and Kamran Talattof, eds (2000) *Modernist and Fundamentalist Debates in Islam*. New York: Palgrave Macmillan.

Moore, Barrington (1966) *Social Origins of Dictatorship and Democracy: Lord and Peasant in the Making of the Modern World*. Boston, MA: Beacon.

Morton, Adam D. (1999) On Gramsci. *Politics* 19(1): 1–8.

Morton, Adam D. (2002) 'La Resurrección del Maíz': Globalisation, Resistance and the Zapatistas. *Millennium: Journal of International Studies* 31(1): 27–54.

Morton, Adam D. (2003a) Social Forces in the Struggle over Hegemony: Neo-Gramscian Perspectives in International Political Economy. *Rethinking Marxism* 15(2): 153–179.

Morton, Adam D. (2003b) Historicising Gramsci: Situating Ideas in and Beyond their Context. *Review of International Political Economy* 10(1): 118–146.

Morton, Adam D. (2003c) The Social Function of Carlos Fuentes: A Critical Intellectual or in the 'Shadow of the State'? *Bulletin of Latin American Research* 22(1): 27–51.

Moten, Abdul Rashid (1997) Democratic and Shura-based System: A Comparative Analysis. *Encounters* 3 (March): 3–20.

Mottahedeh, Roy P. (2001) *Loyalty and Leadership in an Early Islamic Society*. London: I.B. Tauris.

Mouffe, Chantal, ed. (1999) *The Challenge of Carl Schmitt*. London: Verso.

Munck, Ronaldo (2007) *Globalisation and Contestation: The New Great Counter-Movement*. London and New York: Routledge.

Murphy, Craig N. (1994) *International Organisation and Industrial Change: Global Governance since 1850*. New York: Oxford University Press.

Murphy, Craig N. (1998) Understanding IR: Understanding Gramsci. *Review of International Studies* 24(3): 417–425.

Mushakoji, Kinhide (1996) Multilateralism in a Multicultural World: Notes for a Theory of Occultation, in *The New Realism: Perspectives on Multilateralism and World Order*, ed. Robert W. Cox. London: Macmillan for the United Nations University.

Nandy, Ashis (1988) Introduction: Science as a Reason of State, in *Science, Hegemony and Violence: A Requiem for Modernity*, ed. Ashis Nandy, second edn. Oxford: Oxford University Press, pp. 1–23. [First published by United Nations University, Tokyo, 1988.]

Nandy, Ashis (1995) History's Forgotten Doubles. *History and Theory* 34: 44–66.

Nasr, Seyyed Hossein (1975) *Islam and the Plight of Modern Man*. London and New York: Longman.

Nasr, Seyyed Hossein (1997) *Man and Nature: The Spiritual Crisis in Modern Man*. Chicago: ABC International Group.

Nasr, Seyyed Hossein (2002) *The Heart of Islam: Enduring Values for Humanity*. San Francisco: HarperSanFrancisco.

Nef, Jef (1995/1999) *Human Security and Mutual Vulnerability: An Exploration into the Global Political Economy of Development and Underdevelopment*. Ottawa: IDRC Books.

Nelson, Benjamin (1981) *On the roads to Modernity: Conscience, Science, and Civilizations: Selected Writings by Benjamin Nelson*, ed. Toby E. Huff. Totowa, NJ: Rowman and Littlefield.

Neumann, Iver B. (1999) *The Uses of the Other: The 'East' in European Identity Formation*. Minneapolis, MN: University of Minnesota Press.

Newman, Saul (2004) Terror, Sovereignty and Law: On the Politics of Violence. *German Law Journal* 5(5): 569–584.

Norris, Pippa and Ronald Ingelhart (2004) *Sacred and the Secular: Religion and Politics World-wide*. Cambridge: Cambridge University Press.

Nye, Joseph S. Jr. (2002) *The Paradox of American Power: Why the World's Only Superpower Can't Go it Alone*. Oxford: Oxford University Press.

Nye, Joseph S. Jr. (2004) *Soft Power: The Means of Success in World Politics*. New York: Public Affairs.

Odysseos, Louiza and Fabio Petito, eds (2007) *The International Political Thought of Carl Schmitt: Terror, Liberal War and the Crisis of Global Order*. New York and Abingdon, UK: Routledge.

Ogata, Sadako and Johan Cels (2003) Human Security: Protecting and Empowering the People. *Global Governance* 9: 273–282.

O'Hagan, Jacinta (2002) *Conceptualizing the West in International Relations Thought: From Spengler to Said*. Basingstoke, UK: Palgrave Macmillan.

Ortner, Shelley (1984) Theory in Anthropology since the Sixties. *Comparative Studies in Society and History* 26(1): 142–166.

Osborne, Peter (2010) *The Politics of Time: Modernity and Avant Garde*. London: Verso Books.

Osiander, Andreas (2001) Sovereignty, International Relations, and the Westphalian Myth. *International Organization* 55: 251–287.

Parsons, Talcott (1951) *The Social System*. Glencoe: Free Press.

Pasha, Mustapha Kamal (2000) Globalization, Islam, and Resistance, in *Globalization and the Politics of Resistance*, ed. Barry K. Gills. Basingstoke: Macmillan, pp. 241–254.

Pasha, Mustapha Kamal (2010) In the Shadows of Globalization: Civilizational Crisis, the 'Global Modern' and 'Islamic Nihilism'. *Globalizations* 7(1/2): 167–179.

Pasha, Mustapha Kamal (2012) Islam, Nihilism and Liberal Secularity. *Journal of International Relations and Development* 15: 272–289.

Pasha, Mustapha Kamal and Craig N. Murphy, eds (2002) *International Relations and the New Inequality*. Oxford: Blackwell.

Pasha, Mustapha Kamal and Ahmed I. Samatar (1996) The Resurgence of Islam, in *Globalization: Critical Reflections*, ed. James H. Mittelman. Lynne Reiner.

Patman, Robert G. (2006) Globalisation, the New US Exceptionalism and the War on Terror. *Third World Quarterly* 27(6): 963–986.

Philpott, Daniel (2000) The Religious Roots of Modern International Relations. *World Politics* 52: 206–245.

Pipes, Daniel (1983) *In the Path of God: Islam and Political Power*. New York: Basic Books.

Pipes, Daniel (1990) The Muslims are Coming! The Muslims are Coming! *The National Review*, 19 November. www.danielpipes.org/198/the-muslims-are-coming-the-muslims-are-coming (accessed 21 December 2016).

Pipes, Daniel (2002/2003) *Militant Islam Reaches America*. New York: W.W. Norton.

Pomeranz, Kenneth (2000) *The Great Divergence: China, Europe, and the Making of the World Economy*. Princeton, NJ: Princeton University Press.

Prakash, Gyan, ed. (1995) *After Colonialism: Imperial Histories and Postcolonial Displacements*. Princeton: Princeton University Press.

Prozorov, Sergei (2005) X/Xs: Toward a General Theory of the Exception. *Alternatives: Global Local Political* 30: 81–112.

Prozorov, Sergei (2006) Liberal Enmity: The Figure of the Foe in the Political Ontology of Liberalism. *Millennium: Journal of International Studies* 35(1): 75–99.

Pye, Lucian (1963) *Aspects of Political Development: An Analytic Study*. Princeton, NJ: Princeton University Press.

Qutb, Sayyid (1990 [1964]) *Milestones*. Indianapolis, IN: American Trust Publications.

Rahman, Fazlur (1982) *Islam and Modernity: Transformation of an Intellectual Tradition*. Chicago, IL: University of Chicago Press.

Raquibuz Zaman, M. (2002) Islamic Perspectives on Territorial Boundaries and Autonomy, in *Islamic Political Ethics: Civil Society, Pluralism, and Conflict*, ed. Sohail H. Hashmi. Princeton, NJ: Princeton University Press, pp. 79–101.

Ray, Larry (1999) Fundamentalism, Modernity and the New Jacobians. *Economy and Society* 2: 198–221.

Richards, Alan and John Waterbury (1996) *A Political Economy of the Middle East*. Boulder, CO: Westview.

Roberts, Susan, Anna Secor and Matthew Sparke (2003) Neoliberal Geopolitics. *Antipode: A Radical Journal of Geography* 35(5): 886–897.

Robinson, Chase F. (2002) *Islamic Historiography*. Cambridge: Cambridge University Press.

Robinson, William I. (1996) *Promoting Polyarchy: Globalisation, US Intervention and Hegemony*. Cambridge: Cambridge University Press.

Robinson, William I. (1998) Beyond Nation-state Paradigms: Globalisation, Sociology and the Challenge of Transnational Studies. *Sociological Forum* 13(4): 561–594.

Roy, Olivier (1994) *The Failure of Political Islam*. London: I.B. Tauris.

Roy, Olivier (2004) *Globalized Islam: The Search for a New Ummah*. New York: Columbia University Press in association with the Centre d'Etudes et de Recherches Internationales.

Rupert, Mark (1995) *Producing Hegemony: The Politics of Mass Production and American Global Power*. Cambridge: Cambridge University Press.

Rupert, Mark (2000) *Ideologies of Globalisation: Contending Visions of a New World Order*. London: Routledge.

Rupert, Mark (2003) Globalising Common Sense: A Marxian–Gramscian (Re-)Vision of the Politics of Governance/Resistance. *Review of International Studies* 29 (Special Issue): 181–198.

Sabine, George H. (1937) *A History of Political Theory*. London: Harrap.

Said, Edward W. (1978) *Orientalism*. London: Vintage.

Said, Edward W. (1993) *Culture and Imperialism*. New York: Vintage.

Salvatore, Armando (1996) Beyond Orientalism? Max Weber and the Displacements of 'Essentialism' in the Study of Islam. *Arabica: Revue d'Etudes Arabes* 43(3): 457–485.

Sardar, Ziauddin (2002) Mecca. *Granta* 77 (Spring): 223–254.

Sayeed, Khalid B. (1994) *Western Dominance and Political Islam: Challenge and Response.* Albany, NY: State University of New York Press.

Sayyid, Bobby S. (1997) *A Fundamental Fear: Eurocentrism and the Emergence of Islamism.* London: Zed Books.

Schmidt, N. (1967 [1930]) *Ibn Khaldun: Historian, Sociologist and Philosopher.* New York: Columbia University Press.

Schmitt, Carl (1966) *On the Concept of the Political,* trans. George Schwab. Chicago: University of Chicago Press.

Schmitt, Carl (1976 [1932]) *The Concept of the Political,* trans. George Schwab. New Brunswick, NJ: Rutgers University Press.

Schmitt, Carl (1985 [1923]) *The Crisis of Parliamentary Democracy.* Cambridge, MA: The MIT Press.

Schmitt, Carl (1996 [1932]) *The Concept of the Political,* trans. George Schwab. Chicago: University of Chicago Press.

Schmitt, Carl (2003 [1950]) *The Nomos of the Earth in the International Law of the Jus Publicum Europaeum.* New York: Telos Press.

Schmitt, Carl (2005 [1922]) *Political Theology: Four Chapters on the Concept of Sovereignty,* trans. George Schwab. Chicago, IL and London: University of Chicago Press.

Seabrook, Jeremy (2001) The Metamorphosis of Colonialism. *Globalization,* ISSN: 1935-9794. http://globalization.icaap.org/content/v1.1/jeremyseabrook.html

Shapiro, Michael J. (1997) *Violent Cartographies: Mapping Cultures of War.* Minneapolis: University of Minneapolis Press.

Shapiro, Michael (1999) Samuel Huntington's Moral Geography. *Theory and Event* 2(4): 1–11.

Shapiro, Michael J. (2002) Social Science, Geophilosophy and Inequality. *International Studies Review* 4(2): 25–45.

Shari'ati, Ali (1980) *Marxism and Other Western Fallacies: An Islamic Critique.* Berkeley: Mizan Press.

Shayegan, Darius (1997) *Cultural Schizophrenia: Islamic Societies Confronting the West,* trans. John Howe. Syracuse: Syracuse University Press.

Showstack, Anne S. (1987) *Gramsci's Politics,* second edn. Minneapolis, MN: University of Minnesota Press.

Slater, Mark B. (2004) Passports, Mobility and Security: How Smart Can the Border Be? *International Studies Perspectives* 5(1): 71–91.

Smith, Adam (1981 [1776]) *An Inquiry into the Nature and Causes of the Wealth of Nations.* Indianapolis: Liberty Classics.

Smith, Steve (2002a) The End of the Unipolar Moment? September 11 and the Future of World Order. *International Relations* 16(2): 171–183.

Smith, Steve (2002b) The United States and the Discipline of International Relations: 'Hegemonic Country, Hegemonic Discipline'. *International Studies Review* 4(2): 67–85.

Spengler, Oswald (1922) *The Decline of the West,* 2 vols, trans. Charles Francis Atkinson. New York: Alfred A. Knopf.

Spivak, Gayatri C. (1988) Can the Subaltern Speak?, in *Marxism and the Interpretation of Culture,* ed. Cary Nelson and Lawrence Grossberg. Basingstoke, UK: Macmillan Education.

Stepan, Alfred and Graeme B. Robertson (2004) Arab, Not Muslim, Exceptionalism. *Journal of Democracy* 15(4): 140–146.

Stoett, Peter J. (1999) *Human and Global Security: An Explanation of Terms.* Toronto: University of Toronto Press.

Subrahmanyam, Sanjay (1997) Connected Histories: Notes Towards a Reconfiguration of Early Modern Eurasia. *Modern Asian Studies* 31: 735–762.

Suzuki, Shogo (2005) Japan's Socialization into Janus-Faced European International Society. *European Journal of International Relations* 11: 137–164.

Taylor, Charles (1976) Hermeneutics and Politics, in *Critical Sociology*, ed. P. Connerton. Harmondsworth: Penguin, pp. 153–193.

Taylor, Charles (2007a) *A Secular Age*. Cambridge, MA: Harvard University Press.

Taylor, Charles (2007b) Block Thinking, 10 September. www.project-syndicate.org/comm entary/taylor4/English (accessed 31 December 2011).

Taylor, Charles (2008) A Secular Age: Akbar Ganji in Conversation with Charles Taylor. *The Immanent Frame, Social Science Research Council*. http://blogs.ssrc.org/tif/2008/12/23/a kbar-ganji-in- conversation-with-charles-taylor/ (accessed 21 December 2011).

Taylor, Mark C. (1984) *Erring: A Postmodern Altheology*. Chicago: University of Chicago Press.

Thies, Cameron G. (2002) Progress, History and Identity in International Relations Theory: The Case of the Idealist-Realist Debate. *European Journal of International Relations* 8(2) (June): 147–185.

Thomas, Caroline and Peter Wilkin, eds (1999) *Globalization, Human Security, and the African Experience*. Boulder, CO: Lynne Rienner Publishers.

Thomas, Scott (2005) *The Global Resurgence of Religion and the Transformation of International Relations*. New York: Palgrave Macmillan.

Tibi, Bassam (1990) *Islam and the Cultural Accommodation of Change*, trans from the German, Clare Johnson-Krojzlov. Boulder, CO: Westview Press.

Tibi, Bassam (1998/2002) *The Challenge of Fundamentalism: Political Islam and the New World Disorder*. Berkeley and London: University of California Press.

Tibi, Bassam (2001) *Islam between Culture and Politics*. Basingstoke and New York: Palgrave in association with the Weatherhead Center for International Affairs, Harvard University.

Trouillot, Michel-Rolph (1995) *The Silencing of the Past: Power and Production of History*. Boston: Beacon Press.

Tuastad, Dag (2003) Neo-Orientalism and the New Barbarism Thesis: Aspects of Symbolic Violence in the Middle East Conflict(s). *Third World Quarterly* 24(4): 591–599.

Tully, James (1995) *Strange Multiplicity: Constitutionalism in an Age of Diversity*. Cambridge: Cambridge University Press.

Turner, Bryan (1974) *Weber and Islam: A Critical Study*. London and Boston, MA: Routledge and Kegan Paul.

Van der Pijl, Kees (1998) *Transnational Classes and International Relations*. London: Routledge.

Van Munster, Rens (2004) The War on Terrorism: When the Exception Becomes the Rule. *International Journal for the Semiotics of War* 17: 141–153.

Vatikiotis, P.J. (1987) *Islam and the State*. London and New York: Routledge.

Vattimo, Gianni (2002) *After Christianity*. New York: Columbia University Press.

Venkatraman, Amritha (2007) Religious Basis for Islamic Terrorism: The Quran and its Interpretations. *Studies in Conflict and Terrorism* 30(3): 229–248.

Vento, Arnold C. (2000) Rediscovering the Sacred: From Secular to a Postmodern Sense of the Sacred. *Wicazo Sa Review* 15(1): 183–205.

Vico, Giambattista (1970) *The New Science of Giambattista Vico*, trans. T.G. Bergin and M.H. Fisch. Ithaca: Cornell University Press.

Voll, John O. (1982) *Islam: Continuity and Change in the Modern World*. Boulder, CO: Westview Press.

Waardenburg, Jacques (1978) Official and Popular Religion in Islam. *Social Compass* 25(3–4): 318.

Waardenburg, Jacques (1997) Islamic Studies and the History of Religion: An Evaluation, in *Mapping Islamic Studies: Genealogy, Continuity and Change*, ed. Azim Nanji. Berlin and New York: Mouton de Gruyter.

Walker, R.B.J. (1988) *One Worlds/Many Worlds: Struggles for a Just Peace*. Boulder, CO: Lynne Rienner.

Walker, R.B.J. (1993) *Inside/Outside: International Relations as Political Theory*. Cambridge: Cambridge University Press.

Walker, R.B.J. (1999) The Hierarchalization of Political Community. *Review of International Studies* 25: 151–156.

Walker, R.B.J. (2002) After the Future: Enclosures, Connections, Politics, in *Reframing the International: Law, Culture, Politics*, ed. R. Falk, L. Edwin, J. Ruiz and R.B.J. Walker. New York and London: Routledge.

Walker, R.B.J. (2006a) Lines of Insecurity: International, Imperial, Exceptional. *Security Dialogue* 37(1): 65–82.

Walker, R.B.J. (2006b) Polis, Cosmopolis, Politics. *Alternatives: Local Global Political* 28(2): 267–286.

Walker, R.B.J. (2009) *After the Globe, Before the World*. Abingdon, UK: Routledge.

Wallerstein, Immanuel (2006) The Curve of American Power. *New Left Review* 40 (July–August): 77–94.

Waltz, Kenneth N. (1979) *Theory of International Politics*. New York: Addison-Wesley; McGraw-Hill.

Wendt, Alexander (1999) *Social Theory of International Politics*. Cambridge: Cambridge University Press.

Westerlund, David, ed. (2002) *Questioning the Secular State: The Worldwide Resurgence of Religion in Politics*. London: Hurst.

Williams, Randall (2003) A State of Permanent Exception: The Birth of Modern Policing in Colonial Capitalism. *Interventions* 5(3): 322–344.

Williams, Raymond (1977) *Marxism and Literature*. Oxford: Oxford University Press.

Wolf, Eric (1982) *Europe and the People without History*. Berkeley, CA: University of California Press.

Wood, Ellen Meiksins (2003) *Empire of Capital*. London: Verso.

Xing Li (2002) Dichotomies and Paradoxes: The West and Islam. *Global Society* 16(2): 401–418.

Yeğenoğlu, Meyda (1998) *Colonial Fantasies: Towards a Feminist Reading of Orientalism*. Cambridge and New York: Cambridge University Press.

Young, Robert J.C. (2001) *Postcolonialism: An Historical Introduction*. Oxford and Malden, Mass.: Blackwell Publishers.

Zaman, M. Raquibuz (2002) Islamic Perspectives on Territorial Boundaries and Autonomy, in *Islamic Political Ethics: Civil Society, Pluralism, and Conflict*, ed. Sohail H. Hashmi. Princeton: Princeton University Press.

Zaretsky, Eli (2002) Trauma and Dereification: September 11 and the Problem of Ontological Insecurity. *Constellations: An International Journal of Critical and Democratic Theory* 9(1): 98–105.

Zartman, I. William (1992) Democracy and Islam: The Cultural Dialectic. *Annals of the American Academy of Political and Social Science* 524: 181–191.

Žižek, Slavoj, ed. (1994) *Mapping Ideology*. London and New York: Verso.

Žižek, Slavoj (1997) Multiculturalism, or, the Cultural Logic of Multinational Capitalism. *New Left Review* 225 (September–October).

Žižek, Slavoj (2000) *The Fragile Absolute: Or, Why is the Christian Legacy Worth Fighting For?* New York: Verso.

Žižek, Slavoj (2001) *On Belief.* New York: Routledge.

Žižek, Slavoj (2003) *The Puppet and the Dwarf: The Perverse Core of Christianity.* Cambridge, MA: MIT Press.

Žižek, Slavoj (2006) A Permanent State of Exception. Cuba.now.net

Zubaida, Sami (1992) Islam, the State and Democracy: Contrasting Conceptions of Society in Egypt. *Middle East Report* 22(6): 2–10.

Zubaida, Sami (2003) *Law and Power in the Islamic World.* London and New York: I.B. Taurus.

INDEX

Abdel-Malek, A. 130
accountability (*ihtisab*) 103
Agamben, G. 7, 8, 11, 37, 44, 49
agonism and postorientalism 134–9
Al-Azmeh, A. 3, 13, 26–7, 45, 58, 71, 122, 128, 130, 131, 133, 136, 138
antinomies and silence 110–11
'Arab Spring' 63–4
Asad, T. 13, 32, 57, 58, 134
'asabiyya (social solidarity) 146, 147, 148, 149–51
Augelli, E. and Murphy, C.N. 111, 112
authentic/inauthentic dualism 138

Benjamin, W. 7
Bigo, D. 9
Blair, T. 124
Butko, T. 111

Calhoun, C. 54, 58, 61–2
Camilleri, J. 51, 55, 56
capitalism *see* market fundamentalism; materialism/capitalism
Casanova, J. 51, 54, 56, 57, 58
Chatterjee, J. 48, 51, 65, 112
Christianity: and Islam 40–1, 45, 72–3, 133, 135; Protestant settlement 54–5, 57, 65–6
civil society: and social movements 71–2, 75, 77–8, 94, 101; and state 38, 39–40, 77–8, 84–5, 88
civilizational analysis *see* Ibn Khaldun; postorientalism and civilizational discourse

civilizational hierarchy 14, 15
'clash of civilizations' thesis 21, 48, 75, 123, 124, 150, 151; and 'dialogue among civilizations' 102, 124, 125, 140
class conflict: and inequalities 78; vs culture conflict 72–5
closure, political 18, 21–2, 36
colonialism 5–6, 11–12, 30–1, 45–6, 47, 48; crisis of leadership 99; decolonization 76–7, 89; and Islamic resurgence 72, 78; and orientalism 128; political and social schizophrenia 90
core-periphery model 111, 112, 113–14, 115, 116–17
Cox, R.W. 4, 5, 73–4, 109, 110, 113, 114, 115–17, 150
crisis: of leadership 99–105; of Muslim society 148–9
critical IR 109–10; antinomies and silence 110–11; culture or culture(s) 111–12; Gramsci, culture and IR 119–21; hegemony vs dominance 114–19; transnational hegemony vs diffusion 112–14
Crusades 135
culture: adaptation and heterogeneity 14–15; and civilization 145–6; conflicts 69–81; deficiency view 133–4; divergence within ICZs 90; homogeneous space 31–3; and politics, Islam as 71; 'science of culture' 142–4, 149, 151, 152; *see also* critical IR